DC'S GREATEST *Imaginary* STORIES

OTTO BINDER • JOHN BROOME
LEO DORFMAN • BILL FINGER • EDMOND HAMILTON
JIM SHOOTER • JERRY SIEGEL
writers

C.C. BECK • CARMINE INFANTINO
BOB KANE • KURT SCHAFFENBERGER
DICK SPRANG • CURT SWAN
pencillers

C.C. BECK • JOE GIELLA
STAN KAYE • GEORGE KLEIN
SHELDON MOLDOFF • CHARLES PARIS
KURT SCHAFFENBERGER
inkers

DAN DiDIO vp-executive editor
JULIUS SCHWARTZ, MORT WEISINGER editors-original series
ROBERT GREENBERGER senior editor-collected edition
ROBBIN BROSTERMAN senior art director
PAUL LEVITZ president & publisher
GEORG BREWER vp-design & dc direct creative
RICHARD BRUNING senior vp-creative director
PATRICK CALDON senior vp-finance & operations
CHRIS CARAMALIS vp-finance
TERRI CUNNINGHAM vp-managing editor
STEPHANIE FIERMAN senior vp-sales & marketing
ALISON GILL vp-manufacturing
RICH JOHNSON vp-book trade sales
HANK KANALZ vp-general manager, wildstorm
LILLIAN LASERSON senior vp & general counsel
JIM LEE editorial director-wildstorm
PAULA LOWITT senior vp-business & legal affairs
DAVID McKILLIPS vp-advertising & custom publishing
JOHN NEE vp-business development
GREGORY NOVECK senior vp-creative affairs
CHERYL RUBIN senior vp-brand management
JEFF TROJAN vp-business development, dc direct
BOB WAYNE vp-sales

DC'S GREATEST IMAGINARY STORIES

Published by DC Comics. Cover, introduction, and compilation copyright © 2005 DC Comics. All Rights Reserved.

Originally published in single magazine form in BATMAN 127, 151, THE FLASH 128, SUPERMAN 149, 162, 166, SUPERMAN'S GIRL FIREND LOIS LANE 19, 51, SUPERMAN'S PAL JIMMY OLSEN 57, WORLD'S FINEST COMICS 172. Copyright © 1959, 1960, 1961, 1962, 1963, 1964, 1967 DC Comics. All Rights Reserved. CAPTAIN MARVEL ADVENTURES 66, Copyright 1946, DC Comics. All characters, their distinctive likenesses and related elements featured in this publication are trademarks of DC Comics. The stories, characters and incidents featured in this publication are entirely fictional. DC Comics does not read or accept unsolicited submissions of ideas, stories or artwork.

DC Comics, 1700 Broadway, New York, NY 10019
A Warner Bros. Entertainment Company
Printed in Canada. First Printing.
ISBN: 1-4012-0534-8

Cover illustration by Brian Bolland
Publication design by Murphy Fogelnest
Selected color reconstruction by David Tanguay

TABLE OF CONTENTS

NOT A HOAX OR A DREAM!

by CRAIG SHUTT

Let's get one thing straight right from the start: No matter what you thought, all comic-book stories are *not* Imaginary Stories.

Oh, sure, all of the stories about Superman and DC's other super-heroes are fictional tales taking place only within the four-color pages of our favorite comic books — and in our imaginations. But most of them count. Most of them adhere to specific continuities, and the events could have ramifications in our hero's world, unless the situation turns out to be a hoax or a dream that lets the writer out of the tight plot-trap he constructed.

To me, hoaxes and dreams were a gyp. They built impossible situations that made us turn the pages ever faster to see how the hero escaped his juicy predicament. And then — *boing*, we learned there was no real dilemma. Instead, we got an elaborate explanation for why the hoax or dream was necessary. I hated hoaxes and dreams.

But, oh, how I loved Imaginary Stories.

They played fair with readers, explaining the situation right up front. This story isn't part of the character's canon, the editor explained. We just thought we'd show what would happen if this scenario had occurred. In some cases, it was possible that it still *might* happen some day.

These stories burst the continuity chains and let the imagination fly. Lois would never marry Lex Luthor and have a son, and she *definitely* couldn't rocket to Krypton when the doomed planet Earth exploded and become Supermaid. We knew these things wouldn't, couldn't, shouldn't happen. But for this one story, they could — and they did. And we saw how things turned out in quick order.

Indeed, Imaginary Stories often covered a lot of ground rapidly, jumping years between panels to focus on key moments in what otherwise could have been an epic series of adventures. Sadly, these stories often involved major tragedies. It was almost as if the editor was telling

us (or the character), "Be careful what you wish for." The stories also gave writers a chance to create real tearjerkers that typically were avoided in the good-always-triumphs, upbeat world of DC's Silver Age. But on occasion, Imaginary Stories ended happily, just to keep us on our toes.

And we bought in. We knew the conditions under which we were reading, and we accepted them. No, the story wouldn't have an impact on next month's issue — back then, not much did anyway, frankly. But it was going to be a wild ride for this one issue, and it could go *anywhere*.

Mort Weisinger, editor of the Superman family of books, was the king of the Imaginary Story. In part, I think this was because Weisinger's Super-tales aimed for a younger audience and were driven by emotion. Legendary DC editor Julius Schwartz, the mastermind of the Silver Age, seldom used the concept. He told puzzle-solving tales aimed at an older, science-drenched audience. Weisinger's stories came from the heart; Schwartz's tales came from the head. Both were successful approaches, but Imaginary Stories thrived only on the former.

And thrive they did. During the 1960s, Weisinger's Superman comics told dozens of Imaginary Stories. The first to use that name was "Mr. and Mrs. Clark (Superman) Kent!" in SUPERMAN'S GIRL FRIEND LOIS LANE #19, featuring the tale everyone had imagined (especially Lois). It was the first of a four-part series, which showed Lois that she might want to be careful what she wished for.

With three women vying for Superman's heart on a daily basis, it's not surprising that a number of tales showed The Man of Steel committing matrimony. Those hit their peak with "The Three Wives of Superman!" in LOIS LANE #51, in which he serially married Lois, Lana and Lori, only to find...well, read it for yourself.

eisinger's heartfelt approach meant these tales often focused on relationships: who Superman married, if his parents joined him on Earth, if Supergirl arrived on Earth first, etc. Frequently, we read about Superman's children, sometimes without even learning his mate's identity, as in "The Fantastic Story of Superman's Sons!" in SUPERMAN #166. Giving him new relations also was a favorite theme, as evidenced by "Superman and Batman...Brothers!" from WORLD'S FINEST #172.

Death played a key role in Imaginary Stories, as these alternative choices sometimes forced characters to pay the ultimate price. But only occasionally was it the centerpiece, as with "The Death of Superman!" in SUPERMAN #149, one of my all-time favorite Superman tales of any type. Although the story was Imaginary, the emotions expressed by his friends as they filed past his bier felt very real.

On the other hand, one of the most joyous Superadventures ever was "The Amazing Story of Superman-Red and Superman-Blue" in SUPERMAN #162. This was a real wish-fulfillment tale, which

DARTING UP THE STAIRS, THE DISGUISED BRUCE SUDDENLY CONFRONTS THE ONCOMING BANDITS...

HOLD IT, YOU TWO! THAT GUY BEHIND YOU IS PLAYING YOU FOR A CHUMP! HE'S A COP--LEADING YOU INTO A TRAP! I'M THE REAL BLUE BAT!

may be lacking somewhat in true dramatic conflict. But to me, it was one of the best, because few were ever so relentlessly upbeat and satisfying.

f course, the stories also could lapse into total loopiness, thanks in part to their need to progress quickly while leaping gigantic plot holes in a single bound. "Jimmy Olsen Marries Supergirl" from SUPERMAN'S PAL JIMMY OLSEN #57 is one of those. Leaving aside the morality of Linda's plan, the story asks us to believe that neither she nor her husband ever realized she was wearing a wig. It's still one of my favorites.

YOU WIN, KNOR-EL! BY DEFEATING YOUR BROTHER, KAL-EL, YOU'VE GAINED THE RIGHT TO WEAR THIS UNIFORM! FROM NOW ON, YOU'LL BE EARTH'S SUPERMAN!

Batman's editor, Jack Schiff, tried his hand at Imaginary Stories, but they didn't resonate as much. Without the strong supporting cast, Batman's tales were more inner-directed, focusing on his secret identity or origin. The best were a series of stories, ostensibly written by Alfred and beginning in BATMAN #131, that showed Robin as the new Batman with Bruce's son joining the team.

rom panel one, we knew these stories were fiction (if you know what I mean), as was true when Bruce visited his old pal Professor Nichols to learn what would have happened if his parents hadn't died, in "The Second Life of Batman" in BATMAN #127. That wasn't the case with a more interesting tale, "Batman's New Secret Identity!" in BATMAN #151. It frankly would have been stronger had we known it was Imaginary—and that anything really could happen.

As noted, Julie Schwartz seldom dipped into the Imaginary Pool. In FLASH #128, he told "The Origin of Flash's Masked Identity," adding new unmasked (and still untold) tales into Barry Allen's early days. But it was only a daydream. In DETECTIVE COMICS #347, he used a few pages after the story ended to show what would've happened if Batman hadn't survived the adventure. The result (the Earth-2 Batman replaced him) didn't really sparkle.

Wonder Woman's editor, Robert Kanigher, created a series of stories (dubbed "Impossible Tales") in which Diana teamed up with her younger selves as Wonder Girl and Wonder Tot. This led to an amazing gaffe when the unknowing (or uncaring) editors lifted Wonder Girl to star in their new TEEN TITANS series. But the Titans' stories were so good that nobody called them on it (at least until the 1980s).

The appeal of "What If" stories has been strong throughout comics history, as is shown by "Captain Marvel and the Atomic War!" from CAPTAIN MARVEL ADVENTURES #66. It doesn't reveal its Imaginary status until the end, creating a darned scary story for its younger readers (as was intended). It's a powerful, if simple, tale for 1946 — and makes me wonder why I was still ducking and covering from nuclear attacks during the 1950s.

In the 1960s, Imaginary Stories became so commonplace, especially in Weisinger's Superman comics, that improbable cover scenes began offering a standard disclaimer: "Not a hoax, a dream or an Imaginary Story!" Always used in that order, the line became a Silver Age mantra. But as the 1960s waned, DC found Marvel surging into the sales lead. Editors tried to ape Marvel's successful format of continued stories and tighter continuity, which left little room for the single-issue standbys of hoaxes, dreams and (>sigh<) Imaginary Stories.

After falling out of favor in the early 1970s, Imaginary Stories faded away. Superman and Batman's sons teamed up for a fondly remembered series in mid-1970s WORLD'S FINEST issues, while Schwartz celebrated Superman's 300th issue by reimagining Kal-El's life if he'd rocketed to Earth in 1976. And just before he was revamped in 1986, the Man of Steel starred in a well-regarded two-parter, "Whatever Happened to the Man of Tomorrow?", postulating Superman's last adventure. It began with the now-famous lines, "This is an Imaginary Story. Aren't they all?"

Well, no. No, they're not. And today's comics writers and readers understand that. Though Imaginary Stories have disappeared, they have been revived as Elseworlds tales. In that form, Superman, Batman, and the rest of the Justice League continue to be reimagined into a vast array of situations where anything could happen, anyone could die. It all counts, it all matters, it all is deeply felt, at least for that one story.

That's really all a reader could want, isn't it?

Craig Shutt, who bought virtually all of the stories from this collection right off the spinner rack, writes the ASK MR. SILVER AGE column for the COMICS BUYER'S GUIDE monthly magazine. His book Baby Boomer Comics regales readers with the wacky and wonderful characters and stories of 1960s comics that produced the Silver Age.

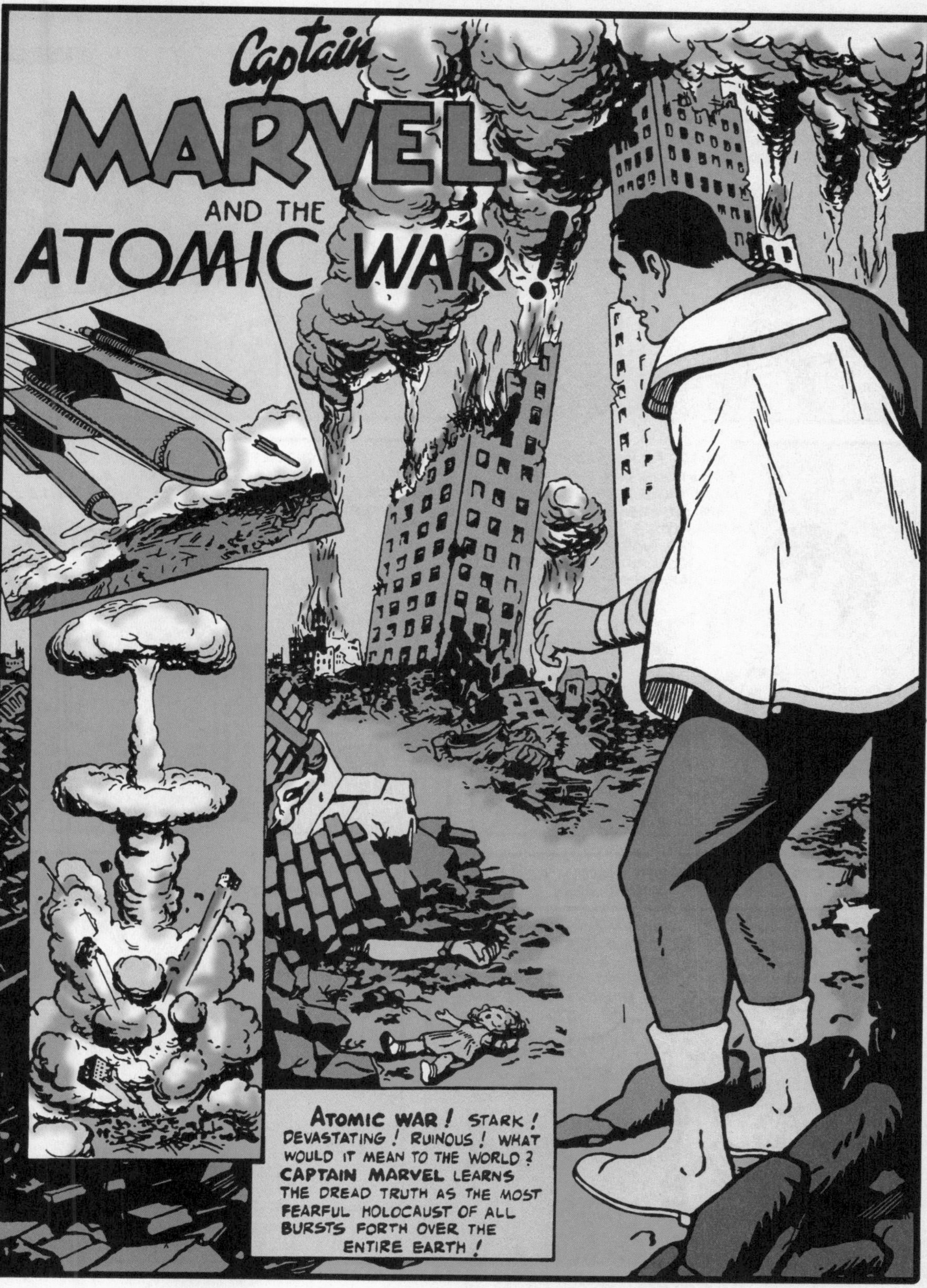
Captain
MARVEL
AND THE
ATOMIC WAR!
ATOMIC WAR! STARK! DEVASTATING! RUINOUS! WHAT WOULD IT MEAN TO THE WORLD? CAPTAIN MARVEL LEARNS THE DREAD TRUTH AS THE MOST FEARFUL HOLOCAUST OF ALL BURSTS FORTH OVER THE ENTIRE EARTH!

ONE FINE MORNING BILLY BATSON, STAR BOY NEWSCASTER FOR STATION WHIZ, MAKES HIS WAY TO WORK, WITH GLADNESS IN HIS HEART!

WHAT A WONDERFUL DAY! WARM SUNSHINE--SOFT BREEZES-- BIRDS SINGING! IT SURE FEELS GOOD TO BE ALIVE!

NOW I KNOW WHY THAT COMPOSER WROTE THE SONG---"OH, WHAT A BEAUTIFUL MORNING!" THIS IS IT!

GOOD MORNING, MR. MORRIS! FINE DAY, ISN'T IT?

STUDIO "C"

SPLENDID, BILLY! SIMPLY SPLENDID!

HELLO, FOLKS! ISN'T THIS A GORGEOUS DAY? I HAVEN'T MUCH NEWS TO REPORT! NO BIG CRIMES, NO FIRES, NO TRAGEDIES! IT SEEMS AS IF THE WORLD HAS REACHED A NICE PEACEFUL STATE OF HAPPINESS AND PROSPERITY!

YES, IT'S A WONDERFUL DAY AND---ER---PARDON ME FOR A MOMENT, PLEASE!

BILLY!... GASP... FLASH BULLETIN--- IT'S HORRIBLE!

BILLY READS THE BULLETIN OFF, HARDLY REALIZING WHAT THE WORDS MEAN!

WE'VE HAD FLASHES BEFORE! WONDER WHY MR. MORRIS IS SO EXCITED!

FLASH! THE CITY OF CHICAGO WAS JUST DESTROYED FIVE MINUTES AGO BY A TERRIFIC EXPLOSION! IT WAS THOUGHT TO BE AN ATOMIC BOMB!

WHAT?---CHICAGO DESTROYED?--- ATOMIC BOMB?--- HOLY MOLEY!

THE DREADFUL MESSAGE SUDDENLY HITS BILLY WITH ITS FULL IMPACT!

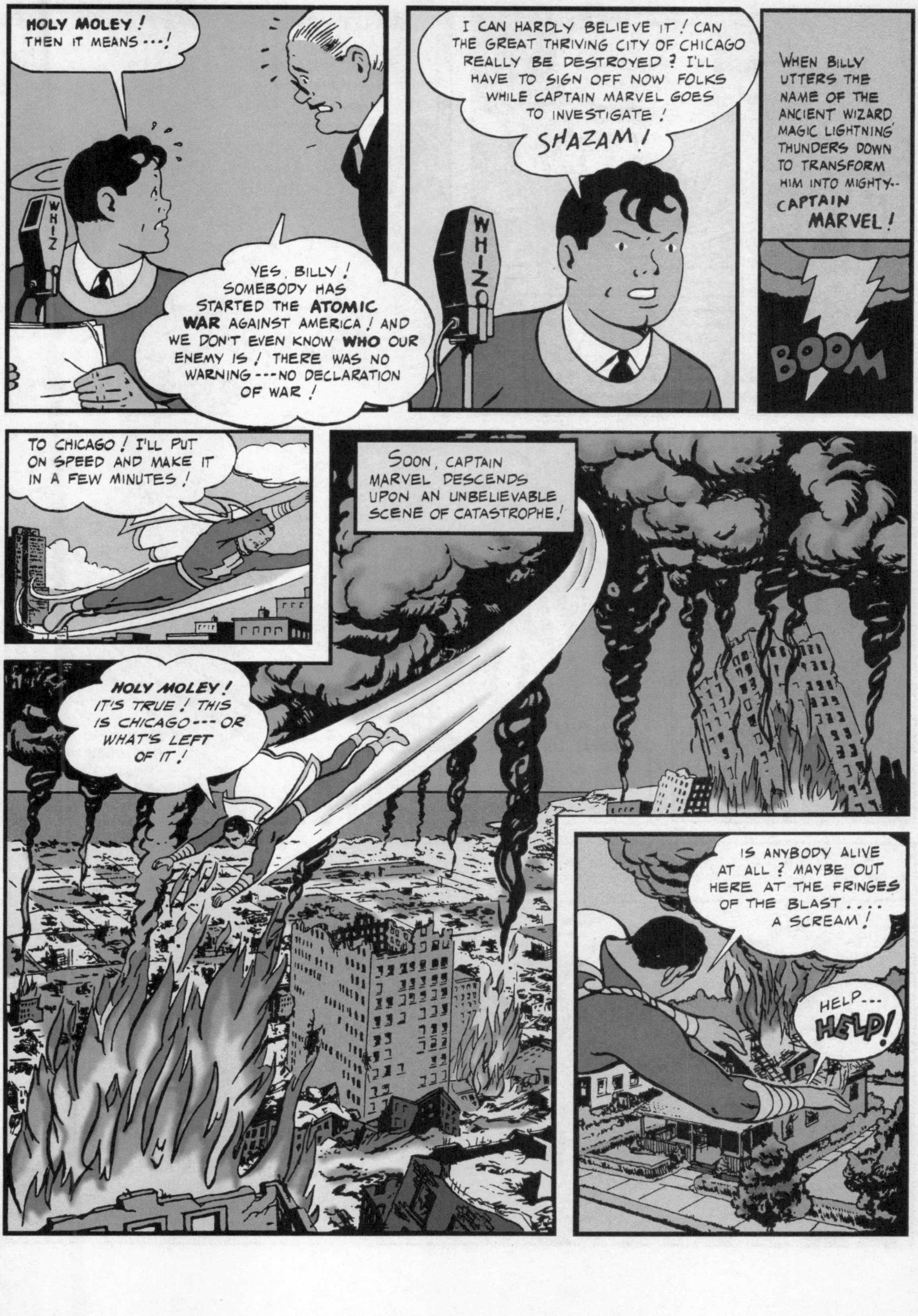

HOLY MOLEY! THEN IT MEANS...!
YES, BILLY! SOMEBODY HAS STARTED THE ATOMIC WAR AGAINST AMERICA! AND WE DON'T EVEN KNOW WHO OUR ENEMY IS! THERE WAS NO WARNING---NO DECLARATION OF WAR!
WHIZ
I CAN HARDLY BELIEVE IT! CAN THE GREAT THRIVING CITY OF CHICAGO REALLY BE DESTROYED? I'LL HAVE TO SIGN OFF NOW FOLKS WHILE CAPTAIN MARVEL GOES TO INVESTIGATE!
SHAZAM!
WHIZ
WHEN BILLY UTTERS THE NAME OF THE ANCIENT WIZARD MAGIC LIGHTNING THUNDERS DOWN TO TRANSFORM HIM INTO MIGHTY-- CAPTAIN MARVEL!
BOOM
TO CHICAGO! I'LL PUT ON SPEED AND MAKE IT IN A FEW MINUTES!
SOON, CAPTAIN MARVEL DESCENDS UPON AN UNBELIEVABLE SCENE OF CATASTROPHE!
HOLY MOLEY! IT'S TRUE! THIS IS CHICAGO---OR WHAT'S LEFT OF IT!
IS ANYBODY ALIVE AT ALL? MAYBE OUT HERE AT THE FRINGES OF THE BLAST.... A SCREAM!
HELP... HELP!

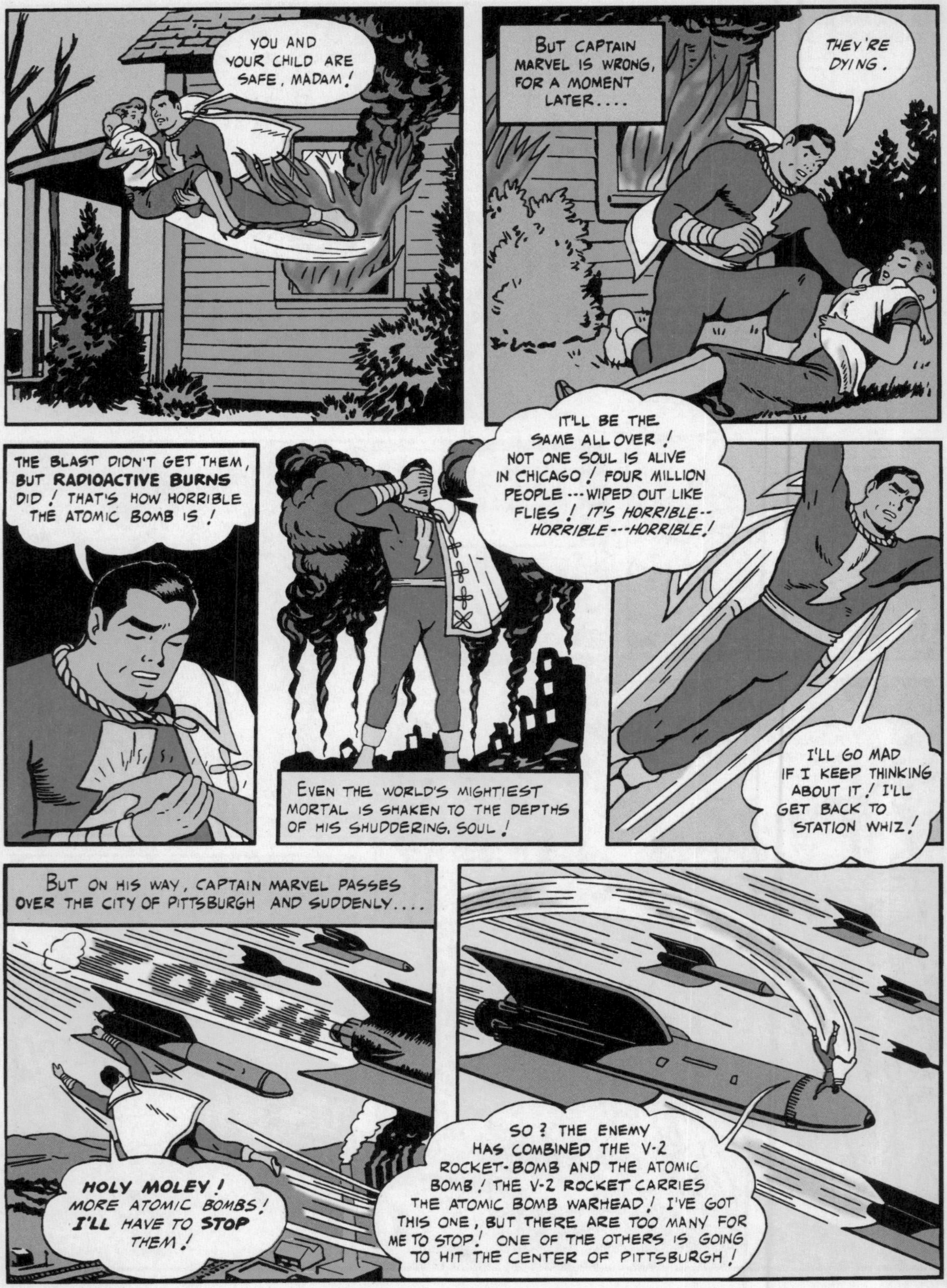

YOU AND YOUR CHILD ARE SAFE, MADAM!
BUT CAPTAIN MARVEL IS WRONG, FOR A MOMENT LATER....
THEY'RE DYING.
THE BLAST DIDN'T GET THEM, BUT RADIOACTIVE BURNS DID! THAT'S HOW HORRIBLE THE ATOMIC BOMB IS!
IT'LL BE THE SAME ALL OVER! NOT ONE SOUL IS ALIVE IN CHICAGO! FOUR MILLION PEOPLE --- WIPED OUT LIKE FLIES! IT'S HORRIBLE-- HORRIBLE---HORRIBLE!
EVEN THE WORLD'S MIGHTIEST MORTAL IS SHAKEN TO THE DEPTHS OF HIS SHUDDERING SOUL!
I'LL GO MAD IF I KEEP THINKING ABOUT IT! I'LL GET BACK TO STATION WHIZ!
BUT ON HIS WAY, CAPTAIN MARVEL PASSES OVER THE CITY OF PITTSBURGH AND SUDDENLY....
ZOOM
HOLY MOLEY! MORE ATOMIC BOMBS! I'LL HAVE TO STOP THEM!
SO? THE ENEMY HAS COMBINED THE V-2 ROCKET-BOMB AND THE ATOMIC BOMB! THE V-2 ROCKET CARRIES THE ATOMIC BOMB WARHEAD! I'VE GOT THIS ONE, BUT THERE ARE TOO MANY FOR ME TO STOP! ONE OF THE OTHERS IS GOING TO HIT THE CENTER OF PITTSBURGH!

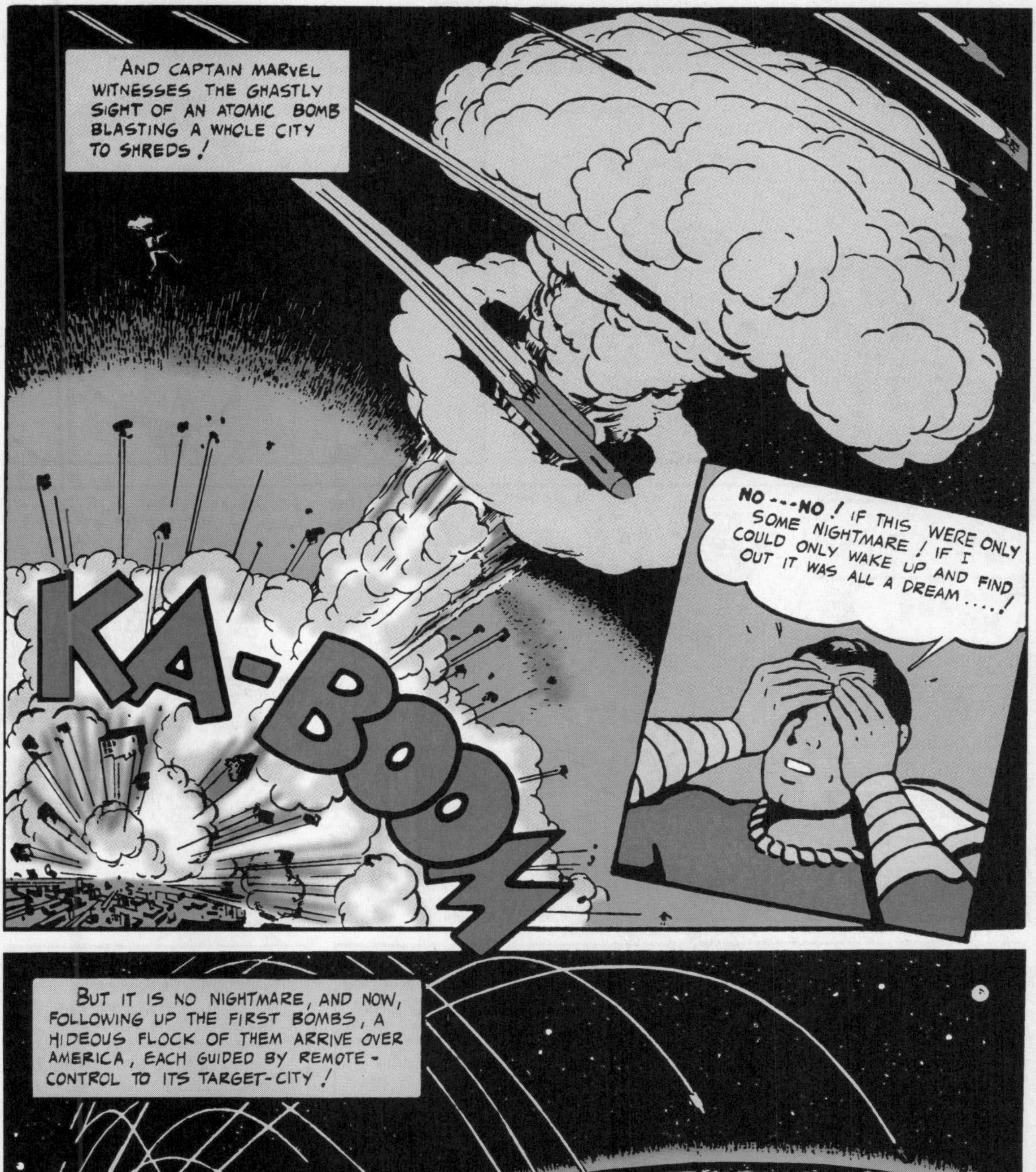
AND CAPTAIN MARVEL WITNESSES THE GHASTLY SIGHT OF AN ATOMIC BOMB BLASTING A WHOLE CITY TO SHREDS !
KA-BOOM
NO---NO ! IF THIS WERE ONLY SOME NIGHTMARE ! IF I COULD ONLY WAKE UP AND FIND OUT IT WAS ALL A DREAM.....!

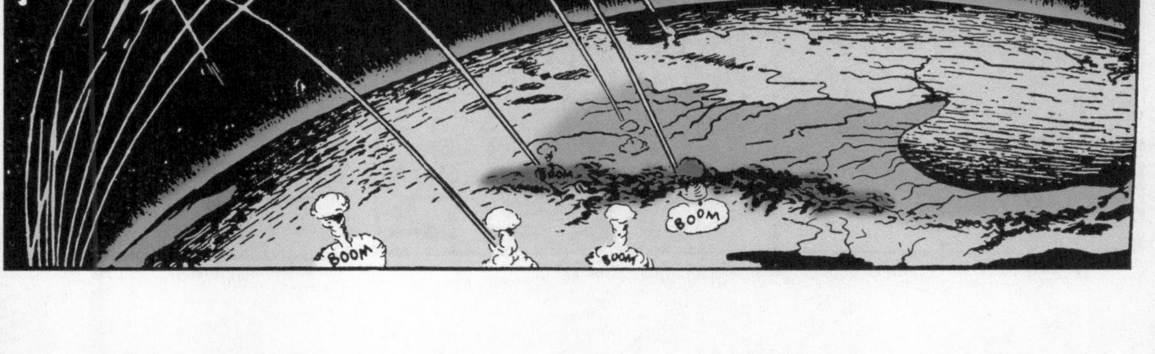
BUT IT IS NO NIGHTMARE, AND NOW, FOLLOWING UP THE FIRST BOMBS, A HIDEOUS FLOCK OF THEM ARRIVE OVER AMERICA, EACH GUIDED BY REMOTE-CONTROL TO ITS TARGET-CITY !
BOOM
BOOM
BOOM
BOOM

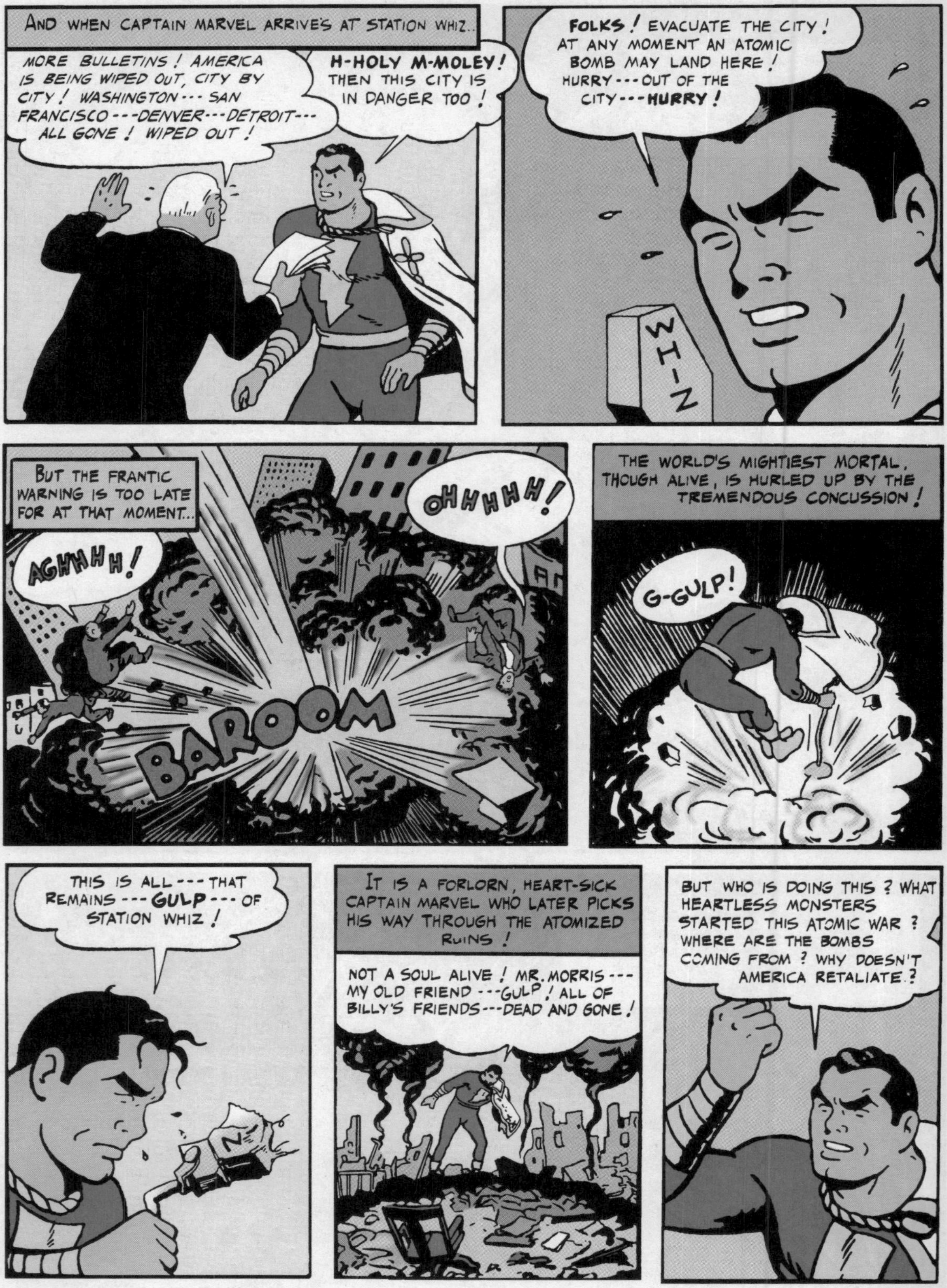
AND WHEN CAPTAIN MARVEL ARRIVES AT STATION WHIZ..
MORE BULLETINS! AMERICA IS BEING WIPED OUT, CITY BY CITY! WASHINGTON--- SAN FRANCISCO---DENVER---DETROIT--- ALL GONE! WIPED OUT!
H-HOLY M-MOLEY! THEN THIS CITY IS IN DANGER TOO!
FOLKS! EVACUATE THE CITY! AT ANY MOMENT AN ATOMIC BOMB MAY LAND HERE! HURRY---OUT OF THE CITY---HURRY!
WHIZ
BUT THE FRANTIC WARNING IS TOO LATE FOR AT THAT MOMENT...
OHHHHH!
AGHHHH!
BAROOM
THE WORLD'S MIGHTIEST MORTAL, THOUGH ALIVE, IS HURLED UP BY THE TREMENDOUS CONCUSSION!
G-GULP!
THIS IS ALL---THAT REMAINS---GULP---OF STATION WHIZ!
IT IS A FORLORN, HEART-SICK CAPTAIN MARVEL WHO LATER PICKS HIS WAY THROUGH THE ATOMIZED RUINS!
NOT A SOUL ALIVE! MR. MORRIS--- MY OLD FRIEND---GULP! ALL OF BILLY'S FRIENDS---DEAD AND GONE!
BUT WHO IS DOING THIS? WHAT HEARTLESS MONSTERS STARTED THIS ATOMIC WAR? WHERE ARE THE BOMBS COMING FROM? WHY DOESN'T AMERICA RETALIATE?

THAT'S WHAT WE NEED YOU FOR, CAPTAIN MARVEL! I THOUGHT WE'D NEVER LOCATE YOU!

I'M GENERAL TOMKINS, OF THE AMERICAN GENERAL STAFF! WE HAVE ATOMIC BOMBS TOO, READY TO GO --- BUT WE DON'T KNOW **WHERE TO SEND THEM!**

WE DON'T KNOW WHO OUR ENEMY IS, EH?

NO! OUR RECONNAISANCE PLANES HAVE BEEN UNABLE TO SEE WHICH DIRECTION THE BOMBS COME FROM, BECAUSE OF THEIR TERRIFIC SPEED! YOU'RE OUR ONLY HOPE, CAPTAIN MARVEL! WE SUSPECT THEY COME FROM THE NORTH, OVER THE NORTH POLE, BUT WE HAVE TO BE SURE! CAN YOU HELP US?

I'M ON MY WAY, SIR!

IF YOU FIGURE IT OUT, REPORT TO US BY THIS RADIO! USE CODE LETTERS ZQZ, AND WE'LL PICK IT UP! THE FATE OF AMERICA DEPENDS ON YOU, CAPTAIN MARVEL!

GRIMLY, CAPTAIN MARVEL HEADS NORTH AND FINALLY....

AN ATOMIC BOMB, COMING STRAIGHT AT ME!

HERE'S ONE BOMB THAT WILL NEVER REACH ITS TARGET!

BOOM

POW

THE WORLD'S MIGHTIEST MORTAL FEARLESSLY EXPLODES THE MIGHTY PROJECTILE IN MID-AIR!

BUT WHILE THE CONCUSSION HURLS HIM BACK, MORE BOMBS WHIZ PAST!

HOLY MOLEY, LOOK AT THE NUMBER OF BOMBS! I'D NEVER BE ABLE TO STOP THEM ALL, BUT I THINK I KNOW NOW WHICH **DIRECTION** THEY'RE COMING FROM!

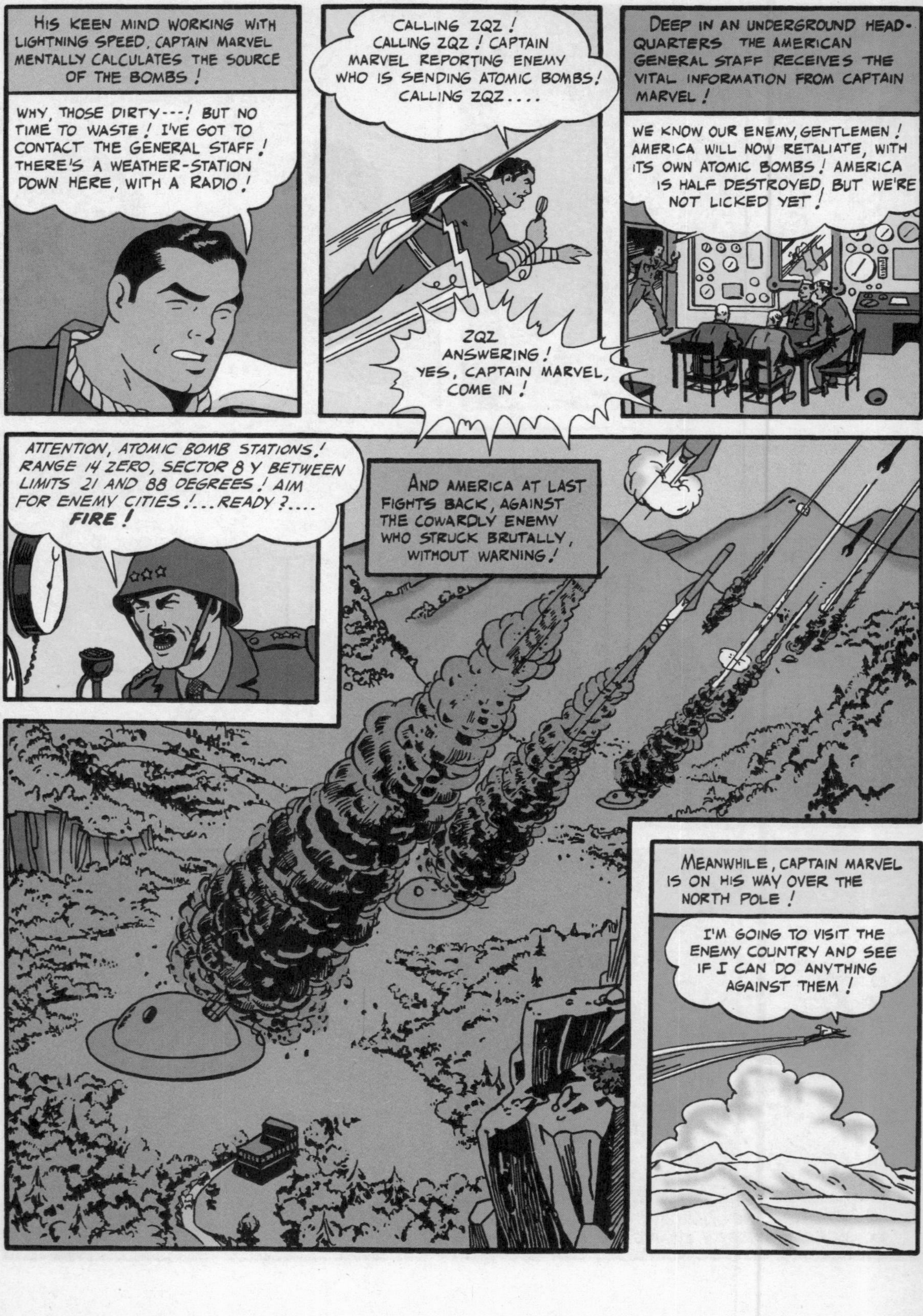

HIS KEEN MIND WORKING WITH LIGHTNING SPEED, CAPTAIN MARVEL MENTALLY CALCULATES THE SOURCE OF THE BOMBS!
WHY, THOSE DIRTY---! BUT NO TIME TO WASTE! I'VE GOT TO CONTACT THE GENERAL STAFF! THERE'S A WEATHER-STATION DOWN HERE, WITH A RADIO!
CALLING ZQZ! CALLING ZQZ! CAPTAIN MARVEL REPORTING ENEMY WHO IS SENDING ATOMIC BOMBS! CALLING ZQZ....
ZQZ ANSWERING! YES, CAPTAIN MARVEL, COME IN!
DEEP IN AN UNDERGROUND HEAD-QUARTERS THE AMERICAN GENERAL STAFF RECEIVES THE VITAL INFORMATION FROM CAPTAIN MARVEL!
WE KNOW OUR ENEMY, GENTLEMEN! AMERICA WILL NOW RETALIATE, WITH ITS OWN ATOMIC BOMBS! AMERICA IS HALF DESTROYED, BUT WE'RE NOT LICKED YET!
ATTENTION, ATOMIC BOMB STATIONS! RANGE 14 ZERO, SECTOR 8 Y BETWEEN LIMITS 21 AND 88 DEGREES! AIM FOR ENEMY CITIES!...READY?.... FIRE!
AND AMERICA AT LAST FIGHTS BACK, AGAINST THE COWARDLY ENEMY WHO STRUCK BRUTALLY, WITHOUT WARNING!
MEANWHILE, CAPTAIN MARVEL IS ON HIS WAY OVER THE NORTH POLE!
I'M GOING TO VISIT THE ENEMY COUNTRY AND SEE IF I CAN DO ANYTHING AGAINST THEM!

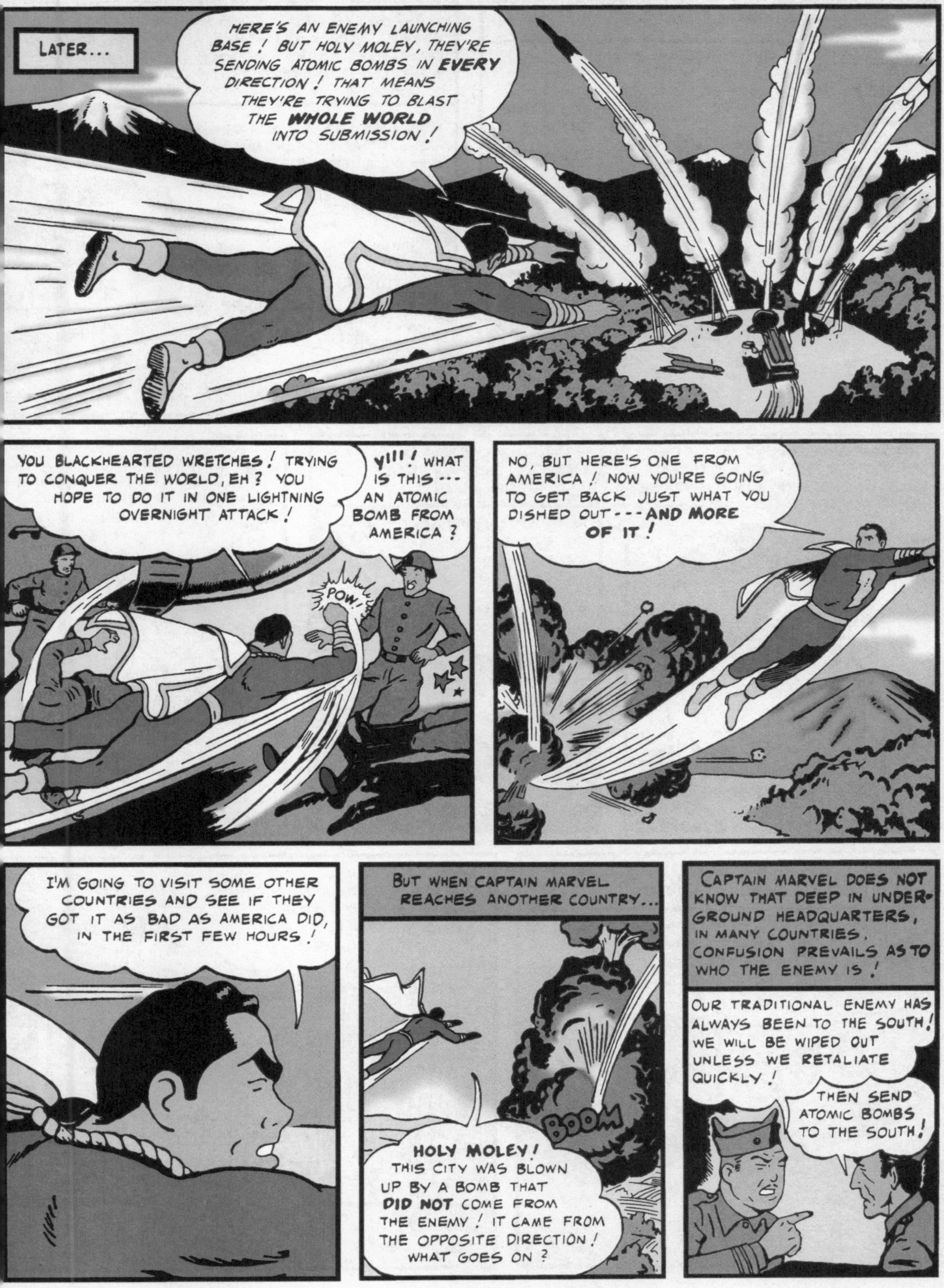
LATER...
HERE'S AN ENEMY LAUNCHING BASE! BUT HOLY MOLEY, THEY'RE SENDING ATOMIC BOMBS IN EVERY DIRECTION! THAT MEANS THEY'RE TRYING TO BLAST THE WHOLE WORLD INTO SUBMISSION!
YOU BLACKHEARTED WRETCHES! TRYING TO CONQUER THE WORLD, EH? YOU HOPE TO DO IT IN ONE LIGHTNING OVERNIGHT ATTACK!
Y!!!! WHAT IS THIS--- AN ATOMIC BOMB FROM AMERICA?
POW!
NO, BUT HERE'S ONE FROM AMERICA! NOW YOU'RE GOING TO GET BACK JUST WHAT YOU DISHED OUT---AND MORE OF IT!
I'M GOING TO VISIT SOME OTHER COUNTRIES AND SEE IF THEY GOT IT AS BAD AS AMERICA DID, IN THE FIRST FEW HOURS!
BUT WHEN CAPTAIN MARVEL REACHES ANOTHER COUNTRY...
BOOM
HOLY MOLEY! THIS CITY WAS BLOWN UP BY A BOMB THAT DID NOT COME FROM THE ENEMY! IT CAME FROM THE OPPOSITE DIRECTION! WHAT GOES ON?
CAPTAIN MARVEL DOES NOT KNOW THAT DEEP IN UNDERGROUND HEADQUARTERS, IN MANY COUNTRIES, CONFUSION PREVAILS AS TO WHO THE ENEMY IS!
OUR TRADITIONAL ENEMY HAS ALWAYS BEEN TO THE SOUTH! WE WILL BE WIPED OUT UNLESS WE RETALIATE QUICKLY!
THEN SEND ATOMIC BOMBS TO THE SOUTH!

AND IN ANOTHER COUNTRY.....

SOMEBODY STARTED AN ATOMIC WAR! WE DON'T CARE WHO! BUT THIS IS OUR CHANCE TO NOW WIPE OUT OUR AGE-OLD ENEMY TO THE WEST! LAUNCH AN ATOMIC WAR ON *THEM*!

AND SO, AS GREED, CONFUSION AND MADNESS SWEEP THROUGH THE WORLD, ALL NATIONS RELEASE THEIR ATOMIC BOMBS AT EACH OTHER! AND BY NIGHTFALL, THE DREAD TRUTH COMES TO CAPTAIN MARVEL!

HOLY MOLEY! THE ATOMIC BOMBS ARE GETTING THICKER AND THICKER! EVERY COUNTRY IS SENDING THEM--- *EVERYWHERE!* STOP, YOU FOOLS-- STOP--!

BOOM

THE WORLD HAS GONE MAD! OH THE POOR BLIND FOOLS! THIS CAN ONLY END IN ONE WAY! IS IT THE SAME ALL OVER THE WHOLE EARTH?

CIRCLING THE WORLD, CAPTAIN MARVEL'S BLOOD FREEZES IN HIS VEINS!

HERE TOO! *GROAN!* THE ATOMIC BOMBS ARE COMING FROM EVERYWHERE, AND HITTING EVERYWHERE!

BOOM

THIS IS HORRIBLE! AND I CAN'T STOP IT! BY NOW EVERY MAJOR CITY ON EARTH IS BOMBED! AND LATER, THE RADIOACTIVE RAYS WILL SPREAD OUT, LIKE A CREEPING PLAGUE AND.... *GROAN!*

ZOOM!

TWENTY FOUR HOURS LATER, AN OMINOUS QUIET COMES OVER THE WORLD!

I HAVEN'T HEARD A SINGLE BLAST IN AN HOUR! HOW DID AMERICA COME OUT? I KNOW ALL THE CITIES ARE GONE, BUT HOW ABOUT THIS FARMHOUSE?

DEAD! ALL DEAD---EVEN THE ANIMALS! RADIOACTIVE RAYS CAME EVEN OUT TO THE REMOTEST FARMS AND VILLAGES!

IT MUST BE THE SAME ALL OVER EARTH! THE ATOMIC BOMBS DESTROYED ALL CITIES! AND THE RADIOACTIVE RAYS KILLED ALL THE OTHER PEOPLE OUTSIDE OF CITIES! EVEN IN THE DEEPEST DUG-OUTS OR CAVES!

EVERYONE DIED IN THIS ATOMIC WAR! I'M---I'M **THE ONLY MAN LEFT ALIVE!**

YES, IT'S THE HORRIBLE TRUTH! **I'M THE ONLY MAN LEFT ALIVE ON EARTH!**

WELL, FOLKS! TAKE A DEEP BREATH AND RELAX! AS YOU ALL KNOW, THIS IS ONLY A TELEVISION BROADCAST FROM STATION WHIZ! WE TRIED OUR BEST TO SHOW YOU WHAT AN ATOMIC WAR WOULD BE LIKE, IF IT EVER CAME!

WE WERE HANDICAPPED BY STUDIO LIMITATIONS! SHOWING THE HORRORS OF AN ATOMIC WAR! THE ATOMIC WAR ITSELF WOULD BE **MUCH WORSE!** GOODBYE, NOW!

GOSH!

GOLLY, DAD! IF AN ATOMIC WAR WOULD BE EVEN WORSE THAN THEY JUST SHOWED, WE'D BETTER NOT HAVE ONE!

RIGHT, SIS! I'M THANKFUL STATION WHIZ PUT THAT TELEVISION PROGRAM ON! IT TEACHES ALL OF US A LESSON!

THE WORLD JUST **CAN'T AFFORD** TO HAVE ANOTHER WAR, BECAUSE IT WOULD WIPE OUT ALL CIVILIZATION AND ALL HUMAN LIFE! *REMEMBER THAT, KIDS!*

GULP! WE SURE WILL!

I GUESS WE'D ALL BETTER LEARN TO LIVE AND GET ALONG TOGETHER --- ONE NATION WITH ALL OTHER NATIONS AND ONE PERSON WITH ALL OTHER PERSONS --- SO THAT THE TERRIBLE ATOMIC WAR WILL NEVER OCCUR!

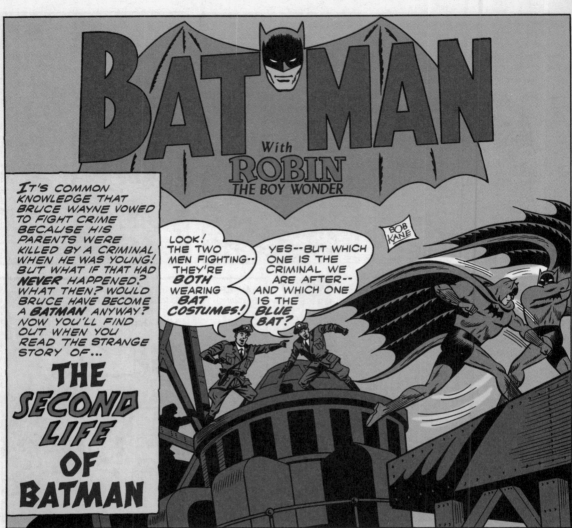

BATMAN
With
ROBIN
THE BOY WONDER

BOB KANE

IT'S COMMON KNOWLEDGE THAT BRUCE WAYNE VOWED TO FIGHT CRIME BECAUSE HIS PARENTS WERE KILLED BY A CRIMINAL WHEN HE WAS YOUNG! BUT WHAT IF THAT HAD *NEVER* HAPPENED? WHAT THEN? WOULD BRUCE HAVE BECOME A *BATMAN* ANYWAY? NOW YOU'LL FIND OUT WHEN YOU READ THE STRANGE STORY OF...

THE SECOND LIFE OF BATMAN

LOOK! THE TWO MEN FIGHTING-- THEY'RE *BOTH* WEARING *BAT* COSTUMES!

YES--BUT WHICH ONE IS THE CRIMINAL WE ARE AFTER-- AND WHICH ONE IS THE *BLUE BAT*?

ONE NIGHT, IN THE MANSION OF SOCIALITE BRUCE WAYNE AND HIS WARD, DICK GRAYSON-- WHO ARE SECRETLY *BATMAN* AND *ROBIN*...

BRUCE, I WONDER WHY YOUR OLD FRIEND PROF. NICHOLS WANTS US TO VISIT HIM TONIGHT?

HE PROBABLY HAS A NEW INVENTION TO SHOW US! I WONDER WHAT IT WILL BE THIS TIME?

LATER, IN PROF. NICHOLS' LABORATORY...

BRUCE, HAVE YOU EVER WONDERED WHAT PATH YOUR LIFE *MIGHT* HAVE TAKEN--IF YOU WERE *NOT* AFFECTED BY SOMETHING THAT HAPPENED TO YOU WHEN YOU WERE YOUNGER?

I'VE THOUGHT ABOUT IT MANY TIMES-- BUT I'LL NEVER KNOW!

BUT YOU *WILL* KNOW--RIGHT NOW! PUT THIS ON AND CONCENTRATE--THINK OF THE EVENT THAT INFLUENCED YOUR LIFE--THINK THAT IT *NEVER HAPPENED*--AND MY INVENTION WILL REVEAL TO YOUR MIND'S EYE THE LIFE YOU *MIGHT* HAVE HAD!

I DECIDED TO BECOME A CRIME-FIGHTER WHEN I WAS A YOUNGSTER--WHEN I SAW MY PARENTS SHOT BY A CRIMINAL! BUT WHAT IF THAT HAD *NEVER* HAPPENED...?

ABRUPTLY, THE PAST LOOMS BEFORE BRUCE--THE PAST *THAT MIGHT HAVE BEEN*...

...DEPICTING BRUCE AS A YOUNG MAN, RECEIVING FRIENDS IN HIS HOME...

BRUCE, I SUPPOSE YOU'LL BE AT THE COSTUME BALL TO HONOR THE OPENING OF THE NEW METROPOLIS AIRPORT! WE'RE ALL TO WEAR COSTUMES THAT REPRESENT FLYING CREATURES!

I KNOW! AND WON'T YOU BE SURPRISED WHEN YOU SEE *MY* COSTUME!

NEXT NIGHT, AT THE UNIQUE BALL GIVEN AT THE AIRPORT...

BRUCE HASN'T ARRIVED YET! I WONDER WHAT KIND OF FLYING CREATURE HE'S COMING AS?

LOOK--HERE'S BRUCE WAYNE--AS *SUPERMAN!* WELL, *SUPERMAN DOES* FLY! HA, HA!

I THINK IT'S A DISGRACE THAT A FRIVOLOUS PERSON LIKE BRUCE SHOULD COME AS *SUPERMAN!* EVER SINCE BRUCE'S PARENTS DIED IN THE AUTO CRASH LAST YEAR, HE'S DONE NOTHING BUT IDLE IN NIGHT CLUBS!

OHH--IT'S THE *BLUE BAT*, THE CRIMINAL WHO'S BECOME THE HEAD OF THE UNDERWORLD!

SUDDENLY...

HOLD IT, EVERYBODY! JUST GIVE YOUR MONEY AND YOUR JEWELS TO MY MEN AND NOBODY WILL GET HURT!

THIS THEN *MIGHT HAVE BEEN* THE ORIGIN OF THE BAT-COSTUME--A DISGUISE TO HIDE THE SECRET IDENTITY OF A *CRIMINAL!*

2

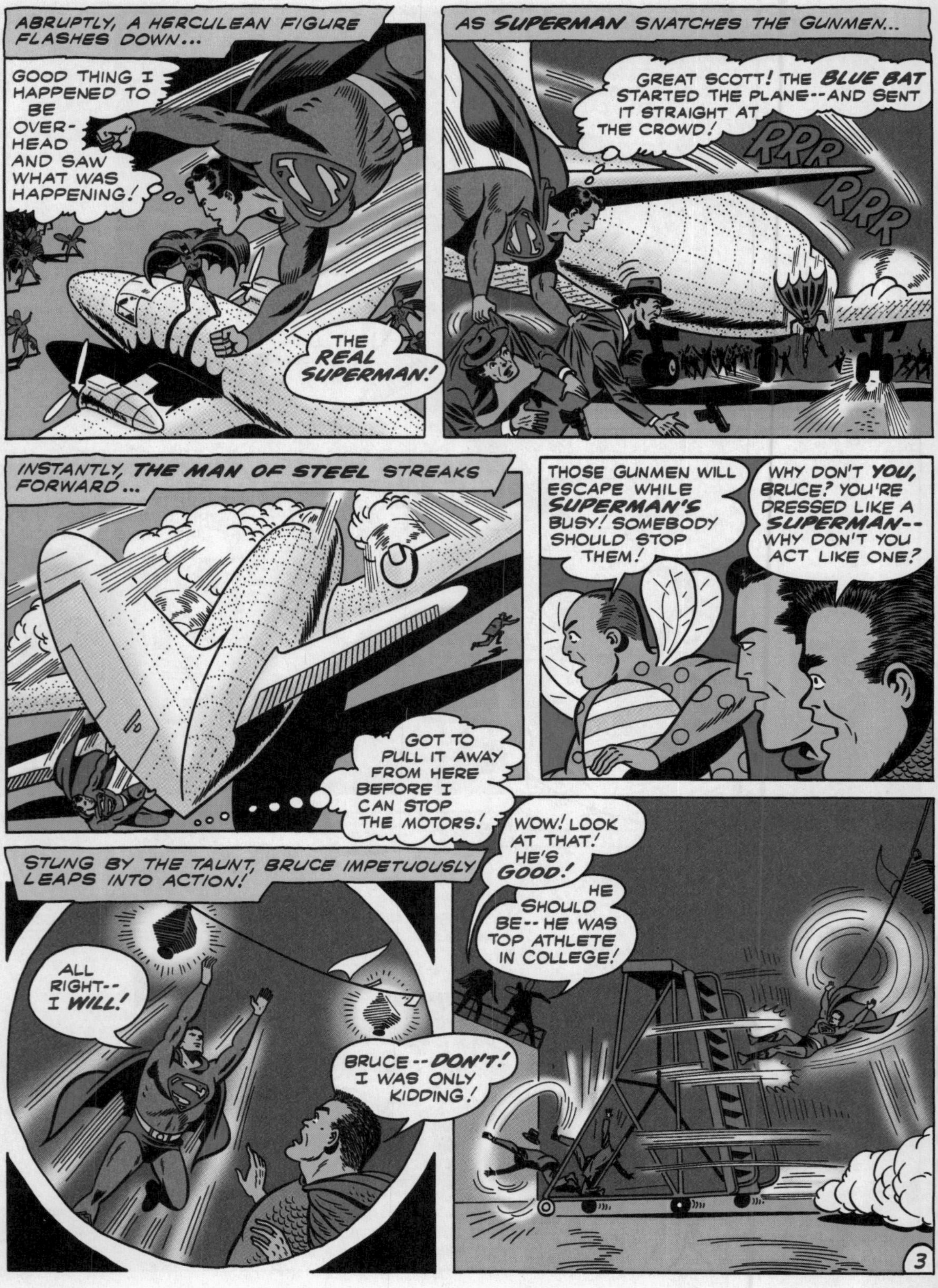
ABRUPTLY, A HERCULEAN FIGURE FLASHES DOWN...
GOOD THING I HAPPENED TO BE OVER-HEAD AND SAW WHAT WAS HAPPENING!
THE REAL SUPERMAN!
AS SUPERMAN SNATCHES THE GUNMEN...
GREAT SCOTT! THE BLUE BAT STARTED THE PLANE--AND SENT IT STRAIGHT AT THE CROWD!
RRR
RRR
INSTANTLY, THE MAN OF STEEL STREAKS FORWARD...
GOT TO PULL IT AWAY FROM HERE BEFORE I CAN STOP THE MOTORS!
THOSE GUNMEN WILL ESCAPE WHILE SUPERMAN'S BUSY! SOMEBODY SHOULD STOP THEM!
WHY DON'T YOU, BRUCE? YOU'RE DRESSED LIKE A SUPERMAN--WHY DON'T YOU ACT LIKE ONE?
STUNG BY THE TAUNT, BRUCE IMPETUOUSLY LEAPS INTO ACTION!
ALL RIGHT--I WILL!
BRUCE--DON'T! I WAS ONLY KIDDING!
WOW! LOOK AT THAT! HE'S GOOD!
HE SHOULD BE--HE WAS TOP ATHLETE IN COLLEGE!
3

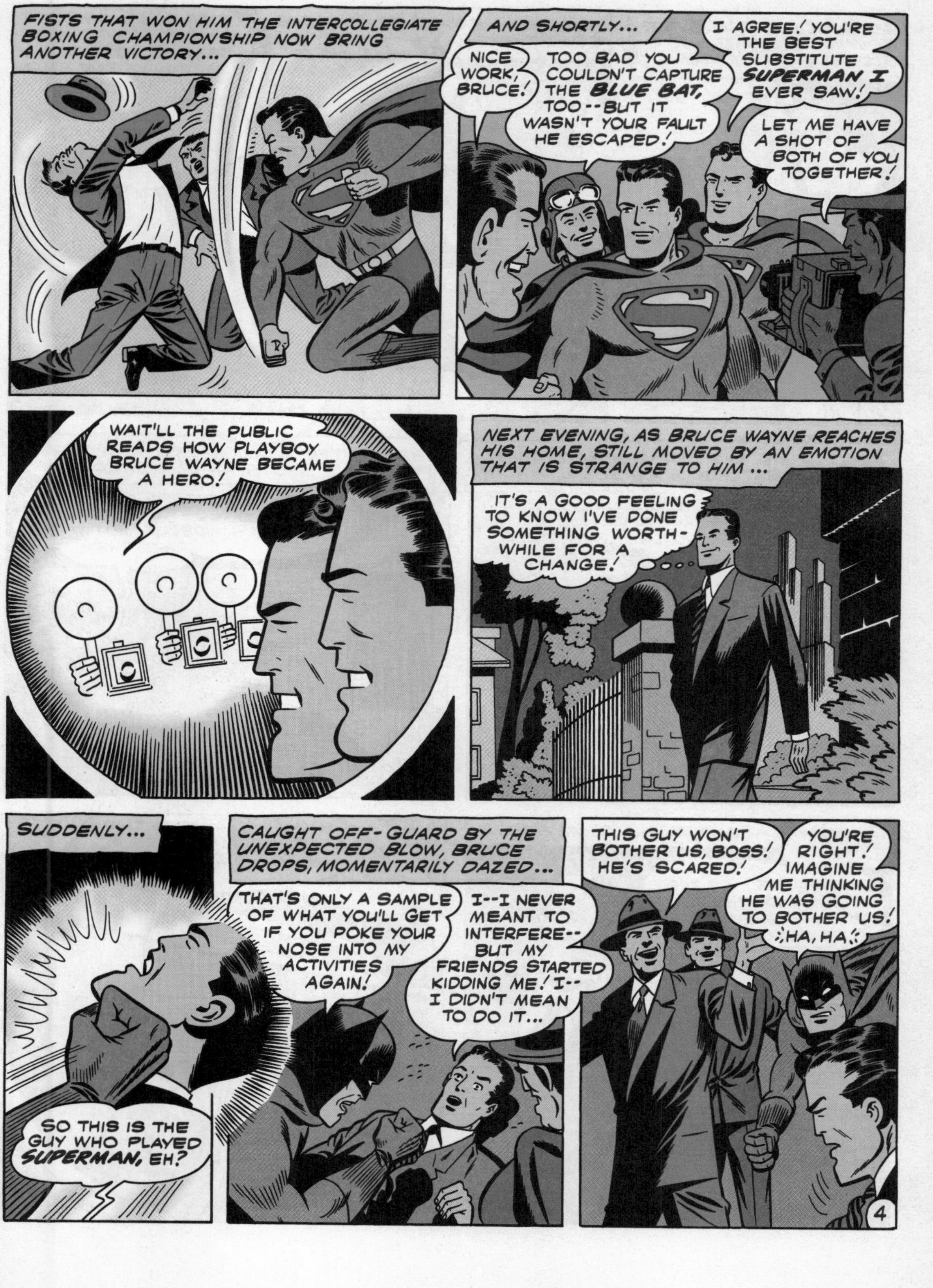
FISTS THAT WON HIM THE INTERCOLLEGIATE BOXING CHAMPIONSHIP NOW BRING ANOTHER VICTORY...
AND SHORTLY...
NICE WORK, BRUCE!
TOO BAD YOU COULDN'T CAPTURE THE BLUE BAT, TOO--BUT IT WASN'T YOUR FAULT HE ESCAPED!
I AGREE! YOU'RE THE BEST SUBSTITUTE SUPERMAN I EVER SAW!
LET ME HAVE A SHOT OF BOTH OF YOU TOGETHER!
WAIT'LL THE PUBLIC READS HOW PLAYBOY BRUCE WAYNE BECAME A HERO!
NEXT EVENING, AS BRUCE WAYNE REACHES HIS HOME, STILL MOVED BY AN EMOTION THAT IS STRANGE TO HIM...
IT'S A GOOD FEELING TO KNOW I'VE DONE SOMETHING WORTH-WHILE FOR A CHANGE!
SUDDENLY...
SO THIS IS THE GUY WHO PLAYED SUPERMAN, EH?
CAUGHT OFF-GUARD BY THE UNEXPECTED BLOW, BRUCE DROPS, MOMENTARILY DAZED...
THAT'S ONLY A SAMPLE OF WHAT YOU'LL GET IF YOU POKE YOUR NOSE INTO MY ACTIVITIES AGAIN!
I--I NEVER MEANT TO INTERFERE--BUT MY FRIENDS STARTED KIDDING ME! I--I DIDN'T MEAN TO DO IT...
THIS GUY WON'T BOTHER US, BOSS! HE'S SCARED!
YOU'RE RIGHT! IMAGINE ME THINKING HE WAS GOING TO BOTHER US! HA, HA!
4

AS BRUCE WATCHES THE CRIMINALS LEAVE, HE GLOWERS WITH RAGE...

"SCARED," EH? IF ONLY THERE WERE SOME WAY I COULD FIND THE BLUE BAT'S HIDEOUT, I'D BREAK UP HIS MOB-- SINGLE-HANDED!

SUDDENLY, BRUCE REMEMBERS SOMETHING ...

WHEN ONE OF THOSE THUGS WALKED AWAY, SOME SAND SPILLED OUT OF HIS TROUSER CUFF!

FINE SAND MIXED WITH COARSE GRAVEL! MOST BEACHES AROUND HERE HAVE FINE SAND ONLY! THIS MIXTURE MIGHT HAVE COME FROM ROCKY POINT, WHERE THERE ARE HIGH BREAKERS! HMM!

FEELING HIS WAR WITH THE BLUE BAT HAS NOW BECOME A PERSONAL MATTER, BRUCE RUSHES TO HIS GARAGE...

I'LL REMOVE THIS SPECIAL COUNTRY CLUB INSIGNIA WHICH WOULD QUICKLY IDENTIFY ME! I WANT TO HANDLE THE BLUE BAT MYSELF-- BUT I DON'T WANT ANY PUBLICITY AGAIN!

THEN, AFTER A QUICK RIDE TO ROCKY POINT, HE SPOTS AN OLD SHED...

EMPTY! BUT THERE'S A SPARE BLUE BAT COSTUME! THIS IS THE MOB'S HIDEOUT! BUT WHERE ARE THEY?

GLANCING ABOUT FOR A CLUE, BRUCE FINDS...

A DRAWING -- OF THE INTERIOR OF THE NEW DAM BEING BUILT OUTSIDE TOWN! THEY MUST BE PLANNING TO ROB THE HUGE PAYROLL!

HMM! I'VE AN IDEA THIS COSTUME MAY COME IN HANDY--IF I WEAR IT!

5

GARBED AS THE *BLUE BAT*, BRUCE SPEEDS ALONG THE HIGHWAY WHEN HE SPOTS...

HIGHWAY POLICE! I THINK *I'LL LET THEM SEE ME* IN THIS COSTUME!

LOOK -- THE *BLUE BAT!* AFTER HIM!

IT WORKED! THEY'RE FOLLOWING ME AS I HOPED! NOW I'LL PUT ON SOME SPEED -- SO THEY CAN'T CATCH UP TO ME UNTIL *AFTER* I REACH THE *BLUE BAT!*

REACHING THE DAM, BRUCE RACES INTO THE GENERATOR ROOM AND SIGHTS HIS QUARRY...

THEY'RE CROSSING OVER THE GENERATORS-- SO THEY WON'T BE SEEN WHEN THEY COME DOWN ON THE OTHER SIDE TO THE PAYROLL ROOM! HMM-- I'VE AN IDEA THAT MAY JUST WORK...

DARTING UP THE STAIRS, THE DISGUISED BRUCE SUDDENLY CONFRONTS THE ONCOMING BANDITS...

HOLD IT, YOU TWO! THAT GUY BEHIND YOU IS PLAYING YOU FOR A CHUMP! HE'S A COP-- LEADING YOU INTO A TRAP! I'M THE *REAL BLUE BAT!*

HEARING APPROACHING FOOTSTEPS, BRUCE MAKES HIS MOVE!

YOU FOOLS! DON'T LISTEN TO HIM! HE'S TRYING TO TRICK YOU! I'M THE *REAL BLUE BAT!*

HOW CAN WE TELL? BOTH OF YOU LOOK LIKE TWINS!

THE POLICE HAVE ARRIVED! I'VE STALLED THE *BLUE BAT'S* MEN LONG ENOUGH!

6

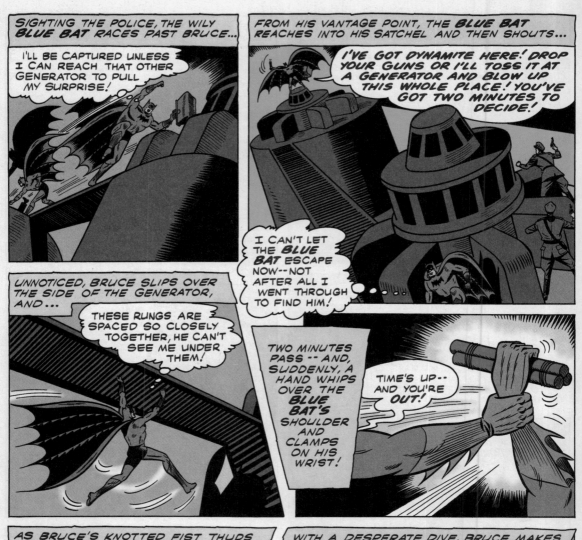

SIGHTING THE POLICE, THE WILY *BLUE BAT* RACES PAST BRUCE...

I'LL BE CAPTURED UNLESS I CAN REACH THAT OTHER GENERATOR TO PULL MY SURPRISE!

FROM HIS VANTAGE POINT, THE *BLUE BAT* REACHES INTO HIS SATCHEL AND THEN SHOUTS...

I'VE GOT DYNAMITE HERE! DROP YOUR GUNS OR I'LL TOSS IT AT A GENERATOR AND BLOW UP THIS WHOLE PLACE! YOU'VE GOT TWO MINUTES TO DECIDE!

I CAN'T LET THE *BLUE BAT* ESCAPE NOW--NOT AFTER ALL I WENT THROUGH TO FIND HIM!

UNNOTICED, BRUCE SLIPS OVER THE SIDE OF THE GENERATOR, AND...

THESE RUNGS ARE SPACED SO CLOSELY TOGETHER, HE CAN'T SEE ME UNDER THEM!

TWO MINUTES PASS -- AND, SUDDENLY, A HAND WHIPS OVER THE *BLUE BAT'S* SHOULDER AND CLAMPS ON HIS WRIST!

TIME'S UP-- AND YOU'RE OUT!

AS BRUCE'S KNOTTED FIST THUDS AGAINST THE *BLUE BAT'S* JAW...

GREAT SCOTT! THE DYNAMITE-- IT *DROPPED* BEFORE I COULD GRAB IT!

WITH A DESPERATE DIVE, BRUCE MAKES A STABBING REACH FOR THE DEADLY EXPLOSIVE...

PHEW! FOR A MINUTE, I THOUGHT I'D NEVER SEE MY NEXT BIRTHDAY!

7

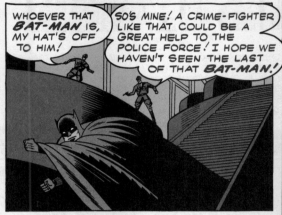
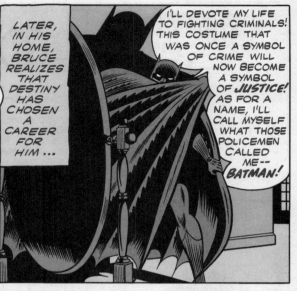

THEN, HIS PERSONAL FEUD FINISHED, THE DISGUISED BRUCE RACES AWAY BEFORE THE POLICE CAN QUESTION HIM...

WHOEVER THAT *BAT-MAN* IS, MY HAT'S OFF TO HIM!

SO'S MINE! A CRIME-FIGHTER LIKE THAT COULD BE A GREAT HELP TO THE POLICE FORCE! I HOPE WE HAVEN'T SEEN THE LAST OF THAT *BAT-MAN!*

LATER, IN HIS HOME, BRUCE REALIZES THAT DESTINY HAS CHOSEN A CAREER FOR HIM ...

I'LL DEVOTE MY LIFE TO FIGHTING CRIMINALS! THIS COSTUME THAT WAS ONCE A SYMBOL OF CRIME WILL NOW BECOME A SYMBOL OF *JUSTICE!* AS FOR A NAME, I'LL CALL MYSELF WHAT THOSE POLICEMEN CALLED ME-- *BATMAN!*

THEN THE PAST *THAT MIGHT HAVE BEEN* FADES -- AND THE BRUCE OF TODAY STARES THOUGHTFULLY INTO SPACE...

WELL--DO YOU KNOW THE TRUTH NOW? WHAT DID YOU SEE?

I--I SAW THAT ALTHOUGH THE CIRCUMSTANCES WERE ALTERED, DESTINY WOULD HAVE STILL CHOSEN THE SAME LIFE FOR ME!

LATER, AFTER LEAVING PROF. NICHOLS, BRUCE TELLS DICK WHAT HE SAW...

GOLLY-- SO EVEN IF YOUR PARENTS WEREN'T KILLED BY A CRIMINAL, YOU'D HAVE BECOME A CRIME-FIGHTER ANYWAY!

YES, DICK--THAT'S THE WAY IT WOULD BE! THERE'D ALWAYS BE A *BATMAN!*

8 THE END

A LOOK AT OTHER GREAT IMAGINARY STORIES

ACTION COMICS #332, 1966
art by Curt Swan & Sheldon Maldoff

JIMMY OLSEN #56, 1961
art by Curt Swan & John Forte

SUPERMAN'S GIRL FRIEND LOIS LANE

FIRST of an IMAGINARY SERIES

HERE IT IS AT LAST...WHAT THOUSANDS OF READERS HAVE WRITTEN IN CLAMORING FOR...AN *IMAGINARY* STORY SHOWING HOW THINGS WOULD BE IF LOIS LANE LEARNED CLARK KENT WERE *SUPERMAN* AND MARRIED HIM! THIS IS ONLY THE FIRST OF MANY SUCH TALES WHICH COULD VERY WELL HAPPEN IN THE FUTURE LIVES OF LOIS LANE AND *SUPERMAN*, BUT PERHAPS NEVER WILL! THE FIRST ADVENTURE IN THIS UNUSUAL SERIES CONCERNING THE MOST FANTASTIC MARRIAGE OF ALL TIME... (WHICH MAY *NEVER* TAKE PLACE, REMEMBER!)...IS ENTITLED...

MR. and MRS. CLARK (SUPERMAN) KENT!

HURRY HOME, DEAR, SUPPER WILL BE READY EARLY TONIGHT!

WOULD OUR NEIGHBORS BE ASTOUNDED IF THEY KNEW MY HUSBAND, CLARK, IS LEAVING OUR HOME THROUGH A SECRET TUNNEL, AS... *SUPERMAN*!

EARLY ONE SUNDAY MORNING IN *METROPOLIS*, SEVERAL YEARS HENCE, ON A DAY THAT *MAY OR MAY NOT* EVER HAPPEN...IN THE SUBURBAN HOME OF MR. AND MRS. CLARK KENT, LOIS KENT AWAKENS...

HE'S STILL SOUND ASLEEP, THE DARLING! I'LL GO MAKE BREAKFAST FOR HIM BEFORE HE AWAKENS!

SOON, IN THE KITCHEN... TO THINK I ONCE CONSIDERED CLARK KENT SOMETHING OF A PEST, LITTLE REALIZING HE WAS SECRETLY THE MIGHTY MAN I ADORED, *SUPERMAN*!

BACK DRIFT LOIS' THOUGHTS, BACK TO THE FATEFUL DAY CLARK HAD PROPOSED...

PLEASE MARRY ME, LOIS!

I CAN'T CLARK! THERE'S SOMEONE ELSE I LOVE, EVEN THOUGH HE MAY NEVER PROPOSE! IT'S...SUPERMAN!

BEFORE LOIS' AMAZED EYES, CLARK HAD PERFORMED AN ASTONISHING TRANSFORMATION...

CLARK KENT... REALLY SUPERMAN! OH, NO, I... I CAN'T BELIEVE IT!

IF YOU STILL WANT ME, THE ANSWER IS YES! BUT WHY DID YOU WAIT SO LONG TO PROPOSE?

I FEARED THAT IF I MARRIED YOU, MY ENEMIES WOULD SEEK TO STRIKE AT ME BY HARMING YOU! BUT I'VE THOUGHT OF A SOLUTION...

AS FAR AS THE WORLD WILL KNOW, YOU'LL BE MARRYING MEEK, MILD CLARK KENT! YOU ALONE WILL SHARE THE SECRET OF MY REAL IDENTITY! THAT WAY YOUR LIFE WILL REMAIN SAFE!

AND SO THEY WERE MARRIED...

POOR THING! SHE'S MARRYING CLARK KENT BECAUSE SHE COULDN'T LAND SUPERMAN!

I HEARD THAT! BUT I DON'T CARE WHAT PEOPLE THINK, AS LONG AS I HAVE SUPERMAN FOR A HUSBAND...EVEN IF THE WORLD DOES BELIEVE HE'S CLARK KENT!

SUDDENLY, LOIS' THOUGHTS RETURN TO THE PRESENT AS MIGHTY ARMS UNEXPECTEDLY SPIN HER ABOUT AND HOLD HER IN A GENTLE GRIP...

HIS ARMS ARE MORE POWERFUL THAN A LOCOMOTIVE...BUT HE HOLDS ME SO GENTLY! OH, HE'S WONDERFUL... WONDERFUL... ≈ SIGH ≈...

2

AFTER BREAKFAST, AS THE TELEPHONE RINGS...

YES, PERRY, I'LL GET WORD TO *SUPERMAN* RIGHT AWAY ABOUT THE EMERGENCY! THANKS FOR CALLING!

AS CLARK CHANGES TO *SUPERMAN*...

DOESN'T PERRY WHITE EVER TAKE A DAY OFF? WHAT EMERGENCY WAS HE TALKING ABOUT, HONEY?

THE CARLYLE OIL FIELD IS ABLAZE! I CAN SEE IT NOW, WITH MY TELESCOPIC VISION! THIS IS A JOB FOR *SUPERMAN!*

SOON, LOIS' DYNAMIC *HUSBAND OF STEEL* ENTERS THE SECRET TUNNEL EXIT IN THEIR HOME...

THAT OIL PROPERTY BELONGS TO OUR RICH NEIGHBORS, THE CARLYLES!

THERE ARE SOME OTHER TASKS I MUST DO, TOO, LOIS, SO DON'T EXPECT ME BACK UNTIL SUPPER-TIME! GOOD-BYE, DEAR!

A SPLIT-INSTANT LATER, *SUPERMAN* FLASHES OUT OF A DISTANT WOODS, AND UP INTO THE SKIES...

YEARS AGO, IN SMALL-VILLE, A SECRET TUNNEL LIKE THIS KEPT PEOPLE FROM LEARNING THAT *SUPERBOY* LIVED WITH MA AND PA KENT AS THEIR SON, CLARK KENT! NOW A SIMILAR TUNNEL HELPS KEEP PEOPLE FROM LEARNING THAT I'M MARRIED TO LOIS!

MOMENTS LATER, AT THE OIL FIELD...

SUPERMAN IS CAPPING THE BLAZING OIL VENT WITH HIS BARE HANDS, DESPITE THE FLAMES!

HE'S SHUTTING OFF THE OXYGEN SUPPLY, SO THE OIL WILL STOP BURNING!

HE PUT THE BLAZE OUT, AND NOW HE'S GOING TO DO THE SAME TO THE OTHER FLAMING WELLS! WHAT A MAN!

I'LL HAVE THINGS UNDER CONTROL HERE IN A JIFFY! THEN I'LL GET ON WITH MY OTHER TASKS!

3

MEANWHILE, IN THE KENT RESIDENCE...

NEWS BULLETIN! SUPER-MAN JUST EXTINGUISHED THE FIRES AT THE CARLYLE OIL FIELD!

THAT'S MY HUSBAND THEY'RE TALKING ABOUT! I'M SO PROUD!

STROLLING, LOIS ENCOUNTERS A NEIGHBOR...

THEY'RE TAKING MY HUSBAND'S LATEST PAINTING TO THE METROPOLIS ART GALLERY WHERE IT WILL BE THE CHIEF EXHIBIT! I'M SO PROUD OF MY HUSBAND!

HOW NICE, MRS. TALBOT!

HER ATTITUDE IS THAT MY HUSBAND IS A NOBODY! GOODNESS, BUT I'D LOVE TO TELL HER THAT MY SUPERMAN CAN DO PRACTICALLY ANYTHING SUPERBLY!

AND AS LOIS WALKS ON...

THAT'S MY HUSBAND, JOHN, RETURNING FROM WASHINGTON, WHERE HE HAD A CONFERENCE WITH THE PRESIDENT! POLITICS IS SO DEMANDING!

BIG DEAL! MY HUSBAND HOBNOBS WITH BIG-SHOTS ALL OVER THE UNIVERSE, SO THERE! BUT CAN I TELL ANYBODY ABOUT IT? NO!

URR, RRRRRRRR

FINALLY, AS LOIS SPEAKS TO ANOTHER NEIGHBOR...

EXCUSE ME, LOIS! I HAVE A VISITOR!

IT'S MRS. WINTHROP CARLYLE, THE RICHEST WOMAN AROUND HERE, AND A BIG WHEEL ON THE TOWN COUNCIL!

WHAT A MORNING! MY HUSBAND'S OIL WELLS WERE ALMOST DESTROYED, AND I'VE BEEN SO BUSY INVITING THE TOWN'S TEN BEST COUPLES TO THE TOWN COUNCIL DANCE! PLEASE COME!

WE'LL GO--WHY NOT INVITE OUR NEW NEIGHBORS, THE KENTS, TOO? THIS IS MRS. KENT!

I'M SORRY, BUT I CAN INVITE...ER...ONLY IMPORTANT PEOPLE! YOUR HUSBAND IS JUST A NEWSPAPERMAN, ISN'T HE, MRS. KENT? YOU CAN SEE WHY I CAN'T POSSIBLY...

WE WOULDN'T GO IF YOU BEGGED!

YOU SNOB! IF MY HUSBAND HADN'T SAVED YOUR HUSBAND'S OIL WELLS, YOU'D BE WIPED OUT!

4

LATER, WHEN **SUPERMAN** RETURNS HOME THROUGH THE SECRET TUNNEL...

GREAT GUNS! WHAT'S GOING ON HERE?

¿SOB¿...I-I'M SO SIZZLING MAD, I RUINED THE MEAL, AND B-BURNT MY FINGER... ¿SOB¿...

¿SOB¿...SOME OF THE NEIGHBORHOOD WOMEN THINK THEY'RE SO GRAND! THEIR HUSBANDS ARE SO BRILLIANT, SO CLEVER, *THEY* SAY! THOSE WITCHES PRACTICALLY CAME RIGHT OUT AND TOLD ME I MARRIED A CREEP!... ¿SOB¿...

¿SOB¿...NO ONE IS MORE WONDERFUL THAN *YOU!* I'VE GOT THE WORLD'S SWEETEST, SMARTEST, STRONGEST MAN...¿SOB¿...BUT THE TROUBLE IS...¿SOB¿ *NOBODY KNOWS IT...* ¿SOB¿...

AW, PLEASE DON'T CRY, HONEY! I WANT THE WHOLE WORLD TO KNOW I MARRIED A WONDERFUL GIRL...BUT WE CAN'T RISK GETTING YOU KILLED...

COME ON, BE BRAVE! LET'S SEE A SMILE! EVEN A LITTLE ONE! SMILE, IF YOU WANT A SUPER- KISS...

¿SNIFF¿

WHAT DO I CARE WHAT OTHER PEOPLE THINK? I'VE GOT A MARVELOUS HUSBAND, AND I'M THE L-LUCKIEST GIRL ON EARTH!

AND DON'T WORRY YOUR PRETTY LITTLE HEAD ABOUT MAKING LUNCH! HERE ARE SOME HAMBURGERS FRIED BY MY X-RAY VISION!

STOP BEING SO DARNED SWEET, OR YOU'LL MAKE ME BAWL AGAIN...

5

NEXT MORNING, AT THE *DAILY PLANET*, WHERE LOIS STILL WORKS...

CLARK MUST HAVE SEEN SOMETHING ON THE TELETYPE THAT REQUIRED HIM TO GO INTO ACTION AS *SUPERMAN!* HE'S CLEANING HIS GLASSES...IT'S THE PREARRANGED SIGNAL THAT HE WANTS ME TO HELP HIM GET AWAY...

SHORTLY, AFTER LOIS PLACES SOME MICROFILMS IN THE NEWSPAPER'S STORAGE VAULT...

NOW TO GO INTO MY ACT SO CLARK CAN SWITCH TO *SUPERMAN!*

HELP! CLARK IS LOCKED IN! I ABSENT-MINDEDLY CLOSED AND LOCKED THE DOOR WHILE HE WAS INSIDE! THE TIME-CLOCK WON'T OPEN FOR AN HOUR! HE'LL SUFFOCATE!

RELAX, LOIS! THERE'S ENOUGH AIR IN THERE FOR HIM UNTIL THE SAFE OPENS!

MEANWHILE, CLARK, WHO HAD NEVER ENTERED THE VAULT, SWIFTLY FLIES TO A SOUTH SEA ISLAND AS *SUPERMAN*...

THE TELETYPED NEWS ITEM WAS CORRECT! THAT ISLAND IS BEGINNING TO SINK INTO THE SEA DUE TO AN EARTHQUAKE!

RAPIDLY BUILDING A GIANT RAFT OUT OF TREES, *SUPERMAN* EVACUATES THE ISLAND'S INHABITANTS BARELY IN TIME...

THERE IT GOES, UNDERWATER! I'LL TAKE THESE PEOPLE TO ANOTHER ISLAND AND BUILD NEW HOMES FOR THEM!

LATER, AS THE TIME-LOCK PERMITS THE *DAILY PLANET'S* STORAGE-VAULT DOOR TO OPEN...

I'M WHIZZING PAST THEM SO SWIFTLY, THEY DON'T SEE ME! NEXT, I'LL QUICKLY CHANGE BACK TO CLARK KENT!

And so...

I'M TERRIBLY SORRY I ACCIDENTALLY LOCKED YOU IN, DEAR!

OH-HHH, MY NERVES!

HOW IRONIC! I USED TO TRICK LOIS AS CLARK, IN ORDER TO GET AWAY INTO ACTION AS *SUPERMAN!* NOW SHE HELPS ME FOOL OTHERS, FOR THE VERY SAME PURPOSE!

6

Panel 1: THAT EVENING, WHILE CLARK AND LOIS WAIT FOR HER SISTER LUCY TO REACH THEIR HOME...

I JUST *LOVE* THIS GORGEOUS *CHAMELEON DRESS* YOU BROUGHT TO ME FROM ANOTHER WORLD!

ITS COLORS CHANGE, DEPENDING ON THE MOOD OF WHOEVER WEARS OR TOUCHES IT! RIGHT NOW IT'S *BLUE*, REFLECTING YOUR HAPPINESS!

Panel 2: HA! I WISH SOME OF THOSE SNOOTY NEIGHBORS COULD SEE ME IN THIS FABULOUS GOWN!

I WISH I COULD OPENLY RAVE ABOUT YOU, THE WAY THE OTHER WOMEN BOAST ABOUT *THEIR* HUSBANDS!

NOW YOUR DRESS IS *RED* BECAUSE YOU'RE *ANGRY!*

AND NOW THE DRESS IS *GREEN...* THE COLOR OF *ENVY!* BETTER REMOVE THE DRESS BEFORE LUCY ARRIVES!

Panel 3: LATER, AS LOIS SHOWS HER SISTER SOME OF HER CLOTHES...

OH, I SIMPLY ADORE *THAT* ONE! LET ME HOLD IT BEFORE ME!

ULP! I TOOK THE *CHAMELEON DRESS* OUT OF THE CLOSET BY MISTAKE! IF LUCY TOUCHES IT, IT WILL CHANGE COLOR AND SHE'LL KNOW IT'S FROM ANOTHER WORLD!

Panel 4: RELUCTANTLY, LOIS SACRIFICES HER FAVORITE GOWN...

YOU'RE TOSSING IT IN THE FIREPLACE! *WHY?!*

IT'S JUST AN OLD RAG I DON'T WANT ANYMORE!

I COULDN'T SAY IT WAS A GIFT FROM *SUPERMAN*, OR LUCY MIGHT HAVE BEGUN TO SUSPECT CLARK MIGHT BE THE *MAN OF STEEL!*

Panel 5: LATER, AFTER AN ENJOYABLE COOK-OUT...

I'VE GOT TO LEAVE FOR SOME VERY IMPORTANT BUSINESS! HAVE FUN, GIRLS!

LUCY AND I WILL PROBABLY GO SEE A MOVIE!

Panel 6: WHEN THE TWO GIRLS ARE ALONE...

I'M GLAD YOU AND CLARK GET ALONG SO WELL! FRANKLY, I THOUGHT YOU'D NEVER GET OVER YOUR CRUSH ON *SUPERMAN...*

CLARK AND I ARE VERY HAPPY!

BECAUSE *HE IS SUPERMAN!* OH, WHAT A SHAME I CAN'T EVEN LET MY OWN SISTER IN ON THE SECRET!

⑦

Later...

TODAY ONLY HOLLYWOOD STAR, GLORIA LAMOUR, IN PERSON! ALSO APPEARING SUPERMAN

GLORIA "FORB

SUPERMAN IN PERSON! LET'S GO IN!

IT'S NO COINCIDENCE, OUR COMING HERE! I THOUGHT I'D CHECK ON MY HUSBAND'S VERY IMPORTANT BUSINESS!

SOON, IN THE THEATER LOBBY...

MISS LAMOUR, IT'S A PLEASURE TO PRESENT THIS PLAQUE TO YOU ON BEHALF OF *METROPOLIS'* THEATER OWNERS FOR YOUR PERFORMANCES IN MANY FINE MOVIES!

OH, THANK YOU!

SMACK

÷GROAN!÷...SHE'S IMPULSIVELY KISSING ME...R-RIGHT IN FRONT OF...L-LOIS!

THE HUSSY! I OUGHT TO TEAR HER HAIR OUT!

ONCE UPON A TIME YOU WOULD HAVE BEEN TERRIBLY UPSET TO SEE ANOTHER WOMAN KISSING *SUPERMAN!* I'VE NEVER SEEN YOU LOOK SO CALM!

IT'S THE CALM BEFORE THE STORM! WAIT'LL THAT HARD-WORKING HUSBAND OF MINE GETS HOME! I'LL SLAUGHTER HIM!

WHEN LOIS' SUPER-SPOUSE NERVOUSLY RETURNS TO HIS LOVE-NEST...

LOIS! BE REASONABLE! I COULDN'T TELL THAT ACTRESS I WAS MARRIED! YOUR *LIFE* DEPENDS UPON OUR KEEPING IT A SECRET!

I KNOW! BUT I STILL *DON'T* LIKE IT!

AFTER LOIS SIMMERS DOWN...

I'M SO UNHAPPY! WON'T PEOPLE *EVER* KNOW WE'RE MARRIED?

MAYBE...SOME DAY! MEANWHILE, THINK HOW DULL LIFE WOULD BE WITHOUT PROBLEMS! BUT AT LEAST, DEAR, WE'VE GOT EACH OTHER!

SEE FUTURE ISSUES OF THIS MAGAZINE FOR MORE STORIES ABOUT THE *IMAGINARY* MARRIAGE BETWEEN LOIS AND *SUPERMAN*...THAT *MAY* COME TRUE... OR MAY *NOT!*

End ⑧

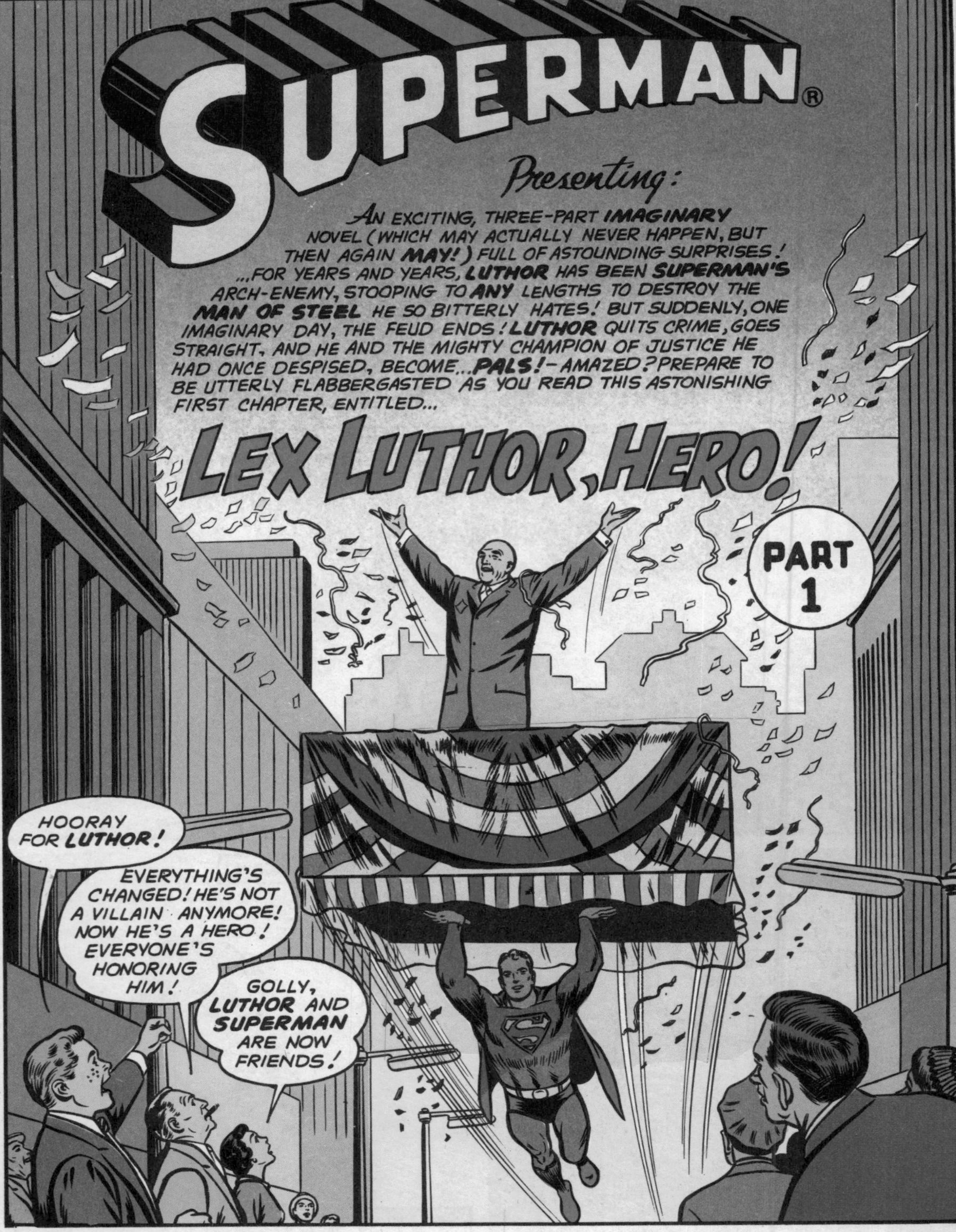
SUPERMAN®
Presenting:
AN EXCITING, THREE-PART IMAGINARY NOVEL (WHICH MAY ACTUALLY NEVER HAPPEN, BUT THEN AGAIN MAY!) FULL OF ASTOUNDING SURPRISES! ...FOR YEARS AND YEARS, LUTHOR HAS BEEN SUPERMAN'S ARCH-ENEMY, STOOPING TO ANY LENGTHS TO DESTROY THE MAN OF STEEL HE SO BITTERLY HATES! BUT SUDDENLY, ONE IMAGINARY DAY, THE FEUD ENDS! LUTHOR QUITS CRIME, GOES STRAIGHT, AND HE AND THE MIGHTY CHAMPION OF JUSTICE HE HAD ONCE DESPISED, BECOME...PALS!—AMAZED? PREPARE TO BE UTTERLY FLABBERGASTED AS YOU READ THIS ASTONISHING FIRST CHAPTER, ENTITLED...
LEX LUTHOR, HERO!
PART 1
HOORAY FOR LUTHOR!
EVERYTHING'S CHANGED! HE'S NOT A VILLAIN ANYMORE! NOW HE'S A HERO! EVERYONE'S HONORING HIM!
GOLLY, LUTHOR AND SUPERMAN ARE NOW FRIENDS!

ONE AFTERNOON AT **METROPOLIS** PRISON, ON AN **IMAGINARY** DAY, THAT MAY **OR MAY NOT** EVER HAPPEN, AS **SUPERMAN'S** ARCH-FOE, CONVICT LEX **LUTHOR**, STROLLS ON AN ERRAND...

THAT STRANGELY GLOWING ROCK MIXED IN WITH ALL THE OTHER BOULDERS, I WONDER ...

KEEP WALKING, **LUTHOR!**

SUDDENLY...

YOU'VE GOT A BIG MOUTH, SYKES! I THINK I'LL SHUT IT!

HOLY CATS! **LUTHOR** SOCKED A GUARD! THEY'LL THROW THE BOOK AT HIM!

YOU'LL LOSE YOUR SOFT JOB IN THE PRISON LIBRARY FOR THIS, **LUTHOR!**

IT WAS WORTH IT! PUT ME TO WORK ON THE ROCK-PILE, FOR ALL I CARE!

WHICH IS EXACTLY WHAT I **WANT!** THAT'S WHY I **REALLY** HIT HIM!

NEXT DAY...

SATISFIED, CON?

YOU BET! NOW I CAN SECRETLY EXAMINE THIS GLOWING ROCK!

HMMM — JUST AS I SUSPECTED! THIS IS NO ORDINARY ROCK! ITS PITTED SURFACE REVEALS IT'S A METEOR FROM OUTER SPACE! I'LL SLIP A HANDFUL OF THE CRUSHED STUFF INTO MY **POCKET,** UNSEEN!

2

THAT NIGHT, IN THE RENEGADE SCIENTIST'S CELL...

THE METEOR GRANULES EMANATE A TWINKLING, MULTI-COLORED BRILLIANCE IN THE DARK, AND FEEL **WARM** TO THE TOUCH! I'VE A STRONG HUNCH THIS IS **ELEMENT "Z"**...!!

"ELEMENT Z" IS A MYSTERIOUS CHEMICAL SUBSTANCE WHICH I'VE LONG-BELIEVED EXISTED ELSEWHERE IN THE UNIVERSE! -- IF "ELEMENT Z" HAS NOW REACHED EARTH, THEN I'M ON THE THRESHOLD OF A TREMENDOUS DISCOVERY...!

NEXT MORNING, IN THE WARDEN'S OFFICE...

LUTHOR, YOU'RE OUT OF YOUR MIND, TO MAKE SUCH A REQUEST!

ALL I ASK, SIR, IS ... LET ME USE THE PRISON HOSPITAL'S LABORATORY FACILITIES FOR 24 HOURS!

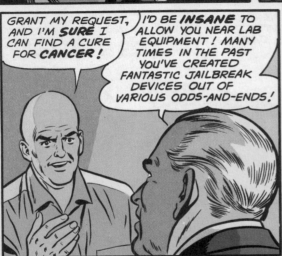

GRANT MY REQUEST, AND I'M SURE I CAN FIND A CURE FOR CANCER!

I'D BE INSANE TO ALLOW YOU NEAR LAB EQUIPMENT! MANY TIMES IN THE PAST YOU'VE CREATED FANTASTIC JAILBREAK DEVICES OUT OF VARIOUS ODDS-AND-ENDS!

BUT, WARDEN! CANCER IS MANKIND'S DEADLIEST DISEASE! IN VIEW OF MY GREAT SCIENTIFIC BACK-GROUND, YOU CAN'T REFUSE TO LET ME TRY!

WHY THIS SUDDEN CONCERN ABOUT MANKIND'S WELFARE, LUTHOR?

ALL YOUR LIFE YOU'VE TRIED TO CRUSH AND RULE MANKIND WITH ONE MAD INVENTION AFTER ANOTHER! YOU'D HAVE SUCCEEDED, TOO, EXCEPT FOR SUPERMAN!

THAT'S WHY THIS EXPERIMENT MEANS SO MUCH TO ME!

Regards from Superman

I REALIZE AT LAST HOW WRONG I'VE BEEN TO USE MY GREAT BRAIN TO FIGHT, RATHER THAN AID, MANKIND! PLEASE GIVE ME THIS CHANCE TO ATONE...!

OKAY! 24 HOURS! -- BUT YOU'LL BE CLOSELY GUARDED EVERY SECOND!

3

ALL DAY LONG, AND ALL THROUGH THE NIGHT, *LUTHOR* DESPERATELY TOILS...

REMEMBER! ONE WRONG MOVE, AND IT'LL BE YOUR LAST!

PLEASE DON'T INTERRUPT! THIS IS A CRUCIAL STAGE OF THE EXPERIMENT!

NEXT MORNING, IN THE WARDEN'S OFFICE...

HERE YOU ARE, SIR! THIS SERUM WILL CURE CANCER!

JUST LIKE *THAT*, EH? ...I'LL HAVE SOME REPUTABLE SCIENTISTS INVESTIGATE YOUR CLAIM. MEANWHILE, RETURN TO THE ROCK-PILE!

LATER, THAT VERY DAY...

;GASP!;--THE INVESTIGATING SCIENTISTS HAVE REPORTED *FANTASTIC* SUCCESS! DOOMED CANCER PATIENTS WERE CURED *INSTANTLY* BY YOUR SERUM! IF THEY *REMAIN* CURED...!

THEY WILL! THE EFFECTS OF "ELEMENT Z" ARE *PERMANENT!*

THAT'S WONDERFUL, JUST WONDERFUL! CONGRATULATIONS, *LUTHOR!* INSTEAD OF LIVING IN INFAMY, YOUR NAME WILL GO DOWN IN HISTORY AS ONE OF THE WORLD'S GREATEST BENEFACTORS! YOU WILL WIN THE NOBEL PRIZE!

I'M...GLAD! BUT I WANT NO REWARD! I JUST WANT TO MAKE UP FOR MY EVIL PAST!

AT THE *DAILY PLANET*, EDITOR PERRY WHITE AND REPORTERS CLARK KENT, LOIS LANE, AND JIMMY OLSEN ARE STUNNED BY THE HEADLINES...

WHAT A SWITCH!

FROM HEEL TO HERO OVERNIGHT!

SO THERE'S SOME *GOOD* IN *LUTHOR*, AFTER ALL!

INCREDIBLE!

DAILY PLANET
LEX LUTHOR DISCOVERS AMAZING CANCER CURE

AS CLARK LEAVES THE OFFICE LATER, HE SLIPS INTO AN EMPTY ALLEY AND, REMOVING HIS OUTER GARMENTS, CHANGES TO THE DYNAMIC IDENTITY OF *SUPERMAN*...

LUTHOR'S MADE A GREAT CONTRIBUTION TO SCIENCE! NOW IT'S *MY* TURN TO BE HELPFUL!

4

FAR OFF INTO OUTER SPACE STREAKS THE *MAN OF STEEL*, COMBING THE COSMOS FOR THE PRECIOUS ELEMENT, UNTIL...

LUTHOR SAYS THE WORLD NEEDS MORE "*ELEMENT Z*", HMMM... MY MICROSCOPIC VISION REVEALS THIS GREAT METEOR SWARM CONTAINS "*ELEMENT Z*"! I RECOGNIZE IT FROM PUBLISHED DESCRIPTIONS OF ITS PROPERTIES...

SWIFTLY, *SUPERMAN* RAMS THE SWARM TOGETHER, FORMING IT INTO A GREAT BALL...

THEY SAY NO ONE IS *COMPLETELY* BAD! I GUESS THAT INCLUDES *LUTHOR*, TOO!

PRESENTLY, AS HE FLIES THE COLOSSAL SPHERE TO THE UNITED NATIONS ON EARTH...

I OFFER THIS AS A GIFT TO ALL MANKIND SO THERE WILL BE ENOUGH ELEMENT "Z" TO CURE EVERY CANCER SUFFERER!

THANKS, *SUPERMAN!*

DAYS LATER, AS *LUTHOR* IS SUMMONED BEFORE THE PRISON'S PAROLE BOARD...

FRANKLY, *LUTHOR*, SOME OF US QUESTION THE SINCERITY OF YOUR REFORMATION...

MAY *I* SPEAK, GENTLEMEN?

SUPERMAN!

BY ALL MEANS, PLEASE DO SPEAK, *SUPERMAN!* WE'D LIKE THE OPINION OF THE MAN WHOM *LUTHOR* TRIED TO DESTROY SO OFTEN!... *SHOULD* HE BE FREED?

AS I UNDERSTAND IT, *LUTHOR* SAYS HE REPENTS HIS EVIL PAST...

...AND WANTS TO SPEND THE REST OF HIS LIFE *HELPING* HUMANITY, INSTEAD OF HARMING IT! — HE HAS CONQUERED CANCER WHO CAN SAY WHAT OTHER BLESSINGS HIS MARVELOUS INTELLECT CAN PERFORM FOR MANKIND? I SAY *LUTHOR* SHOULD GET A CHANCE TO GO STRAIGHT!

MINUTES AFTERWARD...

PAROLE GRANTED!

...; CHOKE; ...THIS IS THE *HAPPIEST* MOMENT OF MY LIFE!

SUPERMAN...DESPITE THE TERRIBLE THINGS I'VE DONE TO YOU... YOU WENT TO BAT FOR ME, BEFORE THE PAROLE BOARD! I DON'T KNOW HOW TO THANK YOU! I...

NOW THAT YOU'VE CHANGED, LET'S BE FRIENDS...

LATER, AS *LUTHOR* LEAVES THROUGH THE PRISON'S GATES...

IF THERE'S ANY WAY I CAN HELP YOU GET A NEW START...

I'D APPRECIATE IT IF YOU WOULD FLY ME TO MY FORMER SECRET HEADQUARTERS!

SHORTLY, WITH *LUTHOR* POINTING OUT THE WAY, THE TWO EX-FOES STREAK DOWN TOWARD AN *IMPRESSIVE* BUILDING...

THIS ABANDONED MUSEUM USED TO BE MY HIDEOUT! HIDDEN TV CAMERAS IN THE EYES OF THAT COLOSSAL STONE STATUE SIGNALLED WHENEVER YOU FLEW NEARBY!

AMAZING!

AND AS THEY ALIGHT...

A SHAKE OF "CAESAR'S" HAND OPENS A SECRET DOORWAY INTO... *LUTHOR'S LAIR!* SINCE I'M QUITTING CRIME FOREVER, I'M NOW GLAD TO SHOW THIS TO YOU!

TO BE DEMOLISHED AT SOME FUTURE DATE

⑥

SOON, INSIDE...

HOW WARPED I USED TO BE! BEHOLD MY **HALL OF HEROES**! **ATILLA THE HUN...GENGHIS KHAN... CAPTAIN KIDD...AL CAPONE**! I CAN'T STAND THE SIGHT OF THEM ANY MORE! PLEASE DESTROY THE STATUES!

OKAY— IF THAT'S ALL YOU WANT!

ATILLA THE HUN   GENGHIS KHAN   CAPTAIN KIDD   AL CAPONE

I'M HAPPY TO SEE THE LAST OF THEM!--I'M GOING TO SELL THIS PLACE, RENT A LABORATORY IN AN OFFICE BUILDING, AND OPERATE **OPENLY**, LIKE ANY RESPECTABLE SCIENTIST WOULD!

WONDERFUL!

ATILLA THE HUN GE   HIS KHAN CAPTAIN KIDD AL CAPONE

AFTERWARD...

SO OUR FEUD'S OVER, AT LAST! ..., MAY I ADMIT SOMETHING? THERE WERE TIMES, **LUTHOR** WHEN YOU HAD ME PLENTY WORRIED...

LIKE THAT TIME WHEN I INVENTED AN **ATOMIC-POWERED TOP** AND LET IT DESTROY AN ENTIRE TOWN!

"...THE SUCTION OF ITS SPIN BECAME LIKE A TORNADO! THAT WAS A TOUGH ONE FOR YOU TO HANDLE, EH, **SUPERMAN**...?"

WHIRRRRR

HELP!

HELP!

"IT SURE WAS, **LUTHOR**! I BUILT A CIRCULAR TRACK ON A HUGE RAFT. THEN, AS THE TOP SPUN ONTO THE TRACK AND RODE 'ROUND AND 'ROUND, I GOT THE TOP UNDER CONTROL AND DUMPED IT IN THE OCEAN..."

⑦

"AND I'LL NEVER FORGET HOW YOU ONCE DISGUISED YOURSELF AS A PROFESSOR AND FOCUSED A **DUPLICATOR RAY** ON ME AND FORMED AN IMPERFECT DOUBLE OF MYSELF...**BIZARRO!** YOU CAN'T IMAGINE ALL THE PROBLEMS THAT **IDIOT OF STEEL** HAS GIVEN ME SINCE THEN..."

EARLY ONE AFTERNOON, AFTER **LUTHOR** DISPOSES OF HIS MUSEUM HIDEOUT, AND RENTS A LAB IN AN OFFICE BUILDING...

MY NEXT GOAL, GENTLEMEN OF THE PRESS? I'M GOING TO FIND A CURE FOR... HEART DISEASE!

WONDERFUL! HOW FORTUNATE FOR HUMANITY THAT YOU'VE GIVEN UP CRIME IN ORDER TO MAKE IMPORTANT DISCOVERIES!

SECONDS AFTER, THE REPORTERS LEAVE...

THAT WAS A PRETTY LITTLE SPEECH YOU MADE, **LUTHOR!** ONLY WE DON'T LIKE IT!

DUKE GARNER AND **AL MANTZ**... UNDERWORLD HOODS! YOU MUST HAVE STOLEN IN WHILE I WENT FOR LUNCH! GET OUT! I'M FINISHED WITH CROOKS!

BUT WE'RE NOT FINISHED WITH YOU!... TELL HIM, AL!

EITHER YOU KILL **SUPERMAN**, OR WE KILL YOU!... WHO'S GONNA DIE, GENIUS? YOU...OR **SUPERMAN**?!!

END, PART I

WHAT WILL **LUTHOR** DECIDE? TURN TO THE NEXT CHAPTER! [8]

A LOOK AT OTHER GREAT IMAGINARY STORIES

SUPERMAN #159, 1963
art by Curt Swan
and George Klein

LOIS LANE #89, 1969
art by Neal Adams

SUPERMAN

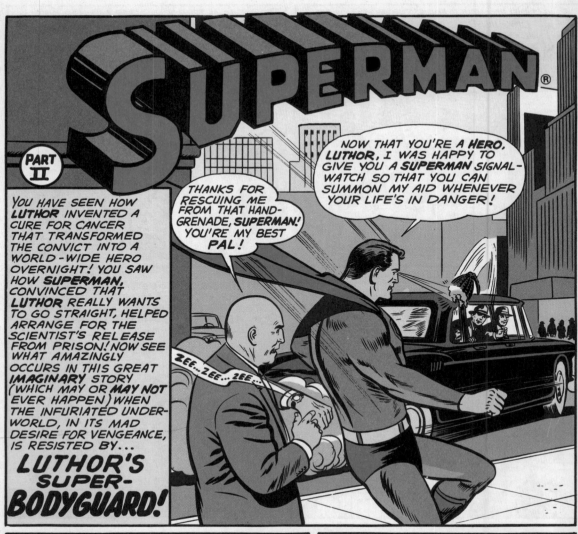

YOU HAVE SEEN HOW *LUTHOR* INVENTED A CURE FOR CANCER THAT TRANSFORMED THE CONVICT INTO A WORLD-WIDE HERO OVERNIGHT! YOU SAW HOW *SUPERMAN,* CONVINCED THAT *LUTHOR* REALLY WANTS TO GO STRAIGHT, HELPED ARRANGE FOR THE SCIENTIST'S RELEASE FROM PRISON! NOW SEE WHAT AMAZINGLY OCCURS IN THIS GREAT *IMAGINARY* STORY (WHICH MAY OR *MAY NOT* EVER HAPPEN) WHEN THE INFURIATED UNDERWORLD, IN ITS MAD DESIRE FOR VENGEANCE, IS RESISTED BY...

LUTHOR'S SUPER-BODYGUARD!

THANKS FOR RESCUING ME FROM THAT HAND-GRENADE, *SUPERMAN!* YOU'RE MY BEST *PAL!*

NOW THAT YOU'RE A *HERO,* *LUTHOR,* I WAS HAPPY TO GIVE YOU A *SUPERMAN* SIGNAL-WATCH SO THAT YOU CAN SUMMON MY AID WHENEVER YOUR LIFE'S IN DANGER!

ZEE... ZEE... ZEE...

AS THE MOBSTERS CONTINUE THEIR TALK WITH *SUPERMAN'S* FORMER ENEMY...

LUTHOR, BECAUSE OF YOUR SCIENTIFIC GENIUS, YOU'RE THE *ONLY* ONE WHO CAN PROBABLY SUCCEED IN DESTROYING *SUPERMAN!*

ALL GANGLAND FEELS THAT IF YOU WON'T KILL *HIM,* THEN YOU'RE PROBABLY DOUBLE-CROSSING US!

YOU KNOW WHAT WE DO TO DOUBLE-CROSSERS!-- WELL, WHO DIES? YOU OR *SUPERMAN!*

I WON'T BETRAY *SUPERMAN!* HE'S MY FRIEND NOW!

HE MADE HIS DECISION, AL. SHOOT HIM!

BUT AS THE TRIGGER-MAN FIRES...

BANG! BANG!

YOU'RE WASTING THOSE BULLETS!

SUPERMAN! FOR THE FIRST TIME IN MY LIFE, I'M GLAD TO SEE BULLETS BOUNCING OFF YOU!

I HAD A HUNCH YOU WOULDN'T BE SAFE FROM YOUR FORMER CRONIES, SO I KEPT YOU UNDER SURVEILLANCE WITH MY SUPER-VISION!

LUCKILY FOR ME!

SUPERMAN REMOVES AN OBJECT FROM HIS CAPE'S SECRET POUCH, THEN...

PROBABLY, THERE WILL BE OTHER ATTEMPTS BY THE UNDERWORLD TO DESTROY YOU! THAT'S WHY I MADE THIS SIGNAL-WATCH! PLEASE ACCEPT IT! IT'S LIKE JIMMY OLSEN'S WATCH, BUT OPERATES ON A DIFFERENT ULTRASONIC FREQUENCY...

WHENEVER YOU'RE IN DANGER, PRESS THE BUTTON ON THE WATCH! I'LL FLASH TO YOUR RESCUE, IN RESPONSE TO THE ULTRASONIC DISTRESS-SIGNAL!

THANK YOU, SUPERMAN! YOU'RE... A WONDERFUL FRIEND!

SHORTLY, AT A MEETING OF GANGLAND BIG-SHOTS...

WE'LL KEEP ON TRYING TO RUB OUT LUTHOR, UNTIL WE SUCCEED!

RIGHT! HE RATTED OUT ON HIS PROMISE TO DESTROY SUPERMAN! FOR THAT, HE'LL DIE!

AGAIN, THE UNDERWORLD STRIKES...

HERE'S A PRESENT, LUTHOR!

A HAND-GRENADE! I MUST PRESS THE BUTTON ON MY SUPERMAN SIGNAL-WATCH, IMMEDIATELY!

ZEE-ZEE-ZEE...

2

INSTANTLY RESPONDING TO THE WATCH'S ULTRA-SONIC SIGNAL, *LUTHOR'S* SUPER-BODYGUARD APPEARS...

THERE! I'VE MELTED THE GRENADE WITH MY *HEAT-VISION!* YOU'VE NOTHING TO FEAR NOW, *LUTHOR!* BUT THOSE ASSASSINS' TROUBLES ARE ABOUT TO *BEGIN!*

SUPER-SWIFTLY, THE *MAN OF STEEL* ALTERS THE CAR'S SHAPE...

LET'S HAVE A BALL, 'BOYS!

HEY!

WHAT'S HE DOIN'?

AWRP!

THEN...

YOU'RE *ROLLING* THE THUGS OFF TO THE POLICE-STATION INSIDE THAT METAL "BALL"!... HA, HA! AM I GLAD YOU'RE NO LONGER MY ENEMY, *SUPERMAN!*

I MAKE A BETTER FRIEND THAN A FOE, EH? HA, HA!

SEVERAL NIGHTS LATER, AS *LUTHOR* ENTERS BUILDING TO ATTEND A CONFERENCE WITH OTHER SCIENTISTS...

THAT SHADOW!...SOMEONE'S GOING TO SHOOT A DART AT ME! IT'S PROBABLY *POISONED!* I'LL USE MY SIGNAL-WATCH

ZEE...ZEE...ZEE...

IN STREAKS *SUPERMAN* INSTANTANEOUSLY, AS HE RECEIVES *LUTHOR'S* DISTRESS-SIGNAL...

GAA!...SUPERMAN'S S-SWALLOWING THE POISONED DART! HE'S GOING TO *EAT* IT! I-I'D BETTER *RUN!*

BUT AS THE GANGSTER RACES UP A RAMP, THE *MAN OF STEEL* BLOWS A GUST OF SUPER-COLD BREATH, SO THAT...

AWP! N-NO!!

I'VE *FROZEN* THE RAIN ON THE RAMP! THE HOODLUM IS SLIDING BACK TOWARD ME!

3

THANKS, SUPERMAN! ONCE AGAIN, YOU'VE SAVED MY LIFE!

GLAD TO HELP YOU, ANYTIME!

THIS LIGHT TAP WILL PUT THE KILLER TO SLEEP UNTIL I GET HIM TO THE POLICE STATION!

SOON AFTERWARD, SUPERMAN MEETS WITH HIS COUSIN, SUPERGIRL, WHO ALSO CAME FROM THE DESTROYED PLANET KRYPTON, AND IS HIS SECRET EMERGENCY WEAPON...

I'M SO HAPPY THAT LUTHOR'S GONE STRAIGHT!

MY BIG PROBLEM IS TO KEEP HIM ALIVE!

I CAN'T POSSIBLY WATCH OVER LUTHOR EVERY INSTANT! SOME DAY THE UNDERWORLD MAY GET HIM BEFORE HE CAN SIGNAL ME FOR HELP, AND MANKIND WILL LOSE A GREAT SCIENTIST!

THERE MUST BE SOME SOLUTION! LET'S TALK OVER DIFFERENT IDEAS!

AFTER THEY CONSIDER AND DISCARD VARIOUS PLANS...

I'VE GOT IT! HE'D BE SAFE IN AN OUTER SPACE SATELLITE LABORATORY!

WHAT A BRILLIANT INSPIRATION!

AT ONCE, SUPERMAN BUILDS THE ASTOUNDING LABORTORY, THEN AFTER HE PLACES IT IN ORBIT ABOVE EARTH...

HOW HAPPY LUTHOR LOOKS AS I'M TAKING HIM TO HIS NEW LAB!

SOON, INSIDE THE SATELLITE-LAB.

CHOKE:...AGAIN I MUST EXPRESS MY GRATITUDE TO YOU, SUPERMAN! NOW NOTHING WILL STOP ME FROM MAKING IMPORTANT DISCOVERIES IN BEHALF OF MANKIND!

I'M... GLAD!

PRESENTLY, INFURIATED UNDERWORLD CHIEFS HOLD A WAR COUNCIL...

SATELLITE OR NO SATELLITE, WE CAN STILL KILL *LUTHOR*, BUT IT'LL COST A FORTUNE!

PRICE IS NO OBJECT! *KILL HIM!*

WEEKS LATER, AS *SUPERMAN* FLIES ALONG ON PATROL...

GREAT SCOTT! MY TELESCOPIC SIGHT REVEALS AN INCREDIBLE THREAT TO *LUTHOR'S* LIFE!

UP INTO OUTER SPACE DESPERATELY FLASHES THE *MAN OF STEEL*...

THAT MISSILE-BOMB WILL EXPLODE *LUTHOR'S* LABORATORY, UNLESS I DESTROY THE MISSILE FIRST!

DELIBERATELY, *SUPERMAN* MEETS THE MISSILE IN A HEAD-ON COLLISION...

JUST IN TIME!... I'M UNHARMED! HMM... GANGLAND MAY HAVE MANY SUCH MISSILE-LAUNCHING BASES! I MUST DO SOMETHING TO PERMANENTLY CANCEL OUT THE MISSILE-THREAT!

SWIFTLY, *SUPERMAN* CONSTRUCTS AN INVULNERABLE SHIELD ABOUT THE SATELLITE-LAB...

NOTHING, NOT EVEN A HYDROGEN-BOMB EXPLOSION, CAN PIERCE THIS SUPER-HARD, SEMI-TRANSPARENT SUBSTANCE I INVENTED! AND ONLY *LUTHOR* CAN OPERATE THAT EXIT-HATCH IN THE SHIELD....!

SHORTLY, IN THE SATELLITE LAB...

THE SIGNAL-WATCH'S ULTRASONIC WAVES CAN'T TRAVEL THROUGH OUTER SPACE! IF YOU EVER URGENTLY NEED ME, FIRE THIS JET-ROCKET, WHICH RESEMBLES YOU, INTO EARTH'S UPPER ATMOSPHERE!

I'LL DO THAT!

A WEEK LATER, OUT THROUGH THE INVULNERABLE SHIELD'S EXIT-HATCH, FLASHES THE DISTRESS-ROCKET...

HIGH IN OUR PLANET'S ATMOSPHERE, THE ROCKET EXPLODES WITH A COLOSSAL ROAR THAT IS HEARD ABOUT THE WORLD AND SIMUTANEOUSLY, ITS FRAGMENTS DISSOLVE INTO MULTI-COLORED FLARES...

BWOOOOOMMM

LUTHOR'S EMERGENCY-SIGNAL!... HE NEEDS ME!!

LUTHOR HAS OPENED THE ESCAPE-HATCH SO I CAN ENTER! SOMETHING MUST BE TERRIBLY WRONG! WHAT'S HAPPENED? HAS GANGLAND DISCOVERED SOME ASTOUNDING NEW WAY TO MENACE LUTHOR??

MOMENTS LATER, INSIDE THE SATELLITE...

WHAT'S WRONG, LUTHOR? I SAW YOUR DISTRESS-SIGNAL AND CAME AT ONCE!

WRONG?... NOTHING'S WRONG, FOR ME...

UNEXPECTEDLY, LUTHOR TOUCHES A BUTTON WHICH REMOVES LEAD-LIDS FROM BEFORE THE LENSES OF CONCEALED RAY-PROJECTORS...

I'M FINE! BUT YOU'RE IN SUPER-TROUBLE!

OW!... G-GREEN KRYPTONITE RAYS!

GREEN KRYPTONITE IS... THE ONE SUBSTANCE... TH-THAT C-CAN... DESTROY ME!

AS THE MAN OF STEEL COLLAPSES...

I'M H-HORRIBLY WEAKENED AND... PAINED...BY THE RAYS!...:GASP:... TURN THEM OFF! HAVE Y-YOU GONE OUT OF YOUR MIND?

HA, HA, HA!

6

SECONDS LATER, AS *LUTHOR* STRAPS THE *MAN OF STEEL* TO A BENCH, WITH BANDS OF METAL CONTAINING *KRYPTONITE*...

HA, HA! OH, HOW SIMPLE IT WAS TO OUTWIT YOU!

THEN, AS *LUTHOR* PULLS A SWITCH...

SEE, *SUPERMAN!* THAT WALL IS RISING! THERE'S A THICK GLASS PARTITION BEHIND IT, SEPARATING US FROM YOUR DEAR FRIENDS... LOIS LANE, JIMMY OLSEN, AND PERRY WHITE!...THEY CAN'T POSSIBLY BREAK THROUGH THAT GLASS AND RESCUE YOU!

BEHIND THE GLASS PARTITION...

LUTHOR HASN'T REFORMED! HE'S AS EVIL AS EVER! HE'S GOING TO KILL *SUPERMAN!*

DON'T GIVE UP HOPE, LOIS!

SUPERMAN'S GOTTEN OUT OF TIGHTER FIXES THAN THIS!

SMIRKING, *LUTHOR* GLOATS...

WASN'T IT KIND AND *CONSIDERATE* OF ME TO KIDNAP YOUR FRIENDS, SO THEY COULD WITNESS THIS... HA, HA... TOUCHING MOMENT?...HA, HA! YOU'VE BEGUN TO *TURN GREEN* AS KRYPTONITE FEVER RAGES WITHIN YOU!

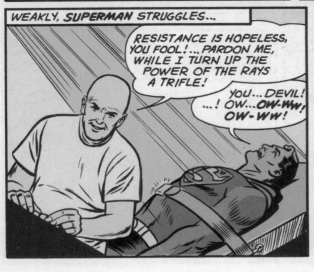

WEAKLY, *SUPERMAN* STRUGGLES...

RESISTANCE IS HOPELESS, YOU FOOL!...PARDON ME, WHILE I TURN UP THE POWER OF THE RAYS A TRIFLE!

YOU...DEVIL! ...! OW...*OW-WW!* OW-WW!

CLEVER DEVIL, YOU MEAN!... I DISCOVERED THAT CANCER-CURE, IN ORDER TO BE RELEASED FROM JAIL! I PRETENDED TO HAVE REFORMED, SO I COULD LULL YOU INTO A FALSE SENSE OF SECURITY! THE PURPOSE? TO CATCH YOU OFF-GUARD AND LURE YOU INTO THIS DEATH-TRAP!!

7

THOSE GANGLAND ATTEMPTS AGAINST MY LIFE WERE ON THE LEVEL! THE UNDERWORLD DIDN'T SUSPECT I WAS PLAYING A CUNNING ROLE! HOW THEY HATED ME! BUT THEY'LL FEEL DIFFERENTLY ABOUT ME NOW, EH?

I WAS A FOOL... *GASP!*... TO TRUST YOU...

INDEED YOU WERE!... NOW TO RAISE THE KRYPTONITE POWER IN THESE RAYS TO FULL-STRENGTH!

OWWW! OHH-HHHH...

AS SUPERMAN TURNS COMPLETELY GREEN AND HIS STRUGGLES CEASE, LUTHOR EXAMINES THE LIMP FORM...

I MUST MAKE SURE YOU AREN'T JUST PRETENDING TO BE DEAD, TO TRICK ME INTO PREMATURELY TURNING OFF THE RAYS! HMM... THIS SUPER XXX-RAY DISCLOSES YOU'RE THE GENUINE SUPERMAN, AND NOT A ROBOT!

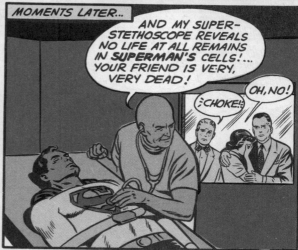

MOMENTS LATER...

AND MY SUPER-STETHOSCOPE REVEALS NO LIFE AT ALL REMAINS IN SUPERMAN'S CELLS!... YOUR FRIEND IS VERY, VERY DEAD!

CHOKE!

OH, NO!

AT LAST!! AFTER ALL THESE YEARS OF VAINLY TRYING, I'VE FINALLY SUCCEEDED IN KILLING SUPERMAN! I'VE DESTROYED THE MIGHTIEST MAN IN THE UNIVERSE! WHAT A GLORIOUS ACHIEVEMENT!

LATER, AFTER LUTHOR LANDS THE SATELLITE LAB ON EARTH...

YOU CAN HAVE SUPERMAN BACK, NOW THAT HE'S DEAD! HA, HA!

MADMAN!

YOU'LL PAY FOR THIS, LUTHOR, YOU... YOU MURDERER!!

8

AFTER *LUTHOR* RE-ENTERS THE SATELLITE-LAB, HE RADIOS AN ANNOUNCEMENT...

PEOPLE OF EARTH! I, *LUTHOR*, HAVE KILLED *SUPERMAN!* THIS IS NO HOAX! IT'S ABSOLUTELY TRUE! ... HA, HA, HA, HA!

DECENT PEOPLE EVERYWHERE ARE SHOCKED AND SADDENED...

I HEARD IT ON THE RADIO! *LUTHOR* KILLED *SUPERMAN!* METROPOLIS' *DAILY PLANET* HAS CONFIRMED *LUTHOR'S* BOAST!

OH, NO!

IT CAN'T... IT *MUSTN'T* BE!...;SOB!;

THE UNDERWORLD IS SHOCKED, TOO, BUT OVER-JOYED...

HO, HO! WHAT A SMART COOKIE THAT *LUTHOR* IS!

HE EVEN HAD US WISE GUYS FOOLED! HE'S TERRIFIC!

HE ONLY PRETENDED TO BE PALS WITH *SUPERMAN*, SO HE COULD KILL HIM!

AS FOR *LUTHOR*, HIS GLEE IS BOUNDLESS.

ONLY *SUPERMAN* STOOD BETWEEN ME AND MY GREAT GOAL TO RULE THIS PLANET! SOON, I'LL BE *KING* OF THE EARTH!

END PART II

WILL *SUPERMAN'S* DEATH GO UNAVENGED TURN TO THE FINAL CHAPTER OF THIS ASTOUNDING, UNFORGETTABLE IMAGINARY TALE!

A LOOK AT OTHER GREAT IMAGINARY STORIES

ACTION COMICS #396-397, 1971
art by Carmine Infantino and Murphy Anderson

50

SUPERMAN

PART III

WHAT IS THE REACTION OF THE WORLD, AND THE ENTIRE UNIVERSE, TO THE DESTRUCTION OF *SUPERMAN*? HOW DO HIS CLOSEST FRIENDS TAKE IT? NOW THAT THE *MAN OF STEEL* IS SLAIN, DOES *LUTHOR* FINALLY RULE EARTH? WILL CRIME AND INJUSTICE FLOURISH WITH *SUPERMAN* GONE? THE FINAL CHAPTER IN THIS AMAZING *IMAGINARY* TALE ANSWERS ALL THESE, AND MANY MORE QUESTIONS, RAISED BY...

The DEATH *of* SUPERMAN!

SOB!

CHOKE!

THE SUN RISES ON A SADDENED WORLD... EVERY DECENT PERSON ON EARTH FEELS A GREAT PERSONAL LOSS AT THE PASSING OF THE *MAN OF STEEL*...

SOON, THE STREETS OUTSIDE *METROPOLIS* CHAPEL ARE CHOKED WITH HUNDREDS OF THOUSANDS OF MOURNERS, EACH SILENTLY AWAITING A FINAL GLIMPSE OF THE SLAIN *SUPERMAN* WHO LIES IN STATE...

INSIDE THE CHAPEL, ONE BY ONE, THEY SLOWLY FILE PAST **SUPERMAN'S** CASKET... AMONG THEM ARE WORLD LEADERS WHO HAVE FLOWN BY JET TO **METROPOLIS**, TO PAY THEIR FINAL RESPECTS...

ON MOVES THE MELANCHOLY PROCESSION... AMONG THE MOURNERS ARE WEIRD ALIEN BEINGS FROM OTHER WORLDS, WHO SPED TO EARTH IN ODD VEHICLES VIA SPACE-WARPS UPON LEARNING THE INCREDIBLE, TRAGIC NEWS...

HE BEFRIENDED ALL—HUMAN, OR OTHERWISE!--HE SAVED MY WORLD FROM DESTRUCTION!

HE COULD HAVE RULED THE UNIVERSE! BUT HE UNSELFISHLY CHOSE TO HELP **OTHERS!**

THE SEA OF FACES SLOWLY EDDIES BY... FACES OF EVERY RACE AND NATIONALITY... YOUNG FACES... OLD FACES... EACH FACE SORROWFUL AT THE PASSING OF A GREAT MAN...

THEN IT IS THE TURN OF GRIEF-STRICKEN LOIS LANE, ASSISTED BY HER SISTER LUCY, TO STAND BEFORE THE COFFIN... AND AS LOIS TAKES A LAST LOOK AT HER FALLEN HERO...

GOODBYE...

THERE'LL NEVER BE ANYONE FOR ME, BUT... YOU! OH, DARLING, I-I HAD SO MUCH LOVE TO GIVE TO YOU... JUST HOW MUCH, EVEN **YOU**, NEVER DREAMED!... ⸮SOB!⸮...GOODBYE! — I'LL... LOVE... YOU... ALWAYS... ⸮SOB!⸮

NEXT, **SUPERMAN'S** FRIENDS, JIMMY OLSEN, PERRY WHITE...AND MERMAID **LORI LEMARIS** FROM **ATLANTIS**... TAKE LAST, LINGERING LOOKS...

I'LL... MISS YOU...

¿CHOKE¿... SO LONG, PAL! NO ONE EVER HAD A TRUER BUDDY THAN YOU!

I'LL NEVER FORGET YOU!

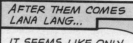

AFTER THEM COMES **LANA LANG**...

IT SEEMS LIKE ONLY YESTERDAY THAT I WAS YOUR CHILDHOOD FRIEND IN SMALLVILLE.' FIRST, I WAS AN AWFUL PEST, THEN I GOT A CRUSH ON YOU. WHEN I GREW UP, THE CRUSH RIPENED INTO LOVE! NOW YOU'RE... GONE! FAREWELL... ¿CHOKE¿

THEN THE **MAN OF STEEL'S** FAITHFUL PET **KRYPTO** PASSES THE COFFIN...

I WILL NEVER KNOW ANOTHER MASTER LIKE YOU! ¿CHOKE¿ —GOODBYE! —WHEN I THINK OF ALL THE ADVENTURES WE HAD TOGETHER...

ON MOVE THE FACES, ONE AFTER ANOTHER... THEN, BEFORE THE SLAIN **MAN OF STEEL**, APPEARS THE TEAR-STAINED FEATURES OF A TEEN-AGED GIRL WHOM NO ONE SUSPECTS IS HIS **SUPERGIRL** COUSIN LINDA, FROM **KRYPTON**...

TOGETHER, WE EXPLORED THE UNIVERSE... BUT EVEN INFINITY WASN'T AS BIG AS YOUR... ¿CHOKE¿ ...GALLANT, NOBLE HEART...

AND NOW, THERE FILES PAST--**THE LEGION OF SUPER-HEROES** FROM THE DISTANT FUTURE...!

WE SALUTE YOU IN DEATH AS WE HONORED YOU IN LIFE, COMRADE!

OF ALL THE SUPER-HEROES, YOU WERE THE **GREATEST**!!

THOUSANDS OF MILES AWAY, IN **SUPERMAN'S** ARCTIC **FORTRESS OF SOLITUDE**, THE **SUPERMAN** ROBOTS, TOO, PAY THEIR FINAL RESPECTS TO THEIR SLAIN MASTER...

THERE'S NOT A ONE OF US WHO WOULDN'T HAVE DIED GLADLY, IN HIS PLACE!

AND INSIDE THE MINIATURE BOTTLE-CITY OF **KANDOR**, IN THE FORTRESS, **VAN-ZEE** AND **SYLVIA** JOIN MILLIONS OF OTHER KANDORIANS IN AN IMPRESSIVE TRIBUTE...

WHY ARE THEY LOWERING THE KRYPTONIAN FLAG, MOMMY?

A GREAT MAN HAS DIED-- ¿CHOKE¿ —**SUPERMAN** WILL NEVER VISIT US... AGAIN... ¿SOB!¿

3

IN SHARP CONTRAST TO THE MOURNING OVER *SUPERMAN'S* DEATH, IS THE GLEE AT A GREAT PARTY SECRETLY TOSSED BY THE UNDERWORLD ON A REMOTE ISLE, TO CELEBRATE THE NEWS WHICH HAS SADDENED DECENT PEOPLE...

EVERYBODY EAT, DRINK AND MAKE MERRY! HA, HA, HA!

HOORAY FOR *LUTHOR!*

HE'S *GREAT!* HE KILLED *SUPERMAN!* WOW!!

CALLOUSLY, *LUTHOR* HAS DECORATED THE GREAT BANQUET HALL WITH EXHIBITS MOCKING THE FINAL DEATH OF *SUPERMAN...*

IT COST ME PLENTY TO GET THESE TROPHIES MADE SO FAST! LIKE 'EM? THE BEAUTIFUL PAINTING RE-ENACTS MY TRIUMPH OVER *SUPERMAN!*

TELL US *AGAIN,* HOW YOU KILLED *SUPERMAN,* LUTHOR!

IT WAS *EASY!* I PRETENDED TO REFORM, SEE? HE FELL FOR IT, THE IDIOT! THEN, WHEN HE WAS OFF-GUARD... *WHAM!...*I FED HIM KILLING DOSES OF *KRYPTONITE!* BYE, BYE, *SUPERMAN!* HA, HA!

TELL US *EVERYTHING!*

HE WRIGGLED AND TWISTED LIKE A WORM ON A HOOK! HE SWEATED, AND TURNED GREEN! THE LAST THING HE EVER SAW WAS MY GRINNING FACE!

UP ON YOUR FEET, EVERYBODY!... WHO'S THE TOP CROOK ON EARTH? —WHO WAS SMART ENOUGH TO CON *SUPERMAN* INTO THE GRAVE?—LET'S HEAR IT, YOU GUYS! *YELL IT OUT!*

LUTHOR!!!

HA, HA, HA!

4

SUDDENLY, THE MERRIMENT CHOKES IN THE MOBSTERS' THROATS AS, ASTOUNDINGLY...

GAAA! IT'S... SUPERMAN!

AWRP!... S-SUPERMAN'S ALIVE!

HE CAN'T BE! I KILLED HIM! I'M POSITIVE OF IT!

SHOUTS OF CONSTERNATION AND BAFFLED RAGE FILL THE AIR AS THE INTRUDING FIGURE SMASHES THE MOCKING DECORATIONS...

IMPOSSIBLE! HE'S GOT TO BE DEAD! ...; CHOKE;

M-MAYBE IT'S A GH-GHOST!

TO THE ASTONISHMENT OF THE CRINGING GANGSTERS, THE SUPER-POWERFUL FORM FLEXES MIGHTY MUSCLES, THEN...

A DISGUISE IS FLYING OFF! IT AIN'T SUPERMAN! IT'S...

...A GIRL WITH S-SUPER-POWERS!

AND NOW THE FLABBERGASTED UNDERWORLD LEARNS...

MY NAME IS... SUPERGIRL! I'M SUPERMAN'S COUSIN FROM KRYPTON! I'VE BEEN HIS SECRET EMERGENCY WEAPON FOR YEARS!... LUTHOR, IN THE NAME OF PLANET KRYPTON, I ARREST YOU FOR MURDER!

YOU CAN STOP WASTING BULLETS! I HAVE ALL OF SUPERMAN'S ASTONISHING POWERS! — GANGDOM MAY HAVE SUCCEEDED IN TREACHEROUSLY KILLING SUPERMAN, BUT I'M GOING TO CARRY ON HIS GREAT WORK!

SOON, IN A KANDORIAN COURTROOM, AFTER SUPERGIRL TRANSPORTS LUTHOR, AND PROSECUTION WITNESSES, INTO THE MINIATURE CITY, VIA A TRANSFER-RAY...

LEX LUTHOR, YOU KILLED A KRYPTONIAN, AND SO YOU WILL BE TRIED BY KRYPTONIANS!

SHORTLY, THE MOST SENSATIONAL TRIAL OF ALL-TIME BEGINS...

THE PRISONER DELIBERATELY MURDERED *SUPERMAN!* THERE CAN ONLY BE ONE VERDICT... ONE PENALTY!

I'LL OUTWIT THEM ALL!

THE PEOPLE OF EARTH WATCH THE PROCEEDINGS ON *TELEVISION*, THROUGH A SPECIAL HOOK-UP WITH KANDORIAN TV...

I HOPE *LUTHOR* GETS WHAT HE DESERVES!

HE WILL!

IN KANDOR, STREET CROWDS WATCH THE COURT-ROOM DRAMA ON PUBLIC VIEWING SCREENS...

BROKEN-HEARTEDLY, LOIS TESTIFIES AT THE TRIAL...

LUTHOR WOULD NEVER HAVE BEEN RELEASED FROM PRISON, IF *SUPERMAN* HADN'T GONE TO BAT FOR HIM! HE REPAID *SUPERMAN'S* KINDNESS, BY *KILLING* HIM! — ⸮SOB⸮

I SAW HIM DO IT! ⸮SOB⸮ — I...I SAW *LUTHOR* DIABOLICALLY MURDER *SUPERMAN* IN COLD BLOOD, USING *GREEN KRYPTONITE* RAYS... ⸮SOB⸮

AS THE TESTIMONY OF JIMMY OLSEN AND PERRY WHITE GOES INTO THE RECORD, *LUTHOR'S* ICY, ARROGANT COMPOSURE STILL DOESN'T CRACK...

THE PUNY ANTS!

6

THEY AREN'T DEALING WITH AN ORDINARY HOOD! THEY'RE UP AGAINST A CRIMINAL MASTERMIND! I'LL WRIGGLE OUT OF PAYING THE PENALTY, WITH THE HIDDEN ACE I'VE GOT UP MY SLEEVE!

WHEN IT IS LUTHOR'S TURN TO TESTIFY...

I'M...GUILTY! BUT I WON'T PAY FOR MY CRIME!

GUILTY? THEN THERE CAN BE BUT ONE PUNISHMENT... THE PRISONER WILL BE SENT INTO THE PHANTOM ZONE, AT ONCE!

AS THE PHANTOM ZONE RAY IS BROUGHT INTO COURT, LUTHOR PLAYS HIS ACE...

PUNISHING ME WON'T BRING SUPERMAN BACK! LET'S COMPROMISE! LET ME GO, AND I'LL BUILD A RAY THAT'LL ENLARGE KANDOR...

...BACK TO THE NORMAL SIZE IT WAS BEFORE SPACE VILLAIN BRAINIAC SHRANK YOUR CITY WITH A REDUCING-RAY! YOU WON'T HAVE TO LIVE IN A BOTTLE ANYMORE! IS IT DEAL?

NATURALLY, THEY WON'T REFUSE! BEING MADE NORMAL-SIZED AGAIN HAS BEEN THEIR GREATEST DESIRE!

BUT TO THE ARCH-CRIMINAL'S ASTOUNDING DISMAY...

WE KANDORIANS DON'T MAKE DEALS WITH MURDERERS! — EXECUTIONER, SEND THIS WRETCH INTO THE PHANTOM ZONE, IMMEDIATELY! HE IS THE GREATEST VILLAIN SINCE ADOLF EICHMANN!

N-NO! Y-YOU CAN'T MEAN THAT!

AN INSTANT LATER, AFTER THE RAY'S BLACK BUTTON IS PUSHED...

JUSTICE HAS BEEN DONE! BECAUSE OF HIS CRIME, LUTHOR WILL REMAIN A PHANTOM FOR ALL ETERNITY! NEVER AGAIN WILL HE HARM THE WORLD OF MEN!

7

SHORTLY AFTERWARD, ON EARTH...

DAILY PLANET
SUPERGIRL TAKES OVER SUPERMAN'S PATROL

☐ Morning News
GIRL OF STEEL CARRIES ON SUPERMAN'S CRUSADE FOR JUSTICE

WHEREVER **SUPERGIRL** FLIES, ACCOMPANIED BY **KRYPTO,** SHE IS APPLAUDED...

GOOD LUCK! WE MISS **SUPERMAN,** BUT WE'RE GLAD YOU'RE TAKING OVER FOR HIM!

{CHOKE{...I NEVER THOUGHT IT WOULD TURN OUT THIS WAY...

NOW I BELONG TO... **SUPERGIRL!**

ALL THE TIME I WAS **SUPERMAN'S** SECRET EMERGENCY-WEAPON, I EAGERLY LOOKED FORWARD TO THE DAY WHEN I COULD OPERATE OPENLY! NOW THAT IT'S FINALLY HAPPENED, I – I FEEL NO HAPPINESS AT THE "GLORY" THAT'S NOW...MINE...

HERE LIES SUPERMAN TREACHEROUSLY SLAIN BY LEX LUTHOR

{CHOKE{...ALL I FEEL IS A GREAT SORROW AT THE PASSING OF THE STRONGEST, KINDEST, M-MOST POWERFUL HUMAN BEING I'VE EVER KNOWN! {SOB{ –M-MY COUSIN **SUPERMAN...**

END PART III

WELL, LET'S NOT FEEL **TOO** BADLY! AFTER ALL, THIS WAS ONLY AN **IMAGINARY** STORY... AND THE CHANCES ARE A **MILLION TO ONE** IT WILL **NEVER** HAPPEN! SEE THE NEXT ISSUE FOR NEW, GREAT STORIES OF THE MIGHTY **SUPERMAN** YOU KNOW!

⑧

A LOOK AT OTHER GREAT IMAGINARY STORIES

LOIS LANE #26, 1961
art by Kurt Schaffenberger

LOIS LANE #36, 1962
art by Kurt Schaffenberger

SUPERMAN'S PAL JIMMY OLSEN

HERE IT IS, AT LAST... THE STORY THOUSANDS OF READERS HAVE DEMANDED... AN *IMAGINARY TALE* IN WHICH YOUNG *DAILY PLANET* NEWSHAWK JIMMY OLSEN MARRIES --SUPERGIRL! NOW YOU CAN FIND OUT THE ASTOUNDING EVENTS (WHICH MAY ACTUALLY NEVER HAPPEN), SHOULD THESE TWO LIKEABLE YOUNG PEOPLE WED! BE WARNED IN ADVANCE, THAT YOU'RE IN FOR AN AVALANCHE OF AMAZING SURPRISES, AND SOME SAD MOMENTS, IN THIS ASTONISHING TWO-PART *IMAGINARY* NOVEL...

JIMMY OLSEN Marries SUPERGIRL!

PART 1

WHAT A SITUATION! *RED KRYPTONITE* HAS GIVEN LINDA AMNESIA, AND IT'S MADE HER FORGET SHE WAS EVER *SUPERGIRL!* SHE AND JIMMY ARE GETTING MARRIED!... NEVER AGAIN WILL *SUPERGIRL* AND I PATROL TOGETHER!

ONE MORNING IN THE *DAILY PLANET,* ON AN *IMAGINARY* DAY WHICH MAY, **OR MAY NOT,** EVER HAPPEN, AS REPORTER JIMMY OLSEN SPEAKS TO EDITOR PERRY WHITE...

HOW ABOUT A RAISE, CHIEF?

NOT UNTIL YOU *EARN IT* WITH SOME UNUSUAL NEWS STORIES...!

LATER, IN JIMMY'S APARTMENT...

I'VE *GOT* IT!... ONCE, WHILE TEMPORARILY SUFFERING FROM AMNESIA, I LIVED AS AN "ORPHAN" IN THE MIDVALE ORPHANAGE!- HM-MM! I'LL GO BACK AND WRITE A HUMAN INTEREST ARTICLE ABOUT SOME OF THE ORPHANS THERE!

AFTER GATHERING THE NEWS FACTS, I'LL PUT ON A SHOW FOR THE KIDS! I'LL BET THEY'D BE REAL THRILLED TO SEE THESE TROPHIES OF MY ADVENTURES WITH *SUPERMAN!*

NEXT DAY, AS JIMMY BRINGS HIS TROPHY KIT TO THE ORPHANAGE...

SUPERMAN ONCE GAVE ME THIS BOTTLE, WHICH CONTAINED *WOLF-MAN POTION.* LIKE A GOOF, I SWALLOWED SOME, AND FOR A TIME I BECAME A *WOLF-MAN* WHENEVER THE MOON CAME OUT!

NEXT, HE EXHIBITS ANOTHER TROPHY...

GOSH, WHAT A STRANGE *SPACE JEWEL!* THOUGH HE'S YELLING INTO IT AS *LOUD* AS HE CAN, THE JEWEL'S MUFFLING HIS SHOUT INTO A *WHISPER!*

HELLO!

HELLO

FANTASTIC!

AFTER JIMMY ENDS HIS SHOW...

HE'S CUTE!

I ADORED EVERY SECOND OF YOUR WONDERFUL SHOW, JIMMY! YOUR CAREER SOUNDS ABSOLUTELY *FASCINATING!* I'M LINDA LEE DANVERS, AND...

HOW LONG HAVE YOU BEEN AN ORPHAN HERE, LINDA?

ACTUALLY, I'M NO LONGER AN ORPHAN! I'VE BEEN ADOPTED BY MR. AND MRS. DANVERS! BUT MY PARENTS ARE NOW ABROAD, ON AN IMPORTANT TRIP! THEY'VE ARRANGED FOR ME TO STAY HERE WHILE THEY'RE GONE! ...MAY I HAVE YOUR *AUTOGRAPH?*

I'LL DO BETTER THAN *THAT!*

I...LIKE YOU A LOT, LINDA! AND SO I'LL DO SOMETHING I'VE *NEVER DONE BEFORE!* I'M GOING TO *GIVE AWAY* ONE OF MY *SUPER-MAN* TROPHIES! HERE! I'LL OPEN THIS LEAD BOX AND GIVE YOU THIS PIECE OF *RED KRYPTONITE!*

ULP!!--I'M T-TRAPPED!

2

AS JIMMY RAMBLES ON, LINDA'S FEARFUL EXPRESSION VANISHES...

RED KRYPTONITE ALWAYS HAS SOME UNPREDICTABLE EFFECT ON ANYONE FROM THE PLANET **KRYPTON**! HOWEVER, IT CAN AFFECT THEM ONLY **ONCE**! — AT ONE TIME, THIS PIECE AFFECTED **SUPERMAN** AND **KRYPTO**!

SINCE THERE ISN'T ANYONE ELSE FROM **KRYPTON** ON EARTH BESIDES **THEM**, IT'S PERFECTLY SAFE FOR ME TO GIVE IT TO YOU! DON'T WORRY, IT CAN'T POSSIBLY HARM **YOU**... HA, HA!

NATURALLY NOT! HA, HA!

MID ORP

WHY DID LINDA'S FEAR SO SUDDENLY DEPART? BECAUSE THE **RED KRYPTONITE** INSTANTLY AFFECTED HER! NOT ONLY HAS IT ROBBED HER OF HER **SUPER-POWERS** BUT IT HAS DESTROYED HER RECOLLECTION THAT SHE'D **EVER** BEEN **SUPERGIRL**!!

VERY ATTRACTED TO LINDA, JIMMY ASKS...

MAY I TAKE YOU TO THE **METROPOLIS** AMUSEMENT PARK, TONIGHT?

I'D LOVE TO GO WITH YOU!

THAT EVENING, AT THE PARK...

GOODNESS! YOU'RE ABSOLUTELY TERRIFIC, JIMMY! YOU'RE HITTING **EVERY ONE** OF THE FLYING **SUPERMAN** TARGETS!

SUPER 3 WINNER

HIT THE FLYING **SUPERMEN** 2 OUT OF 3 HITS WINS SUP

SHE'S NOT ONLY PRETTY, BUT **BRIGHT**! SHE APPRECIATES ME!

3

PRESENTLY, AT THE DANCE PAVILION...

THERE GOES LUCY, DANCING BY WITH A HANDSOME PILOT! WHO CARES? I'D BE A CHUMP TO CHASE HER NOW, AFTER I'VE MET A LIVING DOLL LIKE LINDA! LUCY'S NEVER APPRECIATED ME, BUT LINDA THINKS I'M GREAT!

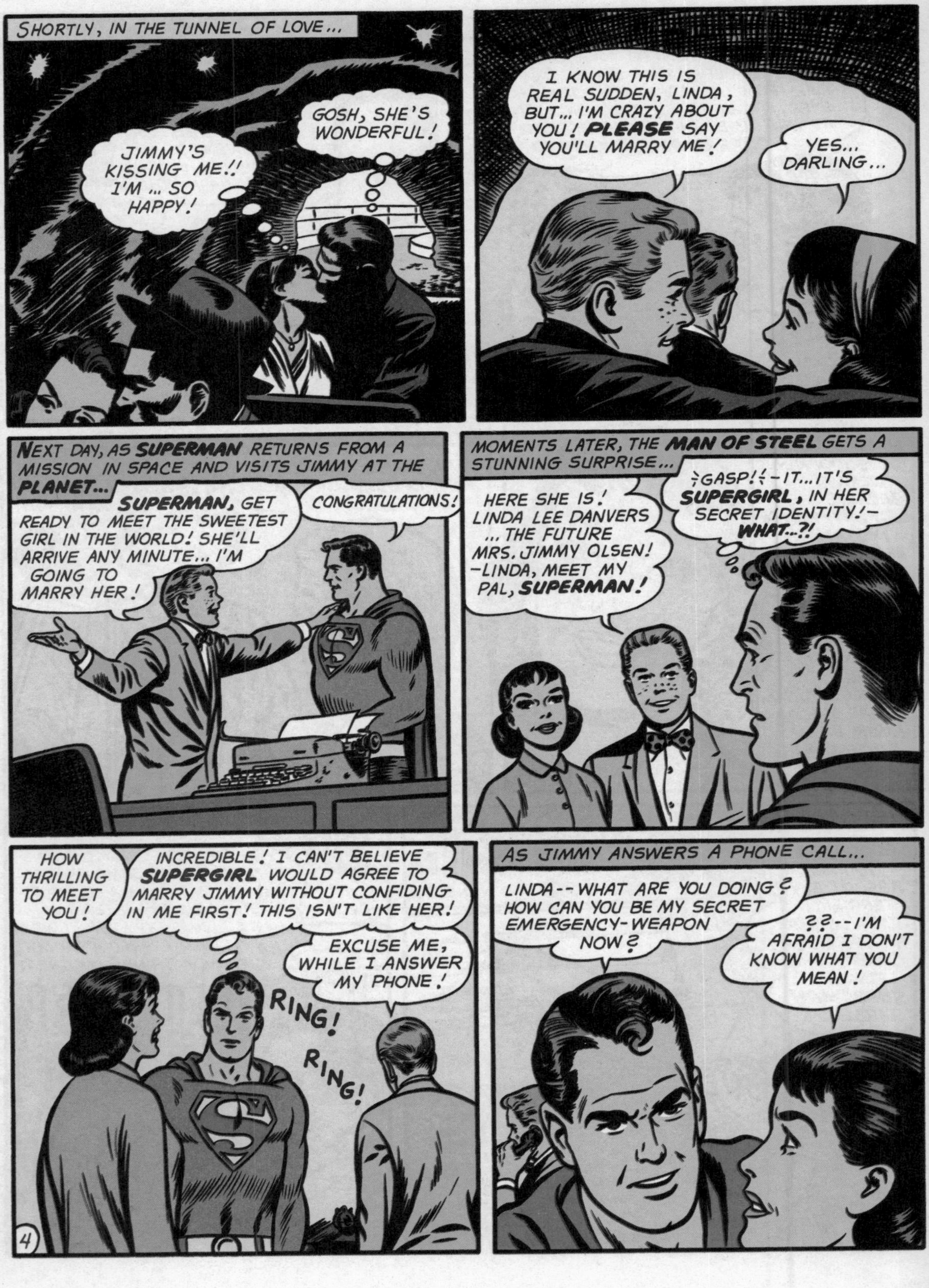
SHORTLY, IN THE TUNNEL OF LOVE...
JIMMY'S KISSING ME.!! I'M ... SO HAPPY!
GOSH, SHE'S WONDERFUL!
I KNOW THIS IS REAL SUDDEN, LINDA, BUT... I'M CRAZY ABOUT YOU! PLEASE SAY YOU'LL MARRY ME!
YES... DARLING...
NEXT DAY, AS SUPERMAN RETURNS FROM A MISSION IN SPACE AND VISITS JIMMY AT THE PLANET...
SUPERMAN, GET READY TO MEET THE SWEETEST GIRL IN THE WORLD! SHE'LL ARRIVE ANY MINUTE... I'M GOING TO MARRY HER!
CONGRATULATIONS!
MOMENTS LATER, THE MAN OF STEEL GETS A STUNNING SURPRISE...
HERE SHE IS! LINDA LEE DANVERS ... THE FUTURE MRS. JIMMY OLSEN! -LINDA, MEET MY PAL, SUPERMAN!
GASP! -IT...IT'S SUPERGIRL, IN HER SECRET IDENTITY!- WHAT..?!
HOW THRILLING TO MEET YOU!
INCREDIBLE! I CAN'T BELIEVE SUPERGIRL WOULD AGREE TO MARRY JIMMY WITHOUT CONFIDING IN ME FIRST! THIS ISN'T LIKE HER!
EXCUSE ME, WHILE I ANSWER MY PHONE!
RING!
RING!
4
AS JIMMY ANSWERS A PHONE CALL...
LINDA--WHAT ARE YOU DOING? HOW CAN YOU BE MY SECRET EMERGENCY-WEAPON NOW?
??--I'M AFRAID I DON'T KNOW WHAT YOU MEAN!

SUDDENLY, LINDA'S PURSE FALLS OPEN, AND AN OBJECT FALLS OUT...

OUCH! RIGHT ON MY TOE!... THAT HURT!

NOW I UNDERSTAND! THIS IS A PIECE OF RED KRYPTONITE I GAVE JIMMY BEFORE SUPERGIRL CAME TO EARTH!...SHE EXCLAIMED WITH PAIN! THE KRYPTONITE HAS MADE HER LOSE HER SUPER-POWERS AND MADE HER FORGET BEING SUPERGIRL!

THAT'S WHY SHE'S MARRYING JIMMY AND DIDN'T TELL ME FIRST! SHE DOESN'T REALIZE SHE'S MY COUSIN! HMM... THEY'RE SO HAPPY... I'LL KEEP MUM, AND DO NOTHING TO SPOIL THEIR HAPPINESS!

AND SO, JIMMY AND LINDA ARE MARRIED...!

TOO BAD CLARK COULDN'T ATTEND THE WEDDING, DUE TO AN URGENT OUT-OF-TOWN ASSIGNMENT!

NOW THAT LUCY'S LOST JIMMY, SHE'S SORRY SHE DIDN'T TAKE HIM MORE SERIOUSLY!

AFTER THEIR HONEYMOON TRIP, THE NEWLYWEDS SETTLE DOWN IN A LOVELY HOME, COMPLETE WITH NEW FURNITURE AND LOADS OF BILLS...

YIPES! IF I DON'T GET A RAISE FROM PERRY, I'LL NEVER BE ABLE TO PAY THESE!

NEXT DAY, AT THE PLANET...

SORRY, I CAN'T INCREASE YOUR SALARY, JIMMY! I HAVEN'T HAD A BIG SCOOP FROM YOU IN WEEKS!

THEN...I QUIT!! I'LL GET A JOB WHERE I'M RESPECTED!

5

BUT WHEN JIMMY MAKES THE ROUNDS...

SORRY, BUT WE'VE GOT NOTHING TO OFFER YOU!

ULP! — I THOUGHT THEY'D SNAP ME UP! ÷CHOKE÷...I'VE GOT A NEW BRIDE, LOTS OF BILLS... AND N-NO JOB!

MEANWHILE, AT THE OLSEN HOME...

I'LL SURPRISE JIMMY BY RE-ARRANGING THE FURNITURE! WHEW! I-I CAN HARDLY BUDGE THIS COUCH! ÷PUFF÷—IT'S...TOO...HEAVY...

UNEXPECTEDLY...

AWP.!! I-I'M NOT ONLY EASILY L-LIFTING IT UP INTO THE AIR...÷GASP÷...I'M FLYING WITH IT!!—I'VE GOT SUPER-POWERS!! WHAT...?!!

NEXT INSTANT, AS MRS. OLSEN ALIGHTS...

GREAT GUNS! IT'S ALL CLEAR NOW! RED KRYPTONITE STOLE SOME OF MY MEMORY, AND ALL MY SUPER-POWERS! THE KRYPTONITE'S EFFECTS HAVE JUST WORN OFF! I'M SUPERGIRL AGAIN, AND REMEMBER... EVERYTHING!!

OH, DEAR! I CAN'T TELL JIMMY RIGHT AWAY THAT HE'S MARRIED TO A SUPER-GIRL! HEAVEN KNOWS WHAT THE SHOCK MIGHT DO TO HIM!-I-I NEED TIME TO DECIDE WHAT TO DO!!

AT DUSK, WHEN HER HUSBAND RETURNS...

WHAT'S UPSETTING YOU, HONEY? WHY ARE YOU PUTTING YOUR SUPERMAN TROPHY KIT IN THE CAR?

I'M UNEMPLOYED! WE DESPERATELY NEED MONEY TO PAY OUR BILLS! I-I'LL RAISE SOME CASH BY SELLING THE TROPHIES...÷CHOKE÷...

6

ABRUPTLY, THE GROUND SHAKES VIOLENTLY...

WHRR-RR!

AN EARTHQUAKE!—JIMMY! EMERGENCY SIRENS ARE WAILING AT THE NEARBY AIRPORT! MAYBE THE EARTHQUAKE WAS WORSE THERE!

JUMP IN! LET'S GO SEE IF WE CAN HELP!

PRESS

SHORTLY, AT THE AIRPORT...

GREAT SCOTT—RUNWAYS 2 AND 3 WERE CRUMPLED BY THE EARTHQUAKE! ONLY RUNWAY NUMBER 1 CAN BE SAFELY USED! A JET AIR-LINER IS DUE TO LAND IN THIRTY SECONDS. THE CONTROL-TOWER'S RADIO TRANSMITTER DOESN'T WORK...

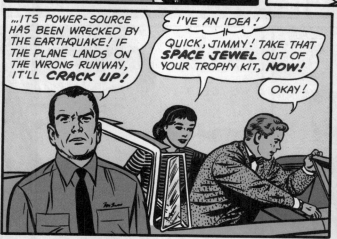

...ITS POWER-SOURCE HAS BEEN WRECKED BY THE EARTHQUAKE! IF THE PLANE LANDS ON THE WRONG RUNWAY, IT'LL CRACK UP!

I'VE AN IDEA! QUICK, JIMMY! TAKE THAT SPACE JEWEL OUT OF YOUR TROPHY KIT, NOW!

OKAY!

AT THE ORPHANAGE, WHEN YOU YELLED INTO THE JEWEL'S FACETED SIDE, YOUR SHOUT BECAME A WHISPER! NOW SPEAK A WARNING INTO THE JEWEL'S OPPOSITE SIDE! MAYBE THAT'LL CAUSE YOUR VOICE TO BE SUPER-MAGNIFIED!

AND AS JIMMY OBEYS...

EMERGENCY INSTRUCTIONS TO JET LINER! LAND ONLY ON RUNWAY ONE!!

HOORAY! THE PILOT HEARD THE WARNING AND IS CHANGING DIRECTION TOWARD RUNWAY ONE!

NO ONE REALIZES THE POWERFUL VOICE IS ACTUALLY MY SUPER-LOUD, DISGUISED, VENTRILOQUISTIC SHOUT!

⑦

AFTER THE PLANE LANDS SAFELY, A PASSENGER GRATEFULLY SPEAKS TO JIMMY...

I'M THE AIRLINE'S PRESIDENT! I INSIST YOU ACCEPT THIS $5,000 CHECK, OLSEN, AS A REWARD!

LUCY'S THE PLANE'S STEWARDESS! HA! SHE LOST A GREAT CATCH WHEN I MARRIED LINDA!

AND WHEN JIMMY VISITS THE *PLANET*...

MY BOY, THE FIRST-HAND ACCOUNT OF HOW YOU SAVED THE PLANE IS *GREAT!* YOU'RE RE-HIRED... AT A HIGHER SALARY!

NATURALLY!

TRIUMPHANTLY, JIMMY RETURNS HOME...

PROUD OF ME, SWEETHEART? ... *HA, HA!* THAT IDEA OF YOURS WAS SUPER!

YOU'RE MARVELOUS!

"SUPER"!—THAT REMINDS ME!... *HOW* SHALL I BREAK THE NEWS TO JIMMY THAT HE'S MARRIED TO A SUPERGIRL?!!

LATER, AS HER HUSBAND DROPS OFF TO SLEEP, LINDA GETS HER BIG INSPIRATION...

I'VE GOT IT! I'LL BREAK IT TO HIM GRADUALLY! FIRST, I'LL LET HIM DISCOVER THAT A *SUPERGIRL* EXISTS!--*THEN*... I'LL TRY TO MAKE HIM FALL IN LOVE WITH HER!

⑧

WILL I SUCCEED? *CAN* I MAKE JIMMY LOVE *SUPERGIRL* MORE THAN HE LOVES... LINDA? I... I'LL TRY!!

END PART I

A LOOK AT OTHER GREAT IMAGINARY STORIES

SUPERMAN #200, 1967
art by Curt Swan
and George Klein

SUPERMAN #300, 1976
art by Curt Swan
and Bob Oksner

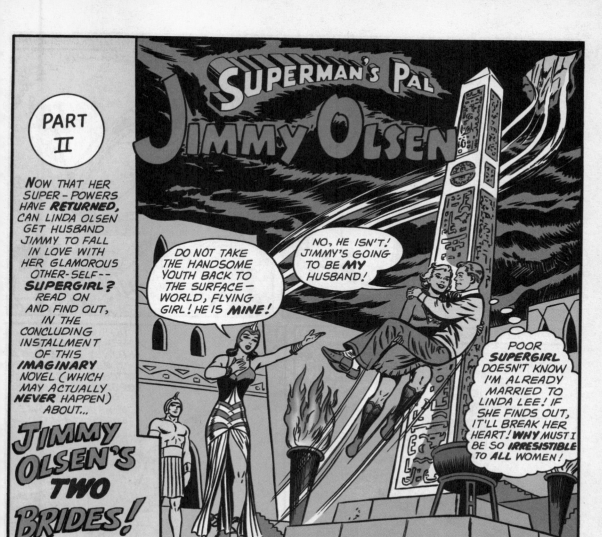

SUPERMAN'S PAL JIMMY OLSEN

PART II

NOW THAT HER SUPER-POWERS HAVE **RETURNED**, CAN LINDA OLSEN GET HUSBAND JIMMY TO FALL IN LOVE WITH HER GLAMOROUS OTHER-SELF-- **SUPERGIRL?** READ ON AND FIND OUT, IN THE CONCLUDING INSTALLMENT OF THIS **IMAGINARY** NOVEL (WHICH MAY ACTUALLY **NEVER** HAPPEN) ABOUT...

JIMMY OLSEN'S TWO BRIDES!

DO NOT TAKE THE HANDSOME YOUTH BACK TO THE SURFACE-WORLD, FLYING GIRL! HE IS **MINE!**

NO, HE ISN'T! JIMMY'S GOING TO BE **MY** HUSBAND!

POOR **SUPERGIRL** DOESN'T KNOW I'M ALREADY MARRIED TO LINDA LEE! IF SHE FINDS OUT, IT'LL BREAK HER HEART! **WHY** MUST I BE SO **IRRESISTIBLE** TO **ALL** WOMEN!

NEXT MORNING, ON ANOTHER **IMAGINARY** DAY (WHICH MAY OR **MAY NOT** EVER HAPPEN), LINDA WATCHES JIMMY FROM AFAR WITH SUPER-VISION...

SOONER OR LATER, HE'LL GET INTO TROUBLE, AS USUAL! THEN I'LL SWITCH TO **SUPERGIRL**...

...AND RESCUE HIM! AFTER HE LEARNS THAT A **SUPER-GIRL** EXISTS, AS **SUPERGIRL** I'LL TELL HIM I LOVE HIM! THEN, WHEN HE FINDS OUT THAT **SUPERGIRL** AND LINDA ARE ONE AND THE SAME, THE SHOCK WON'T BE SO BAD!

PRESENTLY, SHE SEES...

PERRY WANTS AN ARTICLE ON THIS FAIR, WHICH IS CLOSED DOWN BECAUSE OF ITS UNSAFE EQUIPMENT! -GOSH, THIS *SUPERMAN RIDE* LOOKS LIKE FUN! I'LL TURN IT ON AND ENJOY MYSELF!

MOMENTS LATER, LINDA SWIFTLY CHANGES TO THE DYNAMIC *GIRL OF STEEL*...

OH-OH! THE WIRES HOLDING THE *SUPERMAN* FIGURE THAT JIMMY IS RIDING HAVE SNAPPED!

MEANWHILE, AT THE FAIR...

HUH? THAT'S STRANGE! I'M FLYING *WAY* UP INTO THE SKY, JUST AS IF I WAS ASTRIDE THE *REAL SUPERMAN!* WH-WHAT'S GOING ON?!

THEN...

ULP! THE FIGURE BROKE LOOSE, AND N-NOW IT'S *FALLING!* I'D BETTER USE MY WATCH TO SIGNAL FOR *SUPERMAN'S* HELP... NO, IT'S NOT NECESSARY! HERE HE COMES NOW! -;GASP!; IT ISN'T *HIM!!*

IT'S...A *GIRL!* A *SUPERGIRL!* SHE CAN *FLY!* SH-SHE'S SAVING ME JUST THE WAY *SUPERMAN* WOULD!- THIS IS--;GULP!; IMPOSSIBLE!

HI, JIMMY! GLAD TO MEET YOU!

②

AFTER THE *GIRL OF STEEL* SAFELY LANDS JIMMY...

I'M *SUPERGIRL,* FROM THE PLANET *KRYPTON!* I'M *SUPERMAN'S* "SECRET EMERGENCY WEAPON"! SINCE YOU'RE HIS PAL, I'M SURE *YOU* CAN BE TRUSTED NEVER TO REVEAL MY EXISTENCE TO ANYONE!

GASP!

RID

WAIT! THIS DOESN'T MAKE SENSE! YOU'RE MUCH YOUNGER THAN SUPERMAN! HOW CAN BOTH YOU AND HE HAVE COME FROM KRYPTON? HE LEFT KRYPTON WHEN HE WAS A BABY, AND THE PLANET IMMEDIATELY BLEW UP!

"WHEN KRYPTON EXPLODED, BY SHEER LUCK A HUGE CHUNK OF THE PLANET WAS HURLED AWAY INTACT, WITH PEOPLE ON IT! ARGO CITY WAS ON THAT CHUNK, AND A BUBBLE OF AIR CAME ALONG WITH IT!"

"BUT THAT VERY NIGHT..."

GREAT SCOTT! ARGO CITY IS GLOWING... GREEN! THE NUCLEAR EXPLOSION WHICH DESTROYED KRYPTON IS CHANGING THE GROUND INTO KRYPTONITE --WHOSE RADIATIONS CAN KILL KRYPTONIANS!

WE'RE DOOMED, ZOR-EL!

"ZOR-EL, THE BROTHER OF SUPERMAN'S FATHER, JOR-EL, COVERED THE GROUND WITH A LAYER OF LEAD SHEET METAL TAKEN FROM HIS LAB!"

KRYPTONITE RADIATIONS CAN'T PIERCE LEAD! WE WILL LIVE!

"A FEW YEARS AFTERWARD, ZOR-EL AND HIS WIFE HAD A BABY GIRL, KARA-- ME! BUT WHEN I GREW INTO GIRLHOOD..."

METEORS ARE SMASHING HOLES IN THE LEADEN SHIELD, RELEASING KRYPTONITE RADIATIONS, KARA! WE'RE ALL DOOMED...!

③

"MY PARENTS HAD SEEN SUPERMAN ON EARTH THROUGH THEIR SUPER-SPACE TELESCOPE! MOTHER HAD MADE ME A COSTUME LIKE SUPERMAN'S, AND I WAS SHOT TOWARD EARTH IN A ROCKET-SHIP, AS ARGO CITY PERISHED..."

REACHING EARTH, I BECAME MY COUSIN **SUPERMAN'S** SECRET EMERGENCY WEAPON! -- SEEING YOU IN DANGER NOW, I SAVED YOU, EVEN THOUGH IT MEANT REVEALING MY EXISTENCE TO YOU!

DON'T WORRY! I'LL NEVER BETRAY YOUR CONFIDENCE!

I KNOW YOU WON'T! I ADMIRE **EVERYTHING** ABOUT YOU! YOU'RE SMART, CUTE, AND LOADS OF FUN! JUST THE KIND OF MAN I'D LIKE FOR A **HUSBAND!** -- BYE, JIMMY!

JEEPERS! SHE PRACTICALLY ADMITTED SHE **LOVES ME!**

GOLLY, WHAT A GIRL! SHE'S NOT ONLY **PRETTY,** BUT SUPER-POWERFUL, TOO! HM-MM! WHO KNOWS? MAYBE I WOULD NOT HAVE MARRIED LINDA, IF I'D MET **SUPERGIRL** FIRST!

RETURNING HOME, **SUPERGIRL** CHANGES BACK TO LINDA. LATER THAT EVENING...

ANYTHING UNUSUAL HAPPEN TODAY, HONEY?

UH -- NOT ESPECIALLY!

LINDA ISN'T SUPER-POWERFUL, BUT SHE'S THE SWEETEST WIFE ANY FELLOW EVER HAD!

"BLESS HIM! THE DARLING'S KEEPING HIS PROMISE AND NOT REVEALING **SUPERGIRL'S** EXISTENCE, EVEN TO HIS OWN WIFE! I'M **GLAD** HE CAN BE TRUSTED WITH SUCH A TERRIBLY IMPORTANT SECRET!

SEVERAL NIGHTS LATER...

HAVE FUN BOWLING WITH THE BOYS, TONIGHT, SWEETHEART!

I SURE WILL, LINDA DEAR!

4

AN INSTANT AFTER SHE CLOSES THE DOOR...

EXIT LINDA...ENTER **SUPERGIRL!** NOW TO BE **MY OWN COMPETITION** FOR JIMMY'S LOVE!

SHORTLY...

I--CAN'T STOP THINKING ABOUT YOU, JIMMY! I ADORE YOU! PLEASE MARRY ME!

WHAT...?! GOLLY... **SUPERGIRL'S** SO IN LOVE WITH ME IT WOULD BREAK HER HEART TO FIND OUT I'M **ALREADY** MARRIED TO LINDA LEE!

I'LL STALL HER! ER--BEFORE I CAN ANSWER THAT, I'LL HAVE TO KNOW YOU BETTER!

FINE! I SUGGEST WE ADVENTURE TOGETHER ON ANOTHER WORLD, SO WE CAN GET BETTER ACQUAINTED!

SWIFTLY BUILDING A **SPACE-GLOBE**, THE **GIRL OF STEEL** FLIES JIMMY TO ANOTHER PLANET...

A WEIRD CITY... IN RUINS... BELOW, OVER-GROWN BY THE JUNGLE!

5

AS THE DUO FROM EARTH EXPLORES THE ALIEN CITY TOGETHER, SUDDENLY...

SAVE ME, **SUPERGIRL!** HE'S PLAYING WITH ME LIKE A HUMAN YO-YO!

DON'T WORRY, JIMMY! I'LL SAVE YOU! I WON'T LET THAT NASTY MONSTER HARM MY FUTURE HUSBAND!

AT SUPER-SPEED, **SUPERGIRL** PICKS UP A WEIRD STATUE AND HURLS IT PAST THE GROTESQUE CREATURE...

GOOD! I'VE STARTLED THE **THING** INTO DROPPING JIMMY!

QUICKLY PLACING JIMMY BACK INSIDE THE **SPACE-GLOBE**, THE **GIRL OF STEEL** FLIES OFF WITH HIM...

NOW TO SPEED BACK TO OUR OWN WORLD! I'M SORRY THAT MONSTER FRIGHTENED JIMMY!

SOON, ON EARTH...

THINK OVER MY PROPOSAL, JIMMY! REMEMBER, IF YOU BECOME MY HUSBAND, I'LL PROTECT YOU ALWAYS!

SHE'S GOT **EVERYTHING!** I'D MARRY HER IN A MINUTE... BUT I'VE **ALREADY** GOT A WIFE!

WHEN JIMMY RETURNS HOME...

I HOPE YOU LIKE THIS CAKE I'VE BAKED FOR YOU, DARLING!

TWO WONDERFUL GIRLS... EACH MADLY IN LOVE WITH ME! GOSH, I DON'T WANT TO BREAK THE HEART OF **EITHER** OF THEM!

LOVE TO JIMMY

NEXT DAY, ASSIGNED TO WRITE AN ARTICLE ON THE **PURPLE-STONE NATIONAL PARK**, JIMMY VISITS IT...

NO ONE'S WATCHING! I'LL RUN FORWARD, AND PEEK INTO THE PIT, BEFORE THE GUARD NOTICES! THIS WILL MAKE A GREAT SCOOP!

BOTTOMLESS PIT WARNING
KEEP BEHIND RAILS

6

BUT THEN...

AWP! I T-TRIPPED!... I'M FALLING DOWN... DOWN... WOULD SUMMON **SUPERMAN**... BUT I'M ...BLACKING OUT...

MEANWHILE, AT THE PIT'S BOTTOM, IN A COLOSSAL CAVERN WHICH IS PEOPLED BY A SUB-EARTH CIVILIZATION...

YOU HAVE NO CHOICE, *QUEEN TANIA!* YOU *MUST* MARRY ME, YOUR PRIME MINISTER! REFUSE, AND LIKE THE OTHER FOOLS WHO DARED OPPOSE ME, YOU WILL BE TRANSFORMED INTO A SHAPELESS BLOB BY THIS *PUNISHMENT JEWEL* I ALONE POSSESS!

TRAITOR! WHAT YOU REALLY DESIRE IS THE POWER OF MY *THRONE!* AFTER THE WEDDING, YOU WOULD OPPRESS THE CAVERN PEOPLE! BUT YOUR PLOT WILL *FAIL!*

AN ANCIENT PROPHECY FORECAST THAT TREACHERY SUCH AS YOURS WILL BE FOILED BY A HANDSOME YOUTH FROM THE SURFACE-WORLD! I AWAIT MY RESCUER!

THE PROPHECY LIES!

DOWN, DOWN FLOATS THE YOUNG REPORTER...

WHAT LUCK! I'VE COME TO! MY FALL IS BEING BRAKED BY A POWERFUL UP-DRAFT OF AIR!

SHORTLY, AS JIMMY GENTLY ALIGHTS AT THE PIT'S BOTTOM...

¡GASP!¡---SEE! MY DELIVERER HAS ARRIVED FROM THE SURFACE-WORLD AS PROPHESIED!

ACCURSED MEDDLER! THE RAY FROM THIS *PUNISHMENT-JEWEL* WILL MAKE YOU SUFFER A GHASTLY FATE!

⑦

AS HER SUPER-VISION DETECTS HER HUSBAND'S PERIL, LINDA CHANGES TO *SUPERGIRL* AND STREAKS DOWN INTO THE CAVERN...

¡CHOKE!¡-TH-THAT AWFUL RAY HAS TURNED JIMMY INTO A...BLOB!!

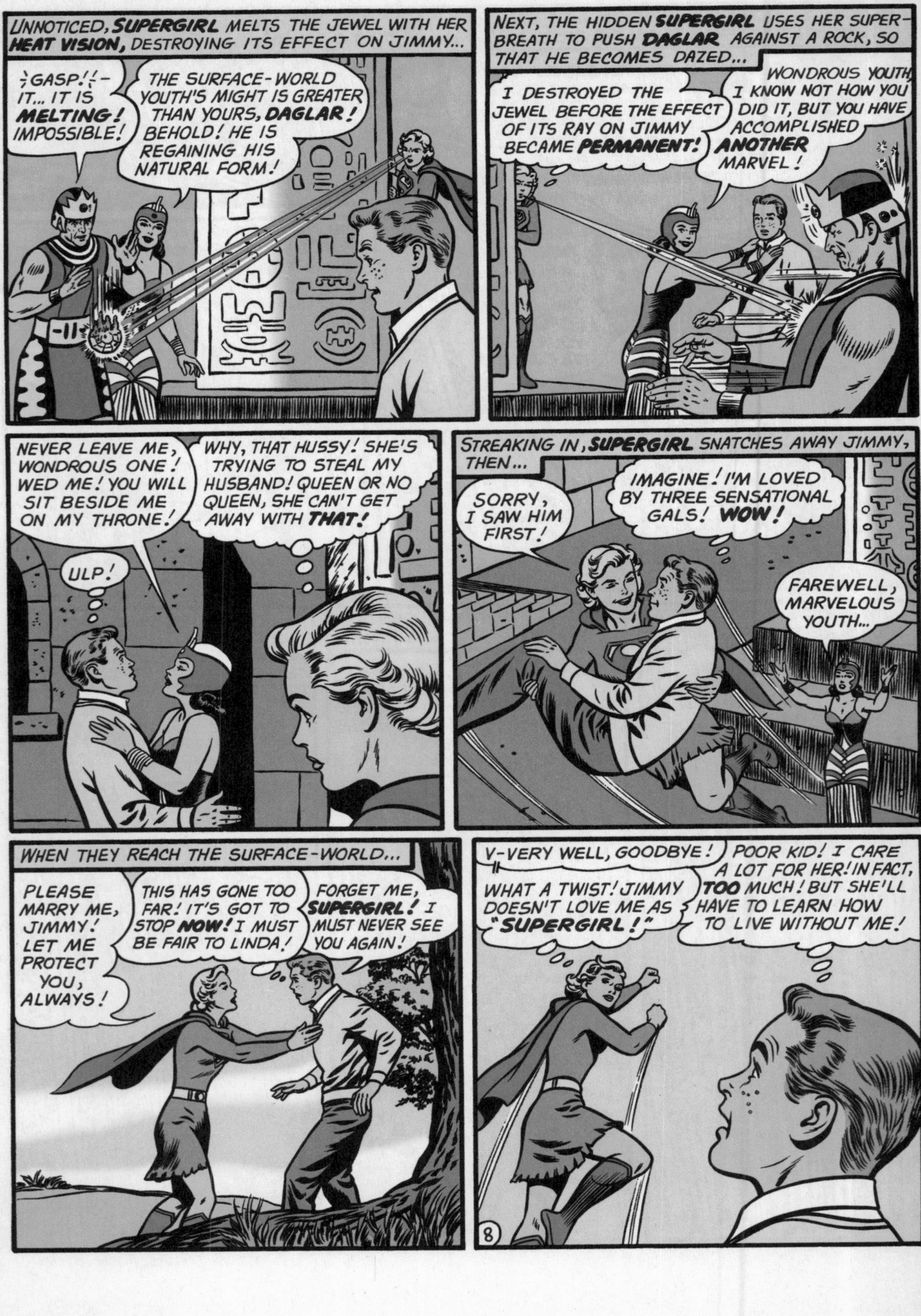
UNNOTICED, SUPERGIRL MELTS THE JEWEL WITH HER HEAT VISION, DESTROYING ITS EFFECT ON JIMMY...
-GASP!- IT... IT IS MELTING! IMPOSSIBLE!
THE SURFACE-WORLD YOUTH'S MIGHT IS GREATER THAN YOURS, DAGLAR! BEHOLD! HE IS REGAINING HIS NATURAL FORM!
NEXT, THE HIDDEN SUPERGIRL USES HER SUPER-BREATH TO PUSH DAGLAR AGAINST A ROCK, SO THAT HE BECOMES DAZED...
I DESTROYED THE JEWEL BEFORE THE EFFECT OF ITS RAY ON JIMMY BECAME PERMANENT!
WONDROUS YOUTH, I KNOW NOT HOW YOU DID IT, BUT YOU HAVE ACCOMPLISHED ANOTHER MARVEL!
NEVER LEAVE ME, WONDROUS ONE! WED ME! YOU WILL SIT BESIDE ME ON MY THRONE!
WHY, THAT HUSSY! SHE'S TRYING TO STEAL MY HUSBAND! QUEEN OR NO QUEEN, SHE CAN'T GET AWAY WITH THAT!
ULP!
STREAKING IN, SUPERGIRL SNATCHES AWAY JIMMY, THEN...
SORRY, I SAW HIM FIRST!
IMAGINE! I'M LOVED BY THREE SENSATIONAL GALS! WOW!
FAREWELL, MARVELOUS YOUTH...
WHEN THEY REACH THE SURFACE-WORLD...
PLEASE MARRY ME, JIMMY! LET ME PROTECT YOU, ALWAYS!
THIS HAS GONE TOO FAR! IT'S GOT TO STOP NOW! I MUST BE FAIR TO LINDA!
FORGET ME, SUPERGIRL! I MUST NEVER SEE YOU AGAIN!
V-VERY WELL, GOODBYE!
WHAT A TWIST! JIMMY DOESN'T LOVE ME AS "SUPERGIRL!"
POOR KID! I CARE A LOT FOR HER! IN FACT, TOO MUCH! BUT SHE'LL HAVE TO LEARN HOW TO LIVE WITHOUT ME!
8

THAT NIGHT, AS LINDA DOES SOME MENDING...

¡CHOKE!--IF ONLY I HAD MADE HIM LOVE ME AS *SUPERGIRL*... THEN IT WOULD HAVE BEEN SO EASY TO TELL HIM I'M *BOTH* GIRLS!

LINDA, YOU'RE TOO GOOD TO ME! I DON'T DESERVE IT!--THERE'S SOMETHING I *MUST* CONFESS!

I'VE MET ANOTHER GIRL--A *SUPERGIRL!* I LOVE *YOU*-- BUT WHEN I'M WITH *HER*, I-I CAN'T HELP THINKING WHAT A SWELL WIFE *SHE'D* MAKE! I FEEL LIKE A SKUNK!

WONDERFUL!

TURN AROUND... JIMMY!

AS JIMMY OBEYS, BEFORE HIS EYES, LINDA USES SUPER-SPEED TO REMOVE HER BROWN WIG AND SWITCH TO HER COSTUME, CHANGING TO HER OTHER IDENTITY!

GREAT SCOTT! MY OWN WIFE IS... LINDA, YOU'RE... *SUPERGIRL!* OOLP!

HE'S FAINTING.!!

AFTER JIMMY REVIVES, AND HIS *WIFE OF STEEL* EXPLAINS EVERYTHING...

I'M M-MARRIED TO A *SUPERGIRL!* WOW! TERRIFIC! *TERRIFIC!!*

THANK GOODNESS I BROKE THE NEWS TO HIM GRADUALLY! OTHERWISE, THE SHOCK *MIGHT* HAVE BEEN TOO MUCH!

YES, THIS STORY HAD A *HAPPY* ENDING, BUT REMEMBER, THIS HAS ONLY BEEN AN *IMAGINARY TALE*, AND MAY *NEVER* HAPPEN! AND BESIDES, LUCY LANE IS STILL AROUND!

The End

A LOOK AT OTHER GREAT IMAGINARY STORIES

SUPERBOY #95, 1962
art by Curt Swan
and George Klein

SUPERMAN #156, 1962
art by Curt Swan
and George Klein

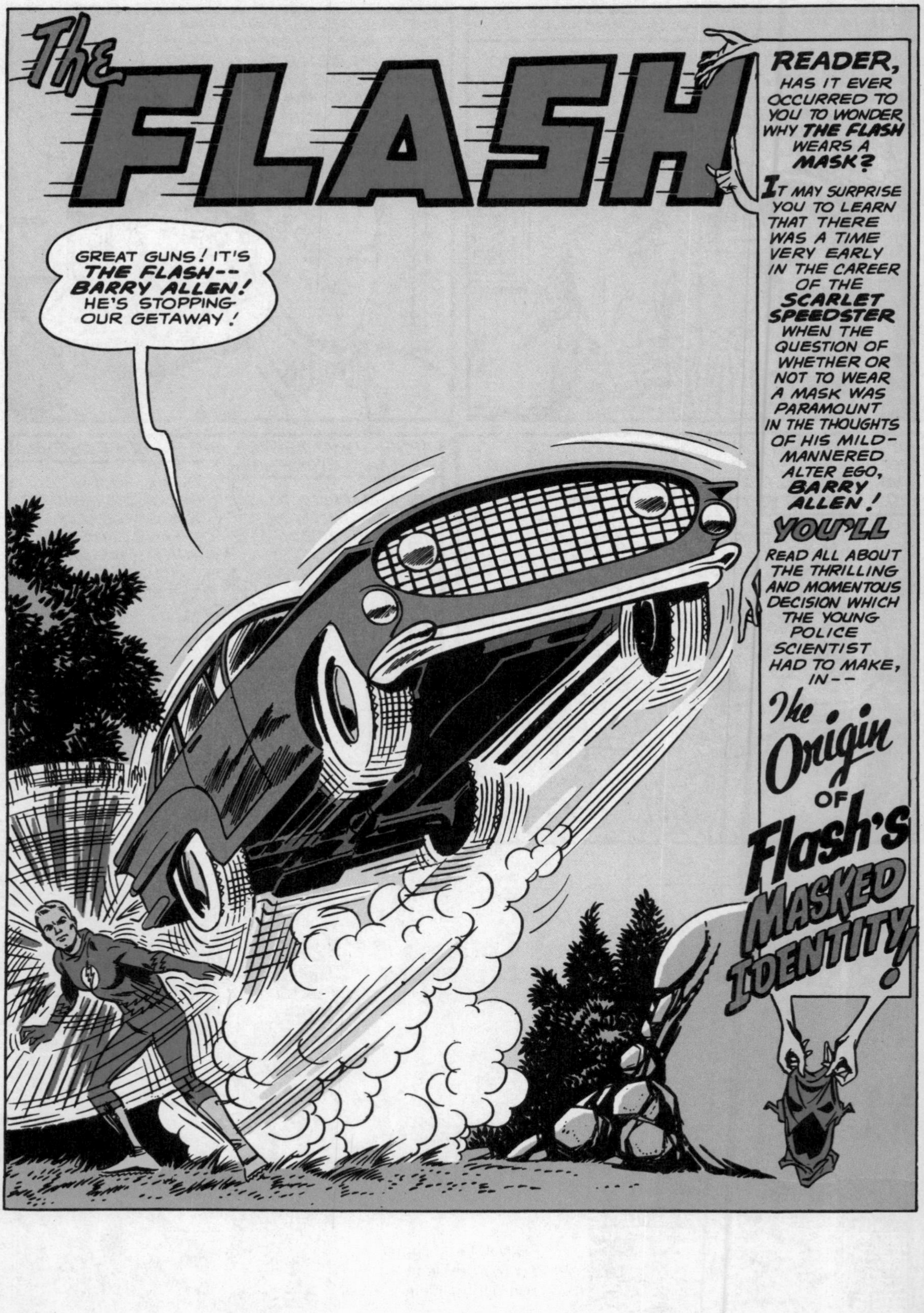

THE FLASH
GREAT GUNS! IT'S THE FLASH-- BARRY ALLEN! HE'S STOPPING OUR GETAWAY!
READER, HAS IT EVER OCCURRED TO YOU TO WONDER WHY THE FLASH WEARS A MASK?
IT MAY SURPRISE YOU TO LEARN THAT THERE WAS A TIME VERY EARLY IN THE CAREER OF THE SCARLET SPEEDSTER WHEN THE QUESTION OF WHETHER OR NOT TO WEAR A MASK WAS PARAMOUNT IN THE THOUGHTS OF HIS MILD-MANNERED ALTER EGO, BARRY ALLEN!
YOU'LL READ ALL ABOUT THE THRILLING AND MOMENTOUS DECISION WHICH THE YOUNG POLICE SCIENTIST HAD TO MAKE, IN--
The Origin of Flash's Masked Identity!

ONE DAY SHORTLY AFTER THE AMAZING ACCIDENT WHICH TURNED *BARRY ALLEN* INTO THE WORLD'S FASTEST HUMAN...

IN THIS OLD COMIC BOOK THE ORIGINAL *FLASH* NEVER BOTHERED TO WEAR A *MASK*-- YET SOMEHOW HIS SECRET IDENTITY REMAINED SAFE! BUT NOW THAT I HAVE *REALLY* BECOME THE *FASTEST MAN ALIVE*-- AS HE WAS CALLED-- I WONDER... CAN I *TOO* GET AWAY WITHOUT WEARING A MASK?

I'VE ALREADY STARTED TO FIGHT CRIME AND INJUSTICE WEARING A MASKLESS UNIFORM LIKE THE OLD *FLASH!* BUT I WRAPPED UP THOSE CASES WITHOUT BEING SEEN! WHAT WOULD HAPPEN IF THE WHOLE WORLD DISCOVERED THAT *BARRY ALLEN* AND *FLASH* WERE THE SAME PERSON? WHAT HARM WOULD IT DO?

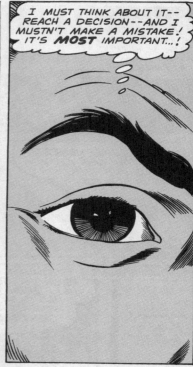

I MUST THINK ABOUT IT-- REACH A DECISION-- AND I MUSTN'T MAKE A MISTAKE! IT'S *MOST* IMPORTANT...!

LATER...

DID YOU SEE TODAY'S PAPER, DR. BAILEY? A POLICE SCIENTIST NAMED *BARRY ALLEN* IS GOING TO ADDRESS THE *NATIONAL SCIENCE CONFERENCE*-- ON HIS ATTAINMENT OF *SUPER-SPEED!*

I'LL LOOK FORWARD TO THAT!

AT A JAM-PACKED CONVENTION HALL IN *CENTRAL CITY,* ONE SPEAKER ELECTRIFIES THE GATHERING OF SAVANTS...

YES, GENTLEMEN... *I AM THE FLASH!!* I HAVE COME HERE TODAY IN ORDER TO REVEAL MY DISCOVERY OF *SUPER-SPEED*-- EVEN THOUGH I DON'T KNOW THE *EXACT DETAILS* OF THE PROCESS MYSELF--

WHAT?!

BEFORE THE SPEAKER CAN CONTINUE...

HE IS THE *FLASH!* I'VE GOT TO GET TO A PHONE-- CALL MY PAPER!

THIS IS *FRONT-PAGE NEWS!*

OUTA MY WAY!

As publicity starts to mount, the scientific gathering remains cool...

WHAT YOU SAY IS VERY INTERESTING, MR. ALLEN! BUT NONE OF US HERE HAS EVER SEEN THE FLASH-- ALTHOUGH OF COURSE WE HAVE HEARD OF HIM! MAY WE ASK--COULD YOU POSSIBLY GIVE US A DEMONSTRATION...

...OF THIS SUPER-SPEED THAT YOU TALK OF? ACTIONS SPEAK LOUDER THAN WORDS IN SCIENCE, YOU KNOW!

EXACTLY! THAT'S WHY I'VE PREPARED A DEMONSTRATION--

At that moment...

GENTLEMEN--A SHOCKING REPORT HAS JUST REACHED US! A HUGE TORNADO HAS BEEN SIGHTED BEARING DOWN ON CENTRAL CITY!

As all present rush out...

THERE IT IS-- IT'S ENORMOUS!

A TORNADO THAT SIZE COULD CAUSE TERRIBLE DAMAGE!

Meanwhile one figure among the savants is already in action...

WHAT'S BARRY ALLEN DOING?

HE PRESSED HIS RING--AND HIS FLASH UNIFORM IS SPURTING OUT!

Instantly, the uniform has enlarged in contact with the air, and BARRY has donned it over his regular clothes...

I'VE GOT TO HALT THAT TORNADO--AND AT THE SAME TIME I'LL GIVE THE SCIENTISTS THE DEMONSTRATION THEY WERE ASKING FOR!

As the **HUMAN ROCKET** hurtles at the ominous **DARK SPIRAL** engulfing all in its path, he swiftly forms a plan to deal with it!

BY CIRCLING AT **SUPER-SPEED**, I'VE SET UP A MASS OF WHIRLING AIR THAT IS ROTATING IN A **CLOCKWISE DIRECTION**-- THE OPPOSITE DIRECTION FROM THAT TORNADO! *

*EDITOR'S NOTE: IN THE NORTHERN HEMISPHERE, DUE TO THE ROTATION OF THE EARTH, THE WINDS OF A TORNADO REVOLVE IN A COUNTER-CLOCKWISE DIRECTION!

AND MOMENTS LATER, IN FULL VIEW OF THE SCIENTISTS...

THAT WHIRLWIND **THE FLASH** SET UP IS **CLASHING** WITH THE TORNADO-- AND **DESTROYING** IT BEFORE IT CAN DO HARM--!

POW!

THAT EVENING...

I'VE SURE HARVESTED A BUMPER CROP OF HEADLINES BY WHAT I DID TODAY! AND I'VE EVEN...

FLASH SAVES CENTRAL CITY

SCARLET SPEEDSTER REVEALED AS POLICE SCIENTIST BARRY ALLEN

...IMPRESSED SOME OF THE DOUBTERS AMONG MY SCIENTIFIC COLLEAGUES!

SCARLET SPEEDSTER REVEALED AS POLICE SCIENTIST BARRY ALLEN

BARRY (THE FLASH) ALLEN WAS HAILED TODAY BY THE NATIONAL SCIENCE CONFERENCE! A TRIUMPH FOR A YOUNG POLICE SCIENTIST...

BUT NEXT MORNING, ON THE WAY TO WORK...

WHAT IN THUNDER? SOMETHING MUST HAVE HAPPENED-- THESE **HUGE CROWDS** IN FRONT OF **POLICE HEADQUARTERS!**

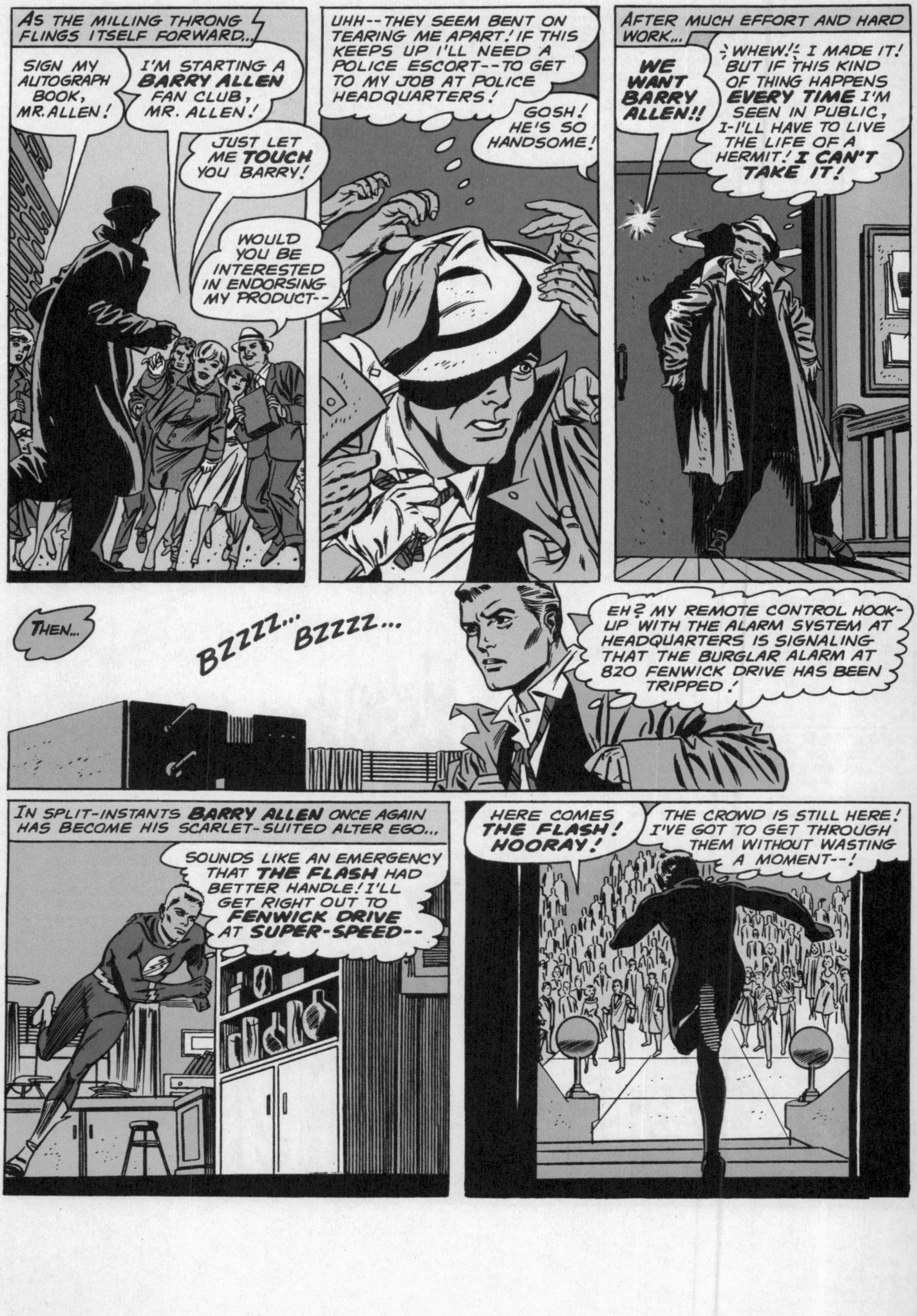

AS THE MILLING THRONG FLINGS ITSELF FORWARD...
SIGN MY AUTOGRAPH BOOK, MR. ALLEN!
I'M STARTING A BARRY ALLEN FAN CLUB, MR. ALLEN!
JUST LET ME TOUCH YOU BARRY!
WOULD YOU BE INTERESTED IN ENDORSING MY PRODUCT--
UHH--THEY SEEM BENT ON TEARING ME APART! IF THIS KEEPS UP I'LL NEED A POLICE ESCORT--TO GET TO MY JOB AT POLICE HEADQUARTERS!
GOSH! HE'S SO HANDSOME!
AFTER MUCH EFFORT AND HARD WORK...
WE WANT BARRY ALLEN!!
WHEW! I MADE IT! BUT IF THIS KIND OF THING HAPPENS EVERY TIME I'M SEEN IN PUBLIC, I-I'LL HAVE TO LIVE THE LIFE OF A HERMIT! I CAN'T TAKE IT!
THEN...
BZZZZ... BZZZZ...
EH? MY REMOTE CONTROL HOOK-UP WITH THE ALARM SYSTEM AT HEADQUARTERS IS SIGNALING THAT THE BURGLAR ALARM AT 820 FENWICK DRIVE HAS BEEN TRIPPED!
IN SPLIT-INSTANTS BARRY ALLEN ONCE AGAIN HAS BECOME HIS SCARLET-SUITED ALTER EGO...
SOUNDS LIKE AN EMERGENCY THAT THE FLASH HAD BETTER HANDLE! I'LL GET RIGHT OUT TO FENWICK DRIVE AT SUPER-SPEED--
HERE COMES THE FLASH! HOORAY!
THE CROWD IS STILL HERE! I'VE GOT TO GET THROUGH THEM WITHOUT WASTING A MOMENT--!

BUT AS THE **HUMAN ROCKET** SEEKS TO PENETRATE THE DENSE WALL OF HUMANITY BEFORE HIM...

THEY'RE SO CLOSELY PACKED I CAN'T GET OUT!

AND I DON'T DARE TRY TO **VIBRATE** THROUGH THEM BY **SUPER-SPEED**...

I HAVEN'T QUITE PERFECTED THAT TRICK AND I MIGHT **HURT SOMEONE** THAT WAY!

FINALLY...

MADE IT--AT LAST! I HOPE THAT DELAY WASN'T **COSTLY!**

IN NO TIME FLAT, ON THE OTHER SIDE OF TOWN...

THIS IS IT...820 FENWICK DRIVE! ARCHIBALD HAYDON, THE RICH ART COLLECTOR, LIVES HERE! BUT I REMEMBER READING THAT HE WAS OUT OF THE CITY, ON VACATION...

DOOR'S OPEN--SOMEONE'S TAMPERED WITH THE LOCK! IT'S BROKEN! AND-- **GREAT SCOTT!**

THERE HAS BEEN A FLOOD OF **ART THEFTS** RECENTLY--AND FROM THE LOOKS OF THOSE BLANK SPACES ON THE WALLS, THE GANG HAS MADE OFF WITH MR. HAYDON'S **ENTIRE COLLECTION!** BUT THEY CAN'T BE FAR AWAY--EH? I JUST THOUGHT OF SOMETHING!

INTO THE KEEN BRAIN OF THE **SCARLET SPEEDSTER** AS HE STREAKS OFF, AN IMAGE SPRINGS...

THAT CAR...THAT WAS LEAVING JUST AS I ARRIVED! I BARELY NOTICED IT AT THE TIME...BUT THE CROOKS MIGHT HAVE BEEN **IN THAT!** GOT TO CHECK--

SPLIT-MOMENTS LATER...

SURE ENOUGH-- THERE THEY ARE!

WHAT IN BLAZES--! IT'S *THE FLASH*!!

INSTANTS AFTER, USING HIS HANDS AT WHIRLWIND SPEED TO SHOOT *COMPRESSED AIR* UNDER THE CAR...

...THE PHENOMENAL SPEEDSTER SUCCEEDS IN RAISING IT COMPLETELY *OFF THE ROAD*, PUTTING IT UNDER *HIS* CONTROL!

AND SOON...

PLUG HIM! HE'S "DRIVING" US TO THAT POLICE STATION UP AHEAD!

PLUG HIM?! HOW CAN I WHEN I CAN HARDLY EVEN SEE HIM!

WITH THE VALUABLE PAINTINGS RECOVERED AND THE GANG BEHIND BARS...

IF THOSE CROWDS BACK AT POLICE HEAD-QUARTERS *DELAYED ME ONE SECOND* MORE, I WOULDN'T HAVE SPIED THE GETAWAY CAR AND THE GANG WOULD HAVE GOTTEN AWAY SCOT-FREE!

THAT SETTLES IT...!

THE *DAYDREAM* I JUST HAD WHILE SITTING HERE PROVES TO ME THAT NO ONE MUST EVER SUSPECT THAT I, *BARRY ALLEN*, AM *THE FLASH*! IT'S *TOO DANGEROUS*! MY ACTIVITIES AS *THE FLASH* WOULD ALWAYS BE HAMPERED!

BY CUTTING A FEW HOLES IN THE COWL OF MY UNIFORM AND THEN PULLING IT OVER MY HEAD, I'VE MADE A *MASK* TO CONCEAL MY *FLASH* IDENTITY!

YES, READER, IT WAS ONLY A DAYDREAM! BUT IT *MIGHT* HAVE BEEN *TRUE*-- EVERY WORD OF IT--IF *BARRY ALLEN* HAD RASHLY REVEALED THE TRUTH ABOUT HIMSELF!

AND IT DOES REVEAL TO US WHY HIS FAMED ALTER EGO MUST ALWAYS GO ABOUT WITH HIS *IDENTITY* A SECRET!

THE END

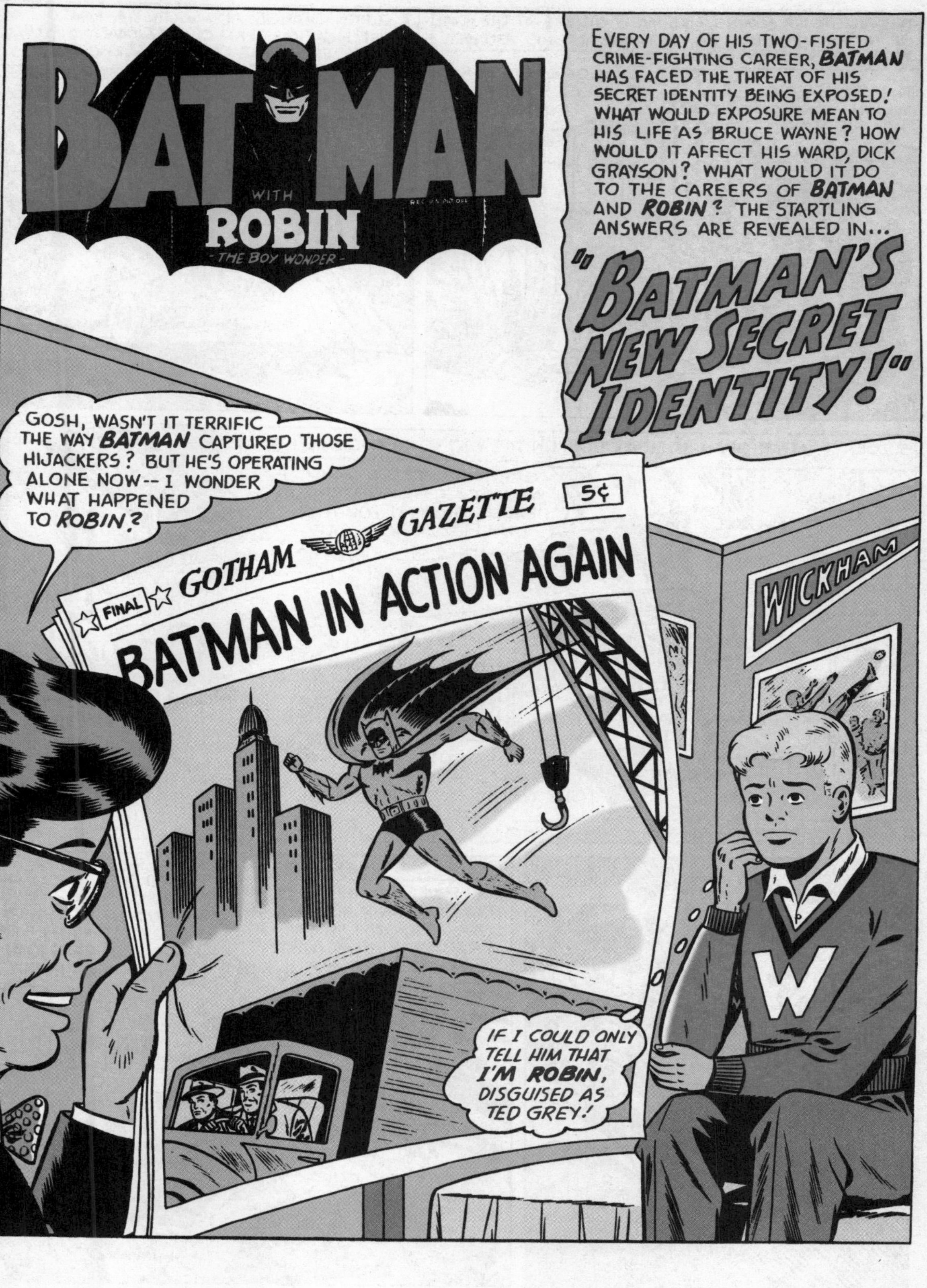
BATMAN
WITH
ROBIN
-THE BOY WONDER-
EVERY DAY OF HIS TWO-FISTED CRIME-FIGHTING CAREER, BATMAN HAS FACED THE THREAT OF HIS SECRET IDENTITY BEING EXPOSED! WHAT WOULD EXPOSURE MEAN TO HIS LIFE AS BRUCE WAYNE? HOW WOULD IT AFFECT HIS WARD, DICK GRAYSON? WHAT WOULD IT DO TO THE CAREERS OF BATMAN AND ROBIN? THE STARTLING ANSWERS ARE REVEALED IN...
"BATMAN'S NEW SECRET IDENTITY!"
GOSH, WASN'T IT TERRIFIC THE WAY BATMAN CAPTURED THOSE HIJACKERS? BUT HE'S OPERATING ALONE NOW-- I WONDER WHAT HAPPENED TO ROBIN?
5¢
GOTHAM GAZETTE
FINAL
BATMAN IN ACTION AGAIN
WICKHAM
IF I COULD ONLY TELL HIM THAT I'M ROBIN, DISGUISED AS TED GREY!

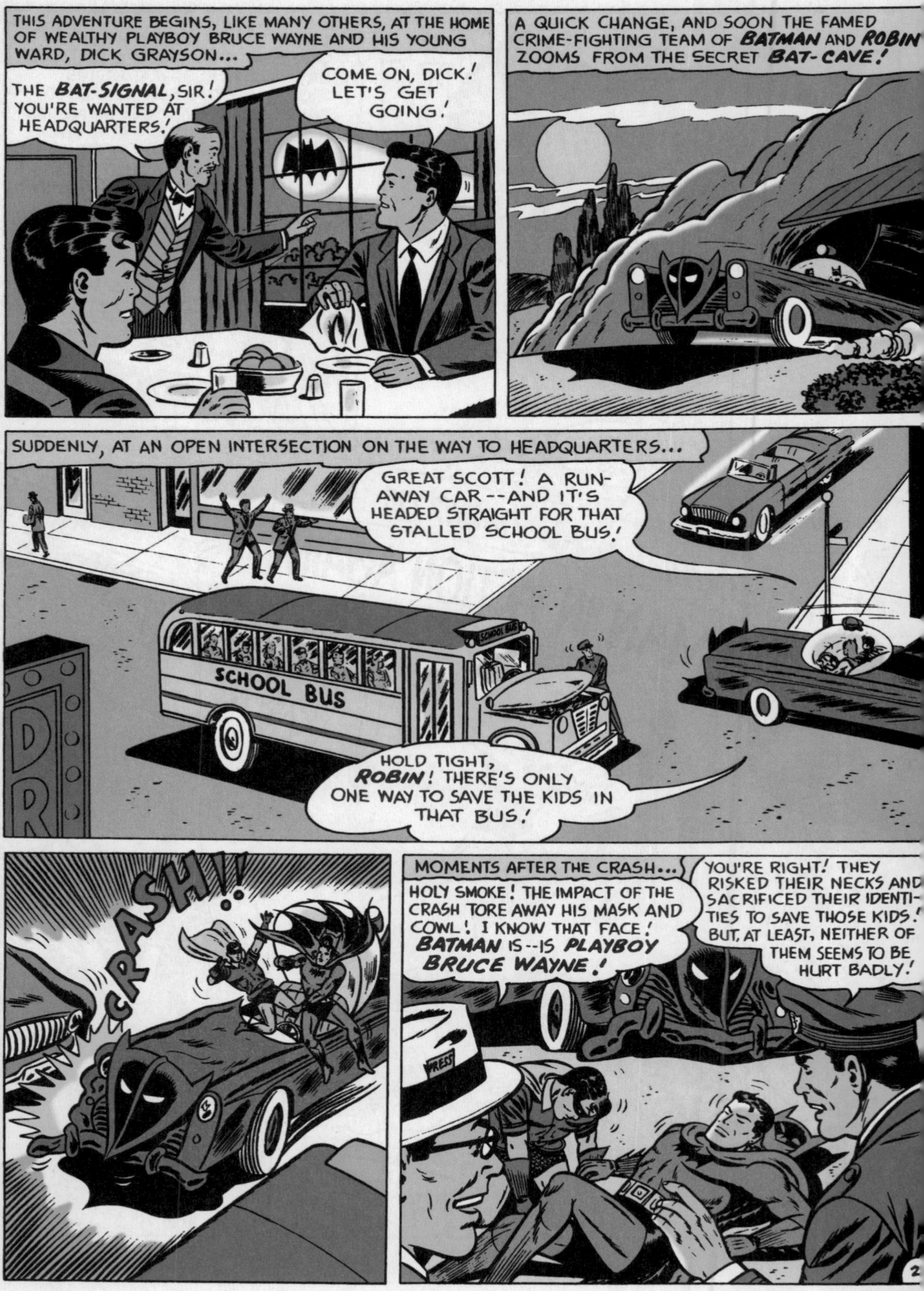

THIS ADVENTURE BEGINS, LIKE MANY OTHERS, AT THE HOME OF WEALTHY PLAYBOY BRUCE WAYNE AND HIS YOUNG WARD, DICK GRAYSON...
THE BAT-SIGNAL, SIR! YOU'RE WANTED AT HEADQUARTERS!
COME ON, DICK! LET'S GET GOING!
A QUICK CHANGE, AND SOON THE FAMED CRIME-FIGHTING TEAM OF BATMAN AND ROBIN ZOOMS FROM THE SECRET BAT-CAVE!
SUDDENLY, AT AN OPEN INTERSECTION ON THE WAY TO HEADQUARTERS...
GREAT SCOTT! A RUN-AWAY CAR--AND IT'S HEADED STRAIGHT FOR THAT STALLED SCHOOL BUS!
SCHOOL BUS
HOLD TIGHT, ROBIN! THERE'S ONLY ONE WAY TO SAVE THE KIDS IN THAT BUS!
CRASH!!
MOMENTS AFTER THE CRASH...
HOLY SMOKE! THE IMPACT OF THE CRASH TORE AWAY HIS MASK AND COWL! I KNOW THAT FACE! BATMAN IS--IS PLAYBOY BRUCE WAYNE!
YOU'RE RIGHT! THEY RISKED THEIR NECKS AND SACRIFICED THEIR IDENTITIES TO SAVE THOSE KIDS! BUT, AT LEAST, NEITHER OF THEM SEEMS TO BE HURT BADLY!
PRESS
2

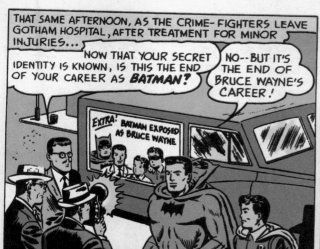

THAT SAME AFTERNOON, AS THE CRIME-FIGHTERS LEAVE GOTHAM HOSPITAL, AFTER TREATMENT FOR MINOR INJURIES...

NOW THAT YOUR SECRET IDENTITY IS KNOWN, IS THIS THE END OF YOUR CAREER AS *BATMAN?*

NO--BUT IT'S THE END OF BRUCE WAYNE'S CAREER!

EXTRA! BATMAN EXPOSED AS BRUCE WAYNE

RETURNING TO THE *BAT-CAVE* BENEATH THE WAYNE HOME...

GOSH, *BATMAN*--ONE THING IS CLEAR! WE'LL CERTAINLY HAVE TO CLOSE UP SHOP AT THIS LOCATION! BUT WHERE DO WE GO FROM HERE?

I'M NOT SURE YET, BUT FIRST, I'LL HAVE TO WIND UP THE AFFAIRS OF BRUCE WAYNE!

NEXT DAY, AT A SPECIAL MEETING OF BRUCE'S BUSINESS ASSOCIATES AT THE WAYNE HOME...

BRUCE, YOU COULD'VE KNOCKED ME OVER WITH A FEATHER WHEN I LEARNED THAT YOU--GOTHAM'S BEST-KNOWN PLAYBOY--WERE REALLY *BATMAN!*

BUT NOW *YOU* KNOW, AND SO DOES THE WHOLE WORLD! LOOK OUTSIDE, GENTLEMEN!

A CONSTANT POLICE GUARD HAS TO PROTECT ME AND ANYBODY ASSOCIATED WITH ME, FROM GANGLAND REPRISALS! SO --FOR EVERYONE'S SAKE--I'VE DECIDED TO SELL OUT ALL MY HOLDINGS AND *CLEAR OUT!*

THAT EVENING, AT THE HOME OF KATHY KANE, ALIAS *BATWOMAN*...

OH, BRUCE-- NOW THAT I FIND YOU AREN'T JUST A PLAYBOY, YOU TELL ME YOU'RE GOING AWAY!

IT HAS TO BE THAT WAY, KATHY! *SIGH* I'LL NEVER SEE YOU AGAIN AS BRUCE WAYNE!

NOW BEGINS THE REAL PROBLEM OF ESTABLISHING A NEW PRIVATE IDENTITY IN ORDER TO OPERATE AS *BATMAN* AGAIN! AND SINCE EVERYBODY WILL BE ON THE ALERT FOR A MAN AND A BOY TOGETHER, *ROBIN* AND I WILL HAVE TO SPLIT UP FOR A WHILE!

3

AFTER SEVERAL DAYS...

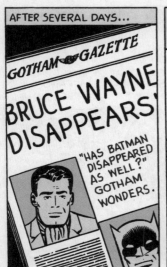

GOTHAM GAZETTE

BRUCE WAYNE DISAPPEARS!

"HAS BATMAN DISAPPEARED AS WELL?" GOTHAM WONDERS.

ONE WEEK LATER, AS A TAXICAB STOPS BEFORE THE ENTRANCE TO WICKHAM HALL, A FAMOUS SCHOOL FOR BOYS...

WHILE I ESTABLISH MY NEW IDENTITY AS BRET WILSON, CAB DRIVER, YOU'RE TO REMAIN HERE AT SCHOOL UNDER THE NAME OF TED GREY. IN TIME, MAYBE IT CAN BE *BATMAN* AND *ROBIN* AGAIN!

I UNDER-STAND, BRUCE--ER--I MEAN, BRET...*CHOKE!* SO LONG...

LATER, AS THE CAB HEADS NORTH TOWARD THE OUT-SKIRTS OF GOTHAM...

THIS CAB-DRIVING SET-UP GIVES ME FREEDOM TO MOVE AROUND AND FUNCTION AS BATMAN! AND WITH NOBODY IN THE CAB, I CAN TUNE IN ON POLICE SHORT-WAVE!

SUDDENLY, CROSSING THROUGH THE GOTHAM FREIGHT TERMINAL...

OH-OH--LOOK LIKE A HI-JACKING OVER AT THAT FREIGHT CAR!

SWERVING THE CAB INTO CONCEALMENT BETWEEN TWO BOXCARS, HE PULLS A LEVER BEHIND THE DASHBOARD AND...

IT TOOK A LOT OF INGENUITY TO WORK OUT THIS NEW SET-UP. THIS'LL BE THE FIRST TIME IT GOES INTO USE! NOW FOR A QUICK CHANGE FROM CABBY BRET WILSON TO -- *BATMAN!*

SECONDS LATER, THE NEW *BATMOBILE* ZOOMS TOWARD THE HIJACKERS JUST MAKING THEIR ESCAPE...

HOLY SMOKE! STEP ON IT! IT'S *BATMAN!* AND I THOUGHT HE'D GONE OUT OF BUSINESS AFTER HIS IDENTITY WAS EXPOSED!

THE **BATMOBILE** GAINS STEADILY ON THE FLEEING TRUCK, UNTIL...

CUT OFF AT THE LAST MOMENT! BUT **THEIR** CAR STALLED ON THE OTHER SIDE! I'VE STILL GOT A CHANCE--WITH THAT CRANE ON THE FLAT CAR!

SECONDS LATER, AT THE CRANE CONTROL-BOX...

THERE -- THAT SHOULD BE JUST ABOUT RIGHT! BUT I'VE GOT TO MOVE FAST--THEY'VE GOT THEIR CAR STARTED AGAIN!

THEN, AS TRAINED MUSCLES PROPEL **BATMAN** AGILELY ACROSS A PRECARIOUS STEEL BRIDGE...

WHEW! LUCKY FOR US **BATMAN** WAS CUT OFF BY THAT LONG FREIGHT TRAIN!

WOW! IT'S **BATMAN** IN ACTION AGAIN! WHAT A SCOOP FOR ME!

CLICK!

HEY-- WHAT--??

THIS IS AN EMERGENCY--SO YOU WON'T MIND IF I USE YOUR **EMERGENCY** BRAKE!

I'LL TAKE CARE OF--

OOF!

AFTER TURNING THE HIJACKERS OVER TO THE POLICE, *BATMAN* RESUMES HIS NEW SECRET IDENTITY, AND SOON AFTER...

HM--ALFRED SHOULD BE OUT HERE ATTENDING TO CUSTOMERS SO PEOPLE WON'T SUSPECT THIS PLACE IS ONLY A BLIND TO COVER *BATMAN'S* SECRET IDENTITY! I'LL HAVE TO SPEAK TO HIM ABOUT IT.

GOTHAM HILLS GARAGE

DESCENDING THE STEPS INTO THE AUTO GREASE-PIT, BRET PRESSES A CONCEALED BUTTON AT THE FAR END AND...

ALFRED--ER--I MEAN--EDWARD--WHERE ARE YOU? WHY AREN'T YOU OUT FRONT?

WHY--BRUCE--ER--I MEAN--BRET--THERE WAS SO MUCH TO DO UNPACKING AND STRAIGHTENING UP THE *BAT-CAVE.* BUT IT'S BEGINNING TO SHAPE UP. WON'T YOUNG MASTER DICK--ER--TED--BE SURPRISED WHEN HE COMES TO VISIT!

AT THAT VERY MOMENT, IN HIS ROOM AT THE WICKHAM BOARDING SCHOOL FOR BOYS...

GOSH--I'M GLAD *BATMAN'S* BACK! BUT I WONDER WHY *ROBIN* ISN'T WITH HIM? SAY--WHAT'RE YOU LOOKING SO GLUM ABOUT, TED?

GOTHAM GAZETTE
BATMAN IN ACTION AGAIN

GUESS I'M NOT HIDING MY FEELINGS VERY WELL...STILL--I CAN'T HELP WONDERING WHEN I'LL BE ABLE TO WORK WITH *BATMAN* AGAIN...

NEXT DAY, DURING A TELEVISED SOCIAL STUDIES LESSON IN THE SCHOOL AUDITORIUM...

WE ARE TAKING YOU ON A TRIP THROUGH THE HUGE GOTHAM FOUNDRY PLANT WHERE YOU CAN SEE THE PROCESS OF IRON AND STEEL MAKING AT FIRST HAND...

--THE MOLTEN STEEL YOU SEE IS BEING POURED INTO OPEN PITS WHERE--

SUDDENLY, INTO THE MIDST OF THE TRANQUIL INDUSTRIAL SCENE, THERE ERUPTS...

--BUT--HOLD IT, FOLKS! SOMETHING UNEXPECTED HAPPENING OVER THERE! IT LOOKS LIKE--YES--IT IS--IT'S *A HOLD-UP!* THOSE MEN ON THAT RAMP ARE FLEEING FROM THE PAYMASTER'S OFFICE--AND THEY'RE BEING PURSUED BY --

-- *BATMAN* AND *BATWOMAN!* YOU'RE WATCHING THEM IN ACTION ON YOUR SCREENS RIGHT NOW IN THIS SENSATIONAL ON-THE-SPOT SCOOP!

WCBX TV

THOSE PAYROLL BANDITS ARE HEADING DOWN THE STAIRS AND OUT ONTO THAT LOADING PLATFORM! THEY'VE GOT TOO MUCH OF A START FOR US TO STOP THEM, *BATMAN!*

THERE'S JUST A CHANCE I CAN STOP THEM WITH THIS IMPROVISED SLED!

7

ROCKETING SWIFTLY DOWN THE LINE OF ROLLERS, THE DARING CRIME-FIGHTER SMASHES INTO THE SURPRISED BANDITS...

THE STUNNED BANDITS ARE QUICKLY SUBDUED BY ARRIVING POLICE, AND THEN...

--AND IT'S ALL OVER, FOLKS! BUT WE'RE BRINGING *BATMAN* AND *BATWOMAN* OVER TO THE MIKE TO SAY A FEW WORDS. HERE THEY ARE...

IF I HADN'T SPOTTED *BATWOMAN* ON HER MOTORCYCLE ON THE WAY HERE AND FOLLOWED HER, I'D NEVER HAVE BEEN IN ON THE FINISH!

I'D JUST GOTTEN A TIP ABOUT THE HOLD-UP, BUT BELIEVE ME, I'M GLAD YOU FOLLOWED ME! IN FACT, I THINK WE MAKE AN IDEAL TEAM, DON'T YOU, *BATMAN*?

WELL --¡CHOKE!-- HE'S GOT *BATWOMAN* NOW TO TAKE MY PLACE! ¡SIGH! GUESS THAT ENDS THE TEAM OF *BATMAN* AND *ROBIN*! I ONLY HOPE SHE PROVES AS GOOD A PARTNER FOR HIM AS ¡CHOKE! I WAS!

CONTINUED IN CHAPTER 2.

8

A LOOK AT OTHER GREAT IMAGINARY STORIES

WORLD'S FINEST COMICS #180, 1968
art by Neal Adams

SUPERMAN #170, 1964
art by Curt Swan and Sheldon Maldoff

CHAPTER 2
DICK GRAYSON'S HOPES ARE SOON FULFILLED AS THE *NEW TEAM* OF *BATMAN* AND *ROBIN* SWINGS INTO ACTION!

BANG!

THAT THUG'S BULLET SEVERED THE ROPE HOLDING THE CARGO! EITHER I SAVE *BATMAN*--OR I GET CRUSHED WITH HIM!

GREAT SCOTT!

I OWE YOU MY LIFE, *BATWOMAN!* YOU-- YOU COULD HAVE BEEN KILLED TRYING TO SAVE ME!

WELL--THAT'S ALL PART OF TEAM-WORK, ISN'T IT?

9

AND IN THE DAYS THAT FOLLOW, HEADLINES POINT UP FURTHER SENSATIONAL TEAM-WORK OF *BATMAN* AND *BATWOMAN*...

BATMAN and BATWOMAN NET STICK-UP GANG ON HIGHWAY

MY WORD -- I WONDER HOW DICK FEELS ABOUT STAYING QUIETLY AT SCHOOL UNDER THE NAME OF TED GREY WHILE ALL THIS ACTION IS GOING ON!

GOTHAM G
BATMAN AND BATWOMAN TRA
BAGS HOLD-UP DU

GOTHAM AMUSEMENT PARK

IN THE RECREATION ROOM OF THE WICKHAM BOYS' SCHOOL...

--AND HERE ARE TV NEWS PHOTOS OF THE RECENT CAPTURE OF ANOTHER PAIR OF DESPERADOES BY *BATMAN* AND *BATWOMAN*...

¡SIGH¡ EVERY- WHERE I TURN -- NEWSPAPERS -- TV -- NEWSREELS -- I FIND NOTHING BUT REMINDERS THAT *BATMAN* HAS NO NEED FOR *ROBIN* ANYMORE. *BATWOMAN* HAS ¡CHOKE¡ TAKEN MY PLACE!

THAT SAME AFTERNOON, AS BRET WILSON'S CAB CRUISES THROUGH A HOODLUM-RIDDEN SECTION OF GOTHAM CITY...

THOSE HIJACKERS I ARRESTED LAST WEEK WOULDN'T TALK, BUT I'M CERTAIN THEY'RE PART OF A LARGE RING -- AND NOW I'VE GOT A TIP THAT TIM NEAL IS A MEMBER OF THE GANG!

TAXI

PRESENTLY, AFTER LINGERING OUTSIDE A CERTAIN POOL-ROOM...

HE'S KNOWN TO HANG OUT AT THIS PLACE -- AND THERE HE IS NOW, SIGNALLING FOR A CAB! MY PATIENCE IS PAYING OFF!

BILLIA

DIRECTED TO A CROSS-TOWN ADDRESS, THE DISGUISED *BATMAN* IS ALL EARS AS HE THREADS HIS CAB THROUGH TRAFFIC...

--AND THE BOYS ARE EXPECTING A FRESH TRUCKLOAD AT THE FARM THIS AFTERNOON...

HM-- THAT MIGHT MEAN THAT THEY'RE USING SOME FARM AS A DROP FOR THEIR LOOT. IF I COULD ONLY FIND SOME WAY OF GETTING TO THAT FARM...

JUST THEN, AT A HIGHWAY CONSTRUCTION SITE BEHIND GOTHAM HILLS GARAGE, EVENTS ARE IN THE MAKING THAT WILL GRANT BRET'S WISH SOONER THAN HE IMAGINES...

THERE GOES THE MOUNTAINSIDE!

BOOM!

MOMENTS AFTER THE DUST SETTLES--CONSTRUCTION MEN MAKE A STARTLING DISCOVERY...

HOLY SMOKE! WE BLASTED OPEN SOME KIND OF UNDERGROUND MUSEUM! WAIT! THIS LOOKS LIKE--SURE--IT'S *BATMAN'S SECRET CAVE!* BUT--WHO ARE YOU?

BLIMEY! EXPOSED! *BATMAN* IS GOING TO BE VERY UNHAPPY OVER THIS DEVELOPMENT!

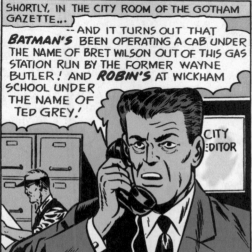

SHORTLY, IN THE CITY ROOM OF THE GOTHAM GAZETTE...

--AND IT TURNS OUT THAT *BATMAN'S* BEEN OPERATING A CAB UNDER THE NAME OF BRET WILSON OUT OF THIS GAS STATION RUN BY THE FORMER WAYNE BUTLER! AND *ROBIN'S* AT WICKHAM SCHOOL UNDER THE NAME OF TED GREY!

CITY EDITOR

AS THE STARTLING NEWS HUMS OUT OVER THE AIR-WAVES, IT IS PICKED UP BY THE RADIO IN BRET'S CAB, WHERE...

--THAT *BATMAN* HAS TAKEN THE IDENTITY OF BRET WILSON, CAB-DRIVER!

HEY--LOOK! ACCORDING TO THAT PLAQUE--THE GUY DRIVING THIS CAB IS BRET WILSON! THAT MEANS HE--HE'S *BATMAN!* WHAT'RE WE WAITING FOR?

BRET WILSON

NEVER MIND THAT CROSS-TOWN TRIP, *BATMAN!* WE'RE GOING TO A NICE QUIET FARM INSTEAD! SO JUST KEEP DRIVING LIKE YOU'RE TOLD IF YOU DON'T WANT THIS GUN TO GO OFF!

MEANWHILE, AT THE HOME OF KATHY KANE...

...IT HAS BEEN DEFINITELY ESTABLISHED THAT *BATMAN* IS CABBY BRET WILSON OPERATING OUT OF THE GOTHAM HILLS GARAGE...

I'D BETTER GET OVER TO THAT GARAGE RIGHT AWAY!

BUT AT WICKHAM SCHOOL, PARTICIPATION IN A TRACK MEET HAS KEPT "TED GREY" IN IGNORANCE OF WHAT HAS HAPPENED UNTIL...

GET SET, TED! IT'S YOUR TURN NEXT! SEE IF YOU CAN'T DO BETTER THAN YOU'VE DONE SO FAR!

HEY--TED! YOU CAN QUIT PRETENDING! YOUR SECRET IS OUT! THE RADIO JUST ANNOUNCED YOU'RE REALLY DICK GRAYSON! IN OTHER WORDS--YOU'RE *ROBIN!*

HUH--THE RADIO? BUT--BUT--WHY? HOW?

A ROAD GANG ACCIDENTALLY BLASTED INTO THE NEW *BAT-CAVE!* THE WHOLE STORY'S BEEN BROADCAST-- INCLUDING THE NAME YOU WERE USING HERE AT SCHOOL!

WHAT? YOU EXPECT US TO BELIEVE TED GREY HERE IS *ROBIN?* AFTER THE POOR SCORE HE'S MADE SO FAR IN THIS TRACK MEET?

SINCE MY IDENTITY'S OUT, AND I DON'T HAVE TO HOLD BACK ANY MORE--I'LL REALLY SHOW THEM SOME BROAD-JUMPING!

GOSH--WHAT A JUMP! HE'S BROKEN THE SCHOOL RECORD!

THAT PROVES IT--HE'S *GOT* TO BE *ROBIN!* GOSH! ALL THIS TIME HE WAS AROUND HERE AND WE NEVER SUSPECTED!

TWENTY MINUTES LATER, HIS NEW IDENTITY DISCARDED, DICK RUSHES TO THE GOTHAM HILLS GARAGE...

ALFRED! AND BATWOMAN, TOO! BUT--WHERE'S BATMAN?

DICK! I'M WORRIED ABOUT BATMAN! WE'VE HAD NO WORD FROM HIM SINCE THE NEW BAT-CAVE WAS DISCOVERED!

DIGGING OUT HIS OLD COSTUME, DICK ONCE AGAIN BECOMES ROBIN, THE BOY WONDER...

SOMETHING MUST HAVE HAPPENED TO HIM! COME ON, BATWOMAN, LET'S START LOOKING!

AT THAT VERY MOMENT, TWENTY MILES SOUTH OF GOTHAM...

AT THE END OF THIS ROAD, TURN RIGHT TO THE FARMHOUSE, BATMAN!

SO THAT'S WHERE YOUR HIDEOUT IS--THE OLD ABANDONED WATERMILL FARM!

SOON AFTER, AS THE CAB APPROACHES THE FARMHOUSE...

A NEW SHIPMENT, I SEE! YOU STORE THE HIJACKED LOOT IN THAT BARN!

THE KNOWLEDGE WON'T DO YOU ANY GOOD, BATMAN! THE FARMHOUSE HERE IS THE END OF THE ROAD FOR YOU!

AND INSIDE THE FARMHOUSE...

SURE ENOUGH--WITHOUT THAT PHONY MUSTACHE, HE'S BRUCE WAYNE! LET'S SEE IF HE HAS HIS BATMAN COSTUME UNDERNEATH!

SO--BATMAN'S REALLY OUR PRISONER! BOYS--I WANT TO ENJOY THIS PLEASURE TO THE FULL--MAKE HIM CHANGE INTO HIS COSTUME!

AFTER A FORCED CHANGE INTO HIS CRIME-FIGHTING GARB...

NOW--GET OUT THERE AND HELP THE BOYS FINISH UNLOADING! I WANT ALL OF YOU IN HERE TO ENJOY THE LITTLE CEREMONY OF FINISHING *BATMAN* OFF ONCE AND FOR ALL!

BUT, MOMENTS LATER...

HEY, BOSS! IT'S BATWOMAN AND ROBIN--THEY'VE LOCATED OUR HIDEOUT!

WHAT?!

WE'LL SOON TAKE CARE OF THAT!

ROBIN GOT MY MESSAGE-- BUT NOW HIS LIFE AND *BATWOMAN'S* ARE IN DANGER!

OUTSIDE...

I GET OFF HERE, *BATWOMAN!*

I'VE GOT TO STOP THOSE MEN IN THE BARN--OR WE'LL BE COMPLETELY OUTNUMBERED!

THIS TRUCK SHOULD DO THE JOB IF I CAN GET IT GOING FAST ENOUGH!

14

WITH A SUDDEN ROAR, THE BIG TRUCK STARTS BACKING SWIFTLY TOWARD THE BARN, AS...

BATWOMAN--SHE'S TRYING TO RUN US DOWN! BACK INSIDE--QUICK!

AS THE MEN FLEE INTO THE BARN, THE HUGE VEHICLE WEDGES ITSELF FIRMLY IN THE DOORWAY...

THAT SHOULD KEEP THEM SEALED UP IN THE BARN!

MEANWHILE ...

ALL RIGHT, BRAT! THIS IS THE END OF THE LINE FOR *YOU*!

YOU FORGOT *ME*!... NEVER DROP A LIGHTED CIGAR ON THE FLOOR--ALL I HAD TO DO WAS TIP MY CHAIR OVER TO IT AND LET THE ROPES BURN THROUGH!

LATER, AFTER THE HIJACK GANG HAS BEEN TAKEN INTO CUSTODY...

--AND IT WAS WHILE THE CAB APPROACHED WINDMILL FARM THAT I MANAGED TO TURN MY *BAT-BELT* TRANSMITTER ON!

AND IF I HADN'T PICKED UP YOUR VOICE ON MY *BAT BELT* RADIO, WE WOULD NEVER HAVE KNOWN YOU WERE AT WINDMILL FARM!

YES--BUT WHERE DO WE GO FROM HERE, NOW THAT OUR IDENTITIES HAVE BEEN EXPOSED AGAIN?

"... NOW THAT OUR IDENTITIES HAVE BEEN EXPOSED AGAIN?"... HMM...

WHY, ALFRED--DON'T TELL ME YOU'RE WRITING ANOTHER ONE OF YOUR STORIES ABOUT THE SECOND BATMAN AND ROBIN TEAM!

NO--BUT REMEMBER HOW CLOSE THE JOKER CAME TO DISCOVERING YOUR IDENTITY RECENTLY! IT SET ME WONDERING! SO I WROTE THIS STORY ABOUT WHAT MIGHT HAPPEN IF YOU HAD TO FIND A NEW IDENTITY!

AND HOW DID WE MAKE OUT, ALFRED?

NOT SO GOOD! YOU'LL HAVE TO START ALL OVER AGAIN LOOKING FOR NEW IDENTITIES!

The End

A LOOK AT OTHER GREAT IMAGINARY STORIES

SUPERMAN #175, 1965
art by Curt Swan
and George Klein

SUPERMAN #194, 1967
art by Curt Swan
and George Klein

SUPERMAN®

AN IMAGINARY NOVEL

"The AMAZING STORY OF SUPERMAN-RED and SUPERMAN-BLUE!"

SUPERMAN BECOMES IMMUNE TO KRYPTONITE! THE BOTTLE CITY OF KANDOR IS RESTORED TO ITS ORIGINAL SIZE! THE PERISHED PLANET, KRYPTON, BECOMES REBORN! ALL CRIME AND EVIL DISAPPEAR! THESE ARE ONLY A FEW OF THE SURPRISES IN THIS IMAGINARY NOVEL!

Part I
"The TITANIC TWINS!"

Part II
"The ANTI-EVIL RAY!"

Part III
"The END OF SUPERMAN'S CAREER!"

ONE MORNING IN **METROPOLIS,** ON AN IMAGINARY DAY WHICH MAY, OR MAY NOT, EVER HAPPEN, THE PUBLISHER OF THE **DAILY PLANET** POSTS A NOTICE...

HOW ABOUT THAT! EVERYONE GOT A RAISE BUT **CLARK!**

THE FOLLOWING EMPLOYEES WILL RECEIVE A SALARY INCREASE:
PERRY WHITE $25 PER WK.
LOIS LANE $10 " "
JIMMY OLSEN $5 " "
CLARK KENT NO INCREASE

FRANKLY, CLARK, THOSE RAISES WERE GIVEN FOR GETTING SCOOPS! YOU'VE GOT TO BE MORE DYNAMIC ...A GO-GETTER!

I GUESS I'M JUST A FLOP, LOIS!

HOW IRONIC! **EVERYONE** GOT A RAISE! BUT I, WHO HELPED THEM GET THOSE SCOOPS IN MY IDENTITY AS **SUPERMAN,** DIDN'T GET A DIME!

TO CELEBRATE, EDITOR PERRY WHITE TREATS THE STAFF TO LUNCH, BUT CLARK BOWS OUT...

SO YOU DON'T FEEL WELL, EH! WELL, TAKE THE REST OF THE DAY OFF!

POOR CLARK! HE'S SO ASHAMED, HE JUST CAN'T FACE US!

THANKS, PERRY! I'VE GOT TO GET TO MY FORTRESS! **SUPERGIRL** INFORMED ME EARLIER THAT THERE WAS IMPORTANT NEWS!

SWITCHING TO HIS **SUPERMAN** COSTUME, HE STREAKS TO HIS ARCTIC HEADQUARTERS...

SUPERGIRL! I CAME AS SOON AS I COULD!

I'M GLAD YOU'RE HERE, **SUPERMAN!** THE PEOPLE OF **KANDOR** ARE ANXIOUS TO CONTACT YOU! I'LL SWITCH ON THE MONITOR SCREEN!

SECONDS LATER, IN THE BOTTLE CITY OF **KANDOR,** AN ELDER STEPS FORWARD...

SUPERMAN! I SPEAK FOR **KANDOR!** WE ARE GRATEFUL FOR YOUR MANY SUPER-DEEDS! BUT FOR YEARS YOU HAVE FAILED TO PERFORM YOUR MOST VITAL TASKS! THE MONITOR SCREEN WILL RECORD YOUR FAILURES!

AS **SUPERMAN** WATCHES...

WHEN THE SPACE-VILLAIN, **BRAINIAC,** SHRANK OUR CITY AND IMPRISONED IT IN A BOTTLE, YOU VOWED TO ENLARGE IT TO NORMAL SIZE! BUT YOU HAVE FAILED!

2

THE RAYS OF **GREEN KRYPTONITE** ARE POISONOUS TO YOU AND TO ALL SUPER-BEINGS FROM **KRYPTON!** YOU PROMISED TO FIND AN ANTIDOTE! SO FAR, YOU'VE FAILED!

CHOKE! HE'S RIGHT! ALL MY EFFORTS WERE USELESS!

YOU HAVE SWORN TO END CRIME AND EVIL OF EARTH! IN THIS VOW YOU HAVE ALSO FAILED!

HEAVEN KNOWS I'VE TRIED! MAYBE I'M UNWORTHY TO BE A **SUPERMAN!**

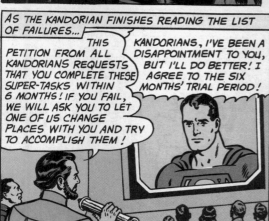

AS THE KANDORIAN FINISHES READING THE LIST OF FAILURES...

THIS PETITION FROM ALL KANDORIANS REQUESTS THAT YOU COMPLETE THESE SUPER-TASKS WITHIN 6 MONTHS! IF YOU FAIL, WE WILL ASK YOU TO LET ONE OF US CHANGE PLACES WITH YOU AND TRY TO ACCOMPLISH THEM!

KANDORIANS, I'VE BEEN A DISAPPOINTMENT TO YOU, BUT I'LL DO BETTER! I AGREE TO THE SIX MONTHS' TRIAL PERIOD!

PRESENTLY, AS THE MONITOR SCREEN FADES...

UNSOLVED SUPER-PROBLEMS

1. RESTORE KANDOR TO NORMAL SIZE

2. FIND ANTIDOTE TO GREEN KRYPTONITE

3. WIPE OUT CRIME AND EVIL

THE KANDORIANS DON'T KNOW IT, BUT I PREPARED THIS CHART OF MY UNACCOMPLISHED TASKS LONG AGO!

GULP! EVEN WITH **YOUR** SUPER-POWERS IT WOULD TAKE A CENTURY TO COMPLETE THOSE JOBS!

THERE'S ONLY **ONE** SOLUTION! THIS **BRAIN-EVOLUTION MACHINE** I'VE BEEN WORKING ON! IF SUCCESSFUL, IT WILL INCREASE MY MENTAL POWER A **HUNDRED TIMES** AND HELP ME COPE WITH THOSE TASKS!

BUT THAT MACHINE IS POWERED BY THE RAYS OF ALL VARIETIES OF KRYPTONITE! IT'S DANGEROUS! SUPPOSE SOMETHING GOES WRONG?

I KNOW THAT THIS LEAD-CRYSTAL GLASS SHIELDS US FROM THE KRYPTONITE! BUT I CAN'T HELP FEARING SOMETHING MAY GO WRONG.!... LET **ME** TAKE YOUR PLACE! THE WORLD CAN'T AFFORD TO LOSE **SUPERMAN!**

I APPRECIATE YOUR LOYALTY, BUT THE RISK MUST BE MINE!

3

QUICKLY, **SUPERMAN** ADJUSTS THE BRAIN MACHINE, THEN...

THE HEADBAND IS IN POSITION! THROW THE SWITCH, **SUPERGIRL!** THEN ADJUST IT TO **MAXIMUM POWER!**

ALL THE LUCK IN THE WORLD, **SUPERMAN!**

¡GULP! HE'S TAKING A TERRIBLE CHANCE!

AS THE CONCENTRATED POWER OF THE KRYPTONITE RAYS TAKES EFFECT...

SUDDENLY...

MY BRAIN, IT SEEMS TO BE GROWING... **EXPANDING!** I UNDERSTAND SO MANY THINGS NOW!

THE **PAIN!** EEEYAHH! MY HEAD IS SPLITTING! TURN IT **OFF!**

IN THE NEXT FANTASTIC SECOND...

POWWWWW

¡GASP! SOMETHING'S GONE TERRIBLY WRONG!

THEN, AN INCREDIBLE SIGHT...

GULP! **TWIN** SUPERMEN! I MUST BE SEEING THINGS!

THIS HAPPENED ONCE BEFORE UNDER THE TEMPORARY INFLUENCE OF **RED KRYPTONITE!**

YES! ONE TWIN WAS GOOD AND THE OTHER WAS EVIL! BUT THIS TIME WE'RE **BOTH GOOD!** THE ONLY DIFFERENCE IS IN OUR COSTUMES!

ACCORDING TO MY CALCULATIONS, THAT BRAIN EVOLUTION MACHINE INCREASED MY MENTAL POWER ONE HUNDRED TIMES!

THE EXPLOSION DOUBLED OUR ATOMIC STRUCTURE, CREATING TWO SUPERMEN... EACH A HUNDRED TIMES SMARTER THAN THE ORIGINAL!

WE'RE IDENTICAL EXCEPT FOR OUR COSTUMES! TO AVOID CONFUSION, I'LL CALL MYSELF **SUPERMAN-BLUE!**

AND I'LL BE **SUPERMAN-RED!** TWO HEADS ARE BETTER THAN ONE! WE'LL USE OUR SUPER-BRAINS TO SOLVE ALL OUR PROBLEMS! OUR FIRST JOB WILL BE TO ENLARGE **KANDOR** TO NORMAL SIZE!

AT SUPER-SPEED, THE TWO SUPERMEN PUT THEIR MAGNIFICENT MENTAL POWERS INTO ACTION...

I GOT **BRAINIAC'S** ENLARGING RAY GUN FROM THE FORTRESS MUSEUM! I'VE NEVER BEEN ABLE TO REPAIR ITS DAMAGED CIRCUITS BEFORE! IT'S CHILD PLAY NOW! BUT WE'LL NEED A RAY-FORCE PELLET TO OPERATE IT!

CHAMBER
TRIGGER MECH.
RELAY.

IT'S SIMPLE, **SUPERMAN-RED!** USING YOUR DRAWINGS, I CAN CALCULATE HOW TO CREATE THE CONCENTRATED FORCE-PELLET THAT **BRAINIAC** USED!

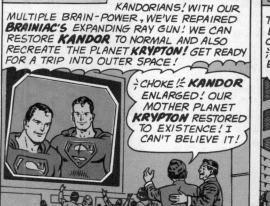

PRESENTLY, THE PEOPLE OF **KANDOR** RECEIVE STARTLING NEWS...

KANDORIANS! WITH OUR MULTIPLE BRAIN-POWER, WE'VE REPAIRED **BRAINIAC'S** EXPANDING RAY GUN! WE CAN RESTORE **KANDOR** TO NORMAL AND ALSO RECREATE THE PLANET **KRYPTON!** GET READY FOR A TRIP INTO OUTER SPACE!

÷CHOKE!÷ **KANDOR** ENLARGED! OUR MOTHER PLANET **KRYPTON** RESTORED TO EXISTENCE! I CAN'T BELIEVE IT!

LEAVING **SUPERGIRL** TO GUARD EARTH, THE TITANIC TWINS STREAK INTO SPACE WITH THE BOTTLE-CITY...

THEY'RE CARRYING OUR BOTTLE TO THE FRINGE OF THE SOLAR SYSTEM! ¡GULP! CAN THEY REALLY ENLARGE **KANDOR** AND RESTORE **KRYPTON?**

IT WOULD BE THE MOST MAGNIFICENT SUPER-FEAT OF ALL HISTORY! BUT IT'S IMPOSSIBLE, OF COURSE!

IN THE METEOR BELT, THE TWO SUPERMEN SEARCH FOR FRAGMENTS OF A MYSTERIOUS ELEMENT UNKNOWN ON EARTH, THEN...

THESE FRAGMENTS ARE MADE OF **HYPER-MAGNETON!** WHEN WE HURL THEM TOGETHER, THEY WILL FUSE INTO A PLANETOID WITH STRANGE MAGNETIC POWERS!

PRESENTLY... IF OUR THEORIES ARE CORRECT, THE STRANGE MAGNETIC BEAMS OF THAT PLANETOID WILL SCATTER THROUGH THE UNIVERSE AND ATTRACT EVERY PIECE OF KRYPTONITE BACK TO THIS SPOT!

5

As the weird power of the magnetic rays draws the shattered remnants of **KRYPTON** from remote corners of space...

Out in space, as the twin Supermen watch...

Just as we calculated! That kryptonite is now harmless to us! The magnetic rays have changed its atomic structure!

When **KRYPTON** exploded, every one of its fragments turned to kryptonite! Now the process is **REVERSED**, and all kryptonite is turning into normal minerals, chemicals and gases!

Taking **BRAINIAC'S** ray-gun from his cloak, **SUPERMAN-RED** focuses it on **KANDOR**...

The enlarging ray is working! **KANDOR** is expanding, breaking out of its bottle!

KRRAASHH

Presently, on the reborn planet...

There it is... **KRYPTON**, complete with its continents, oceans, and even an atmosphere!

There's one task left! We've got to expand **KANDOR** to normal size!

Congratulations, **SUPERMAN-RED**! You've done it! **KANDOR** is normal size at last!

The credit goes to **BOTH** of us, **SUPERMAN-BLUE**!

And so **KANDOR** bursts from its glass prison once again to take its place as a mighty city!

6

104

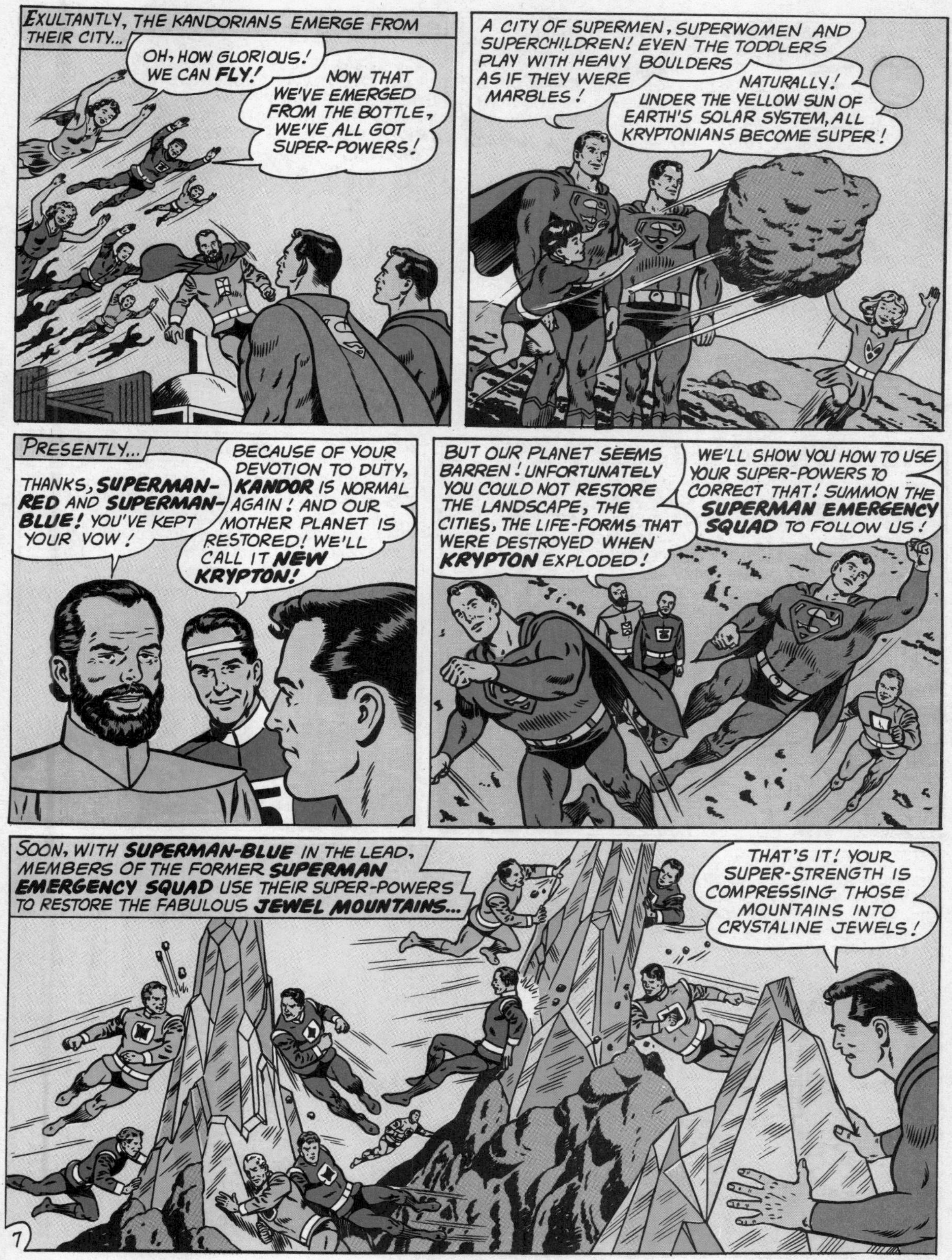
EXULTANTLY, THE KANDORIANS EMERGE FROM THEIR CITY...
OH, HOW GLORIOUS! WE CAN FLY!
NOW THAT WE'VE EMERGED FROM THE BOTTLE, WE'VE ALL GOT SUPER-POWERS!
A CITY OF SUPERMEN, SUPERWOMEN AND SUPERCHILDREN! EVEN THE TODDLERS PLAY WITH HEAVY BOULDERS AS IF THEY WERE MARBLES!
NATURALLY! UNDER THE YELLOW SUN OF EARTH'S SOLAR SYSTEM, ALL KRYPTONIANS BECOME SUPER!
PRESENTLY...
THANKS, SUPERMAN-RED AND SUPERMAN-BLUE! YOU'VE KEPT YOUR VOW!
BECAUSE OF YOUR DEVOTION TO DUTY, KANDOR IS NORMAL AGAIN! AND OUR MOTHER PLANET IS RESTORED! WE'LL CALL IT NEW KRYPTON!
BUT OUR PLANET SEEMS BARREN! UNFORTUNATELY YOU COULD NOT RESTORE THE LANDSCAPE, THE CITIES, THE LIFE-FORMS THAT WERE DESTROYED WHEN KRYPTON EXPLODED!
WE'LL SHOW YOU HOW TO USE YOUR SUPER-POWERS TO CORRECT THAT! SUMMON THE SUPERMAN EMERGENCY SQUAD TO FOLLOW US!
SOON, WITH SUPERMAN-BLUE IN THE LEAD, MEMBERS OF THE FORMER SUPERMAN EMERGENCY SQUAD USE THEIR SUPER-POWERS TO RESTORE THE FABULOUS JEWEL MOUNTAINS...
THAT'S IT! YOUR SUPER-STRENGTH IS COMPRESSING THOSE MOUNTAINS INTO CRYSTALINE JEWELS!
7

MEANWHILE, **SUPERMAN-RED** LEADS A TEAM OF SCIENTISTS IN ANOTHER TASK...

ALL RIGHT, MEN! YOU'VE ALL GOT SEEDLINGS FROM **KANDOR'S** BOTANICAL GARDENS! PLANT THEM AT SUPER-SPEED! WE HAVE MANY OTHER TASKS TO DO!

SOON AFTERWARD... JUST AS I FIGURED! UNDER OUR YELLOW SUN, THOSE KRYPTONIAN SEEDLINGS GREW TO MATURITY IN A FEW MOMENTS, THUS RECREATING **KRYPTON'S** FAMOUS **SCARLET JUNGLE!**

AS THE KRYPTONIANS REBUILD THEIR LOST CITIES...

WITH THESE OLD PLANS TO GUIDE THEM, THE KANDORIANS ARE RECREATING **ARGO CITY!**

THE PLACE WHERE OUR COUSIN, **SUPERGIRL**, WAS BORN! ¿CHOKE!¿ WHO WOULD EVER DREAM IT WOULD BE RESTORED SOME DAY!

AT LAST...

OUR SUPER-TASKS ARE DONE! NOW THAT NEW **KRYPTON** IS REBUILT, WE CAN LIVE OUR NORMAL LIVES AGAIN!

NORMAL LIVES? YOU FORGOT THAT UNDER THE INFLUENCE OF EARTH'S YELLOW SUN YOU ARE ALL SUPER!

YOU CAN ONLY LIVE NORMALLY UNDER A RED SUN LIKE THE ONE **KRYPTON** HAD! IN THIS SOLAR SYSTEM, YOU WILL **ALWAYS** BE A PLANET OF SUPER-BEINGS! IS THAT WHAT YOU WANT?

¿GULP!¿ YOU'RE RIGHT, **SUPERMAN-RED!** THAT IS A GRAVE PROBLEM! WE WILL SUMMON THE COUNCIL TO CONSIDER OUR DECISION!

8

LATER, AS THE COUNCIL MEETS...

WHAT WILL THE DECISION BE? WILL ANOTHER PLANET, POPULATED BY SUPER-BEINGS, BE ADDED TO OUR SOLAR SYSTEM? FOR THE ANSWER, SEE **PART II**

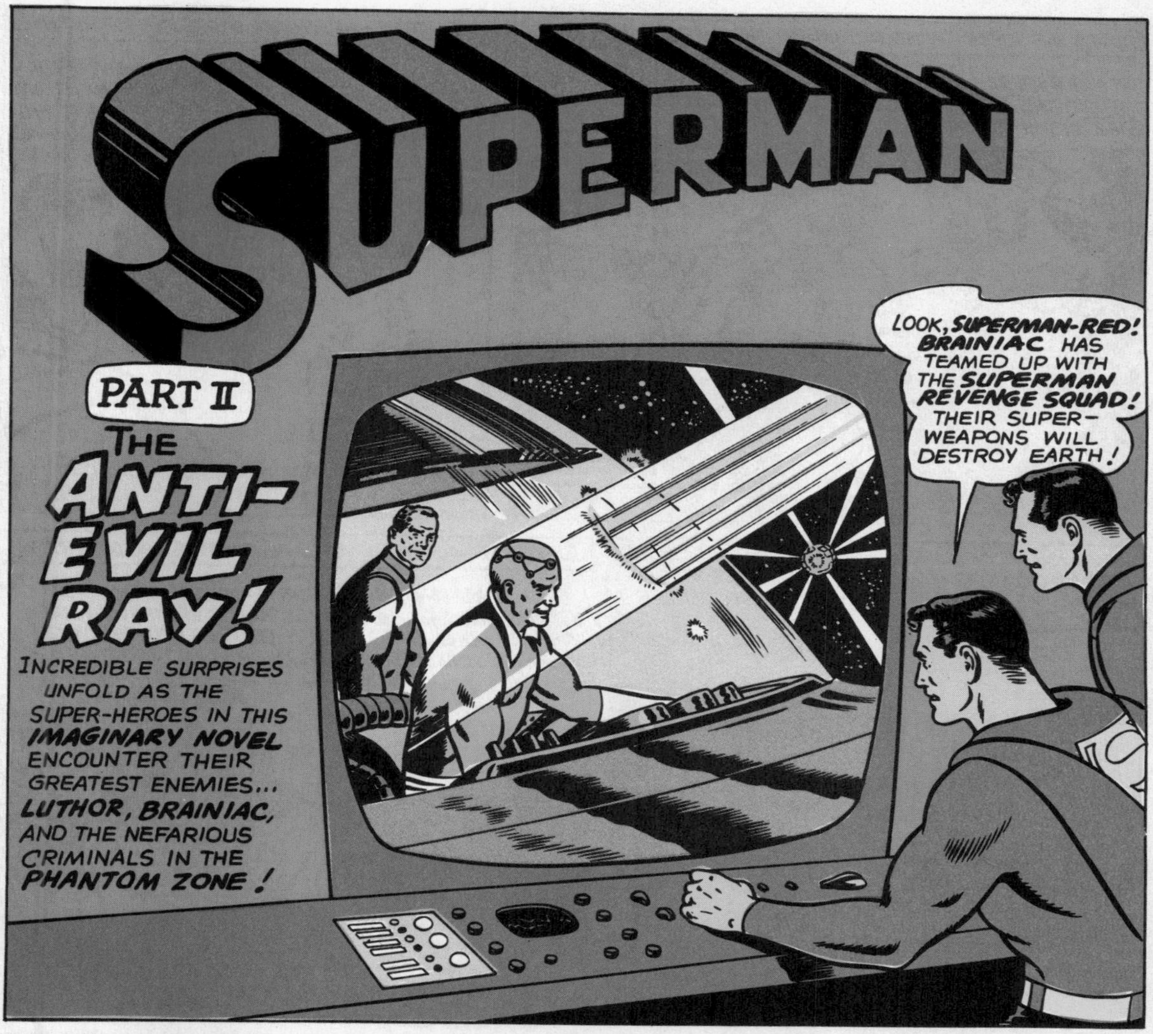
SUPERMAN
PART II
THE ANTI-EVIL RAY!
INCREDIBLE SURPRISES UNFOLD AS THE SUPER-HEROES IN THIS IMAGINARY NOVEL ENCOUNTER THEIR GREATEST ENEMIES... LUTHOR, BRAINIAC, AND THE NEFARIOUS CRIMINALS IN THE PHANTOM ZONE!
LOOK, SUPERMAN-RED! BRAINIAC HAS TEAMED UP WITH THE SUPERMAN REVENGE SQUAD! THEIR SUPER-WEAPONS WILL DESTROY EARTH!

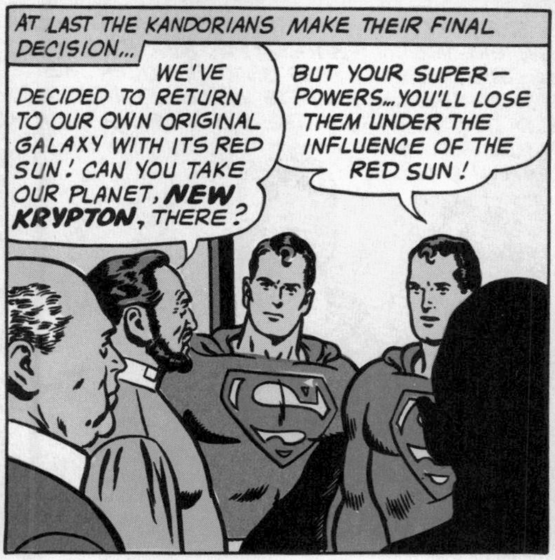
AT LAST THE KANDORIANS MAKE THEIR FINAL DECISION...
WE'VE DECIDED TO RETURN TO OUR OWN ORIGINAL GALAXY WITH ITS RED SUN! CAN YOU TAKE OUR PLANET, NEW KRYPTON, THERE?
BUT YOUR SUPER-POWERS...YOU'LL LOSE THEM UNDER THE INFLUENCE OF THE RED SUN!

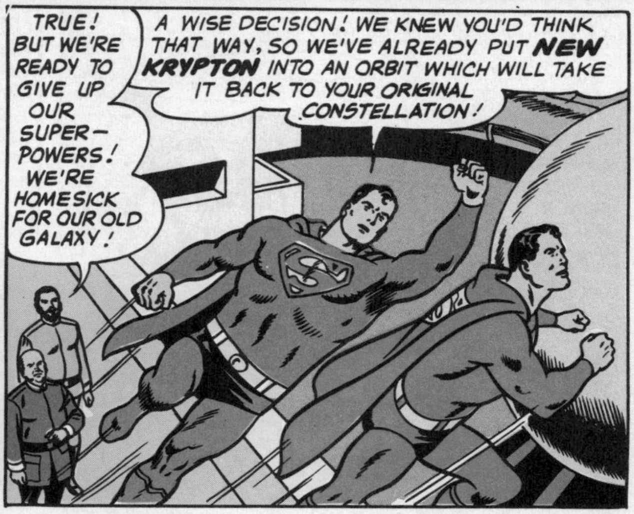
TRUE! BUT WE'RE READY TO GIVE UP OUR SUPER-POWERS! WE'RE HOMESICK FOR OUR OLD GALAXY!
A WISE DECISION! WE KNEW YOU'D THINK THAT WAY, SO WE'VE ALREADY PUT NEW KRYPTON INTO AN ORBIT WHICH WILL TAKE IT BACK TO YOUR ORIGINAL CONSTELLATION!

BUT AS THE SUPER-TWINS RETURN TO THEIR ARCTIC FORTRESS...

GREAT **KRYPTON**! ARE WE SEEING THINGS? THERE'S THE **BOTTLE OF KANDOR** STANDING IN ITS USUAL PLACE!

GASP! THAT'S IMPOSSIBLE! WE JUST FINISHED EN-LARGING IT TO ITS NORMAL SIZE! WE SAW IT WITH OUR OWN EYES! WAS IT ALL SOME KIND OF ILLUSION?

JUST THEN **SUPERGIRL** STEPS OUT OF HIDING...

RELAX, BOTH OF YOU! AFTER WATCHING YOUR SUPER-DEEDS ON THE MONITOR SCREEN, I RE-CREATED A COPY OF THE BOTTLE AS A MEMENTO! WE'LL KEEP IT HERE WHERE **KANDOR** ALWAYS STOOD!

WHEW! FOR A MOMENT WE THOUGHT WE WERE HAVING A NIGHTMARE!

WELL, YOU ACCOMPLISHED YOUR FIRST TWO SUPER-TASKS MAGNIFICENTLY!

BUT WHICH VITAL PROBLEM WILL WE TACKLE NEXT?

UNSOLVED SUPER-PROBLEMS

1. RESTORE KANDOR TO NORMAL SIZE

2. FIND ANTIDOTE TO GREEN KRYPTONITE

3. WIPE OUT CRIME AND EVIL

4. GUARD AGAINST

JUST THEN, A MENTAL VOICE PENETRATES THE FORTRESS...

SUPERMAN-RED, SUPERMAN-BLUE! THIS IS **LORI**, THE MERMAID, CALLING...

LORI'S CONTACTING US BY MENTAL TELEPATHY! THERE MAY BE AN EMERGENCY ON ATLANTIS, THE SUNKEN CONTINENT!

AT THAT MOMENT, IN THE DEPTHS OF THE SEA...

OUR MONITORS OBSERVED THE WONDERS YOU ACCOMPLISHED FOR **KANDOR**! COULD YOU PLEASE USE YOUR POWERS TO HELP **ATLANTIS**?

WE'RE TIRED OF BEING CONSIDERED FREAKS HERE ON EARTH! HELP US FIND A NEW WORLD... A PLANET THAT WILL BE OURS **ALONE**!

LET'S SEE NOW! SOMEWHERE IN OUR SPACE-TRAVEL WE MUST HAVE SEEN A WORLD THAT WAS SUITABLE FOR THE ATLANTEANS!

WAIT! THE IMPROVEMENT OF OUR **MIND-PROBER RAY** WILL HELP US CHECK OVER THE PLANETS WE'VE SEEN THROUGH-OUT THE UNIVERSE!

2

AS THE WEIRD MACHINE IS SWITCHED ON...

BY FOCUSING ITS BEAM ON OUR BRAINS, THE RAY PRODUCES A PICTURE OF OUR MEMORIES ON THAT SCREEN! CONCENTRATE ON ALL THE PLANETS WE'VE EVER SEEN!

I'M WITH YOU, *RED!*

THEN, SUDDENLY...

IT'S FANTASTIC! YOU'RE BOTH CONCENTRATING ON THE SAME PLANET, THE *MEMORIAL WORLD OF KRYPTON* WHICH I ONCE HELPED YOU BUILD!

THAT PLANET IS EXACTLY WHAT WE'RE LOOKING FOR, *SUPERGIRL!*

USING TELESCOPIC VISION, THEY EXAMINE THE CHOSEN PLANET...

THERE'S NO NEED FOR A MEMORIAL NOW THAT *KRYPTON* IS RESTORED! BUT WE MUST FIND SOME WAY OF FLOODING THAT PLANET TO PROVIDE THE WATERY ENVIROMENT THE ATLANTEANS NEED!

THOSE POLAR ICE-CAPS ARE THE ANSWER TO OUR PROBLEM! BUT WE MAY NEED A LITTLE HELP!

WHISTLING A SUPERSONIC SIGNAL, THE SUPER-DUO SUMMONS *KRYPTO*, THE SUPER-DOG, AND...

KRYPTO! WE HATE TO BREAK UP YOUR FUN!

...BUT WE'VE GOT AN IMPORTANT JOB FOR YOU!

ARRFFF! TWIN-SUPERMEN! I DON'T KNOW HOW IT HAPPENED, BUT THEY BOTH SOUND EXACTLY LIKE MY OLD MASTER, SO I GUESS I'D BETTER OBEY!

PRESENTLY, AS THE FANTASTIC PLAN IS PUT INTO OPERATION...

REMEMBER! WE *ALL* FOCUS OUR HEAT VISION ON THE POLAR ICE-CAPS OF THE *MEMORIAL PLANET!*

KRYPTO AND I WILL CONCENTRATE ON THE NORTH POLE! YOU AND *SUPERGIRL* TAKE THE SOUTH... POUR IT ON!

ACROSS THE GULF OF SPACE, THE SEARING BLAST OF THEIR COMBINED HEAT-VISION BEGINS TO MELT THE GLACIAL ICE...

SSSSSSS!

KRAKKK!

MIGHTY TORRENTS POUR INTO THE OCEAN BEDS! AS SEAS OVERFLOW, TITANIC TIDAL WAVES ENGULF THE CITY OF THE MEMORIAL PLANET...

AS THE ATLANTEANS WATCH IN AWE...

THAT WAS AN ASTOUNDING FEAT! BUT HOW CAN WE ATLANTEANS GET TO THAT NEW WORLD YOU'VE CREATED FOR US? WE NEED WATER TO BREATHE! WE'LL DIE IN THE VACUUM OF SPACE!

DON'T WORRY, LORI, WE FIGURED OUT A WAY! WATCH!

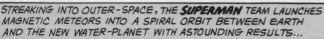

STREAKING INTO OUTER-SPACE, THE **SUPERMAN** TEAM LAUNCHES MAGNETIC METEORS INTO A SPIRAL ORBIT BETWEEN EARTH AND THE NEW WATER-PLANET WITH ASTOUNDING RESULTS...

OUR PLAN WORKED!

SUCCESS! A COLUMN OF WATER IS RISING FROM THE SURFACE OF THE WATER PLANET! SOON IT WILL JOIN WITH THE WATER RISING FROM EARTH, CREATING A SAFE PASSAGE BETWEEN THE PLANETS FOR THE ATLANTEANS!

THIS IS INCREDIBLE! WHAT'S KEEPING THE WATER FROM EVAPORATING INTO THE VACUUM OF SPACE?

IT'S SIMPLE, LORI! THOSE ORBITING METEORITES HAVE ALTERED THE MAGNETIC FIELDS OF EARTH AND THE NEW PLANET, CREATING AN IMMENSE MAGNETIC TUNNEL WHICH HOLDS THE WATER TOGETHER! NOW YOU CAN MIGRATE TO YOUR NEW HOME!

IN AN EPIC EXODUS, THE ATLANTEANS BEGIN THEIR FANTASTIC INTER-PLANETARY JOURNEY...

AN UNDERWATER JOURNEY THROUGH SPACE! OUR DESCENDANTS WILL THINK THIS WONDROUS JOURNEY WAS A MYTH...A LEGEND!

As the Atlanteans take possession of their new home...

An under-water world of our own! We'll call it HYDRA! SUPERMAN-RED, SUPERMAN-BLUE... HOW can we ever thank you!

We were glad to help your people, Lori! We'll come to visit you soon! Goodbye for now!

Our next task is to erase crime and evil from the earth! I've been thinking of an ANTI-EVIL ray! I'll design it at super-speed!

Your mathematical formulae seem correct, BLUE! I'll build a ray projector from your design!

The ray projector is built at super-speed, then...

We'll try our hypnotic anti-evil ray on those giant warrior ants!

It should be an excellent test! This particular species of ants devour each other at every opportunity!

Short moments later, astonishingly...

It's amazing! A few moments of exposure to that ray and those ants stopped eating each other!

Correct, SUPERGIRL! They are now feeding only on plant life and fungus growth! Our hypno-ray works!

Once more the super-twins work at eye-blurring speed, and...

We'll mount our anti-evil hypno-ray projectors into a series of satellites that will orbit the earth!

The ray will erase all thoughts of evil from the minds of the world's criminals!

Using super-strength and super-aim, the incredible duo launch the satellites...

There! They're all circling the earth! Those anti-crime rays will reach every corner of our planet!

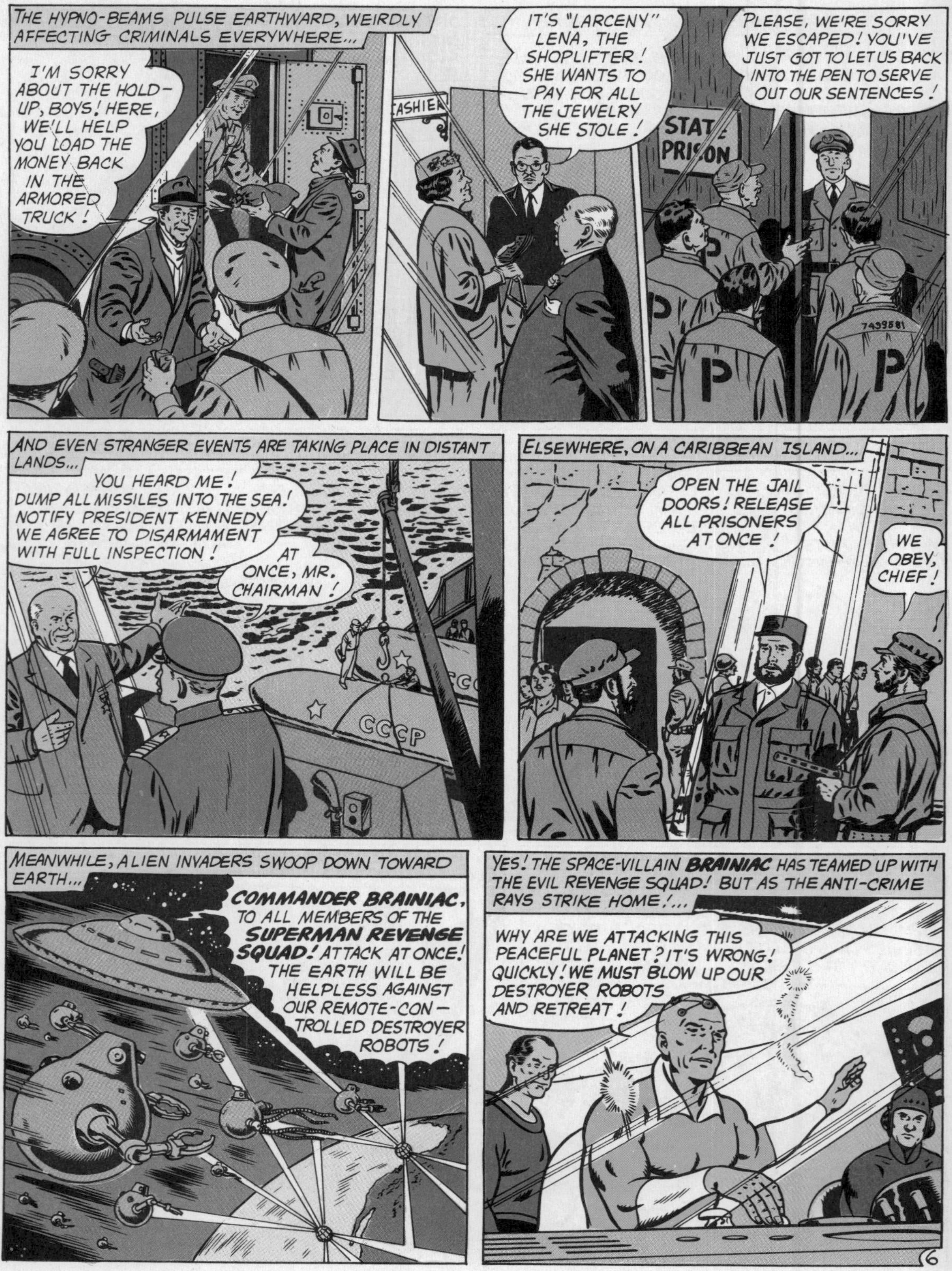

THE HYPNO-BEAMS PULSE EARTHWARD, WEIRDLY AFFECTING CRIMINALS EVERYWHERE...
I'M SORRY ABOUT THE HOLD-UP, BOYS! HERE, WE'LL HELP YOU LOAD THE MONEY BACK IN THE ARMORED TRUCK!
IT'S "LARCENY" LENA, THE SHOPLIFTER! SHE WANTS TO PAY FOR ALL THE JEWELRY SHE STOLE!
CASHIER
PLEASE, WE'RE SORRY WE ESCAPED! YOU'VE JUST GOT TO LET US BACK INTO THE PEN TO SERVE OUT OUR SENTENCES!
STATE PRISON
7499581
AND EVEN STRANGER EVENTS ARE TAKING PLACE IN DISTANT LANDS...
YOU HEARD ME! DUMP ALL MISSILES INTO THE SEA! NOTIFY PRESIDENT KENNEDY WE AGREE TO DISARMAMENT WITH FULL INSPECTION!
AT ONCE, MR. CHAIRMAN!
CCCP
ELSEWHERE, ON A CARIBBEAN ISLAND...
OPEN THE JAIL DOORS! RELEASE ALL PRISONERS AT ONCE!
WE OBEY, CHIEF!
MEANWHILE, ALIEN INVADERS SWOOP DOWN TOWARD EARTH...
COMMANDER BRAINIAC, TO ALL MEMBERS OF THE SUPERMAN REVENGE SQUAD! ATTACK AT ONCE! THE EARTH WILL BE HELPLESS AGAINST OUR REMOTE-CON-TROLLED DESTROYER ROBOTS!
YES! THE SPACE-VILLAIN BRAINIAC HAS TEAMED UP WITH THE EVIL REVENGE SQUAD! BUT AS THE ANTI-CRIME RAYS STRIKE HOME!...
WHY ARE WE ATTACKING THIS PEACEFUL PLANET? IT'S WRONG! QUICKLY! WE MUST BLOW UP OUR DESTROYER ROBOTS AND RETREAT!
6

I THOUGHT WE'D HAVE TO TACKLE THOSE INVADERS! BUT THOSE ANTI-CRIME HYPNO-RAYS DID THE JOB FOR US!

RIGHT! THEY'RE HEADING BACK TOWARD THEIR OWN GALAXY!

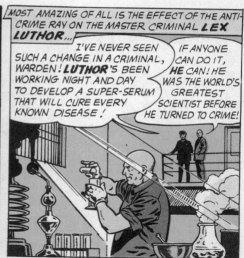

MOST AMAZING OF ALL IS THE EFFECT OF THE ANTI-CRIME RAY ON THE MASTER CRIMINAL LEX LUTHOR...

I'VE NEVER SEEN SUCH A CHANGE IN A CRIMINAL, WARDEN! LUTHOR'S BEEN WORKING NIGHT AND DAY TO DEVELOP A SUPER-SERUM THAT WILL CURE EVERY KNOWN DISEASE!

IF ANYONE CAN DO IT, HE CAN! HE WAS THE WORLD'S GREATEST SCIENTIST BEFORE HE TURNED TO CRIME!

THE NEXT DAY, AS THE SUPERMEN ARE SUMMONED TO METROPOLIS PRISON...

THIS SERUM WILL REPAY ALL THE EVIL I'VE EVER DONE! JUST SCATTER IT IN THE WORLD'S DRINKING WATER, AND IN TWO DAYS IT WILL WIPE ALL DISEASE FROM THE EARTH!

I'VE ANALYZED THIS FLUID WITH MY MICROSCOPIC VISION! IT'S THE MOST EFFECTIVE ANTIBIOTIC EVER INVENTED! WE'LL TRY IT AT ONCE!

SHORTLY, THE TWIN SUPERMEN SPRAY THE SERUM OVER THE EARTH...

A FEW DROPS SHOULD BE ENOUGH TO AFFECT THE ENTIRE MISSISSIPPI VALLEY!

THERE! THIS SHOULD TAKE CARE OF THE AMAZON AREA!

AS THE SERUM TAKES MIRACULOUS EFFECT...

IT'S A MIRACLE! ONE DRINK OF WATER AND MY SIGHT RETURNED!

HELP THE BLIND

IT'S UNCANNY! EVERY HELPLESS CRIPPLE HAS SUDDENLY BEGUN TO WALK AGAIN!

AND IN LUTHOR'S CELL...

LOOK! THE SERUM IS WORKING ON ME, TOO! I'M NO LONGER BALD!

7

END OF PART II

A LOOK AT OTHER GREAT IMAGINARY STORIES

LOIS LANE #64, 1966
art by Kurt Schaffenberger

LOIS LANE #65, 1966
art by Kurt Schaffenberger

SUPERMAN

PART III

THE END OF SUPERMAN'S CAREER!

NOW, AS OUR *IMAGINARY NOVEL* BUILDS TO A DRAMATIC CLIMAX, BOTH *SUPERMAN-RED* AND *SUPERMAN-BLUE* MARRY THE GIRL OF THEIR CHOICE. ONE COUPLE DECIDES TO LIVE ON EARTH, THE OTHER PAIR DECIDES TO SETTLE ON *NEW KRYPTON*. WE ASK YOU-- WHICH COUPLE DO YOU THINK IS HAPPIEST?

CLARK!?! GOOD GRIEF, AM I SEEING DOUBLE?

ULP! THEY'RE TWINS! BUT THAT'S IMPOSSIBLE!

JUST A MINUTE, GIRLS! WE CAN EXPLAIN!

KEEP OUR PARKS CLEAN

AS THE TWIN SUPERMEN STREAK DOWN TO HALT THE ESCAPE OF THE CRIMINALS...

GOOD GRIEF, *SUPERGIRL*, YOU CAN'T RELEASE THOSE KRYPTONIAN DESPERADOES FROM THE *PHANTOM ZONE!*

BUT THEY'RE NOT CRIMINALS ANY LONGER! YOUR ANTI-CRIME RAY HAS REFORMED THEM! THEY WANT TO JOURNEY TO *NEW KRYPTON*, AND LIVE THERE AS USEFUL CITIZENS!

AND I AM GOING TO LEAD THEM THERE! ⌐CHOKE!⌐ YOU SEE, I'M LEAVING EARTH TO LIVE ON MY OLD PLANET!

BUT, *SUPERGIRL!* YOU DON'T KNOW WHAT YOU'RE SAYING! UNDER THE RED SUN OF *NEW KRYPTON*, YOU'LL LOSE ALL YOUR SUPER-POWERS!

EVEN IF I LOSE MY POWERS, IT'S WORTH IT! I'VE NEVER FORGOTTEN MY HOME PLANET! NOW THAT **KRYPTON** IS RESTORED I WANT TO LIVE THERE!

THERE'S ONE PROBLEM! SINCE **KRYPTON**'S RED SUN WILL ERASE YOUR SUPER-POWERS, YOU AND THE OTHERS WILL NEED A SPACE-SHIP TO TAKE YOU THERE!

JUST THEN...

ULP! A SPACE-SHIP MATERIALIZING OUT OF NOWHERE!

AND THERE'S A TIME-TRAVEL CABINET BESIDE IT! I THINK THE **LEGION OF SUPER-HEROES** IS ABOUT TO VISIT US!

YES! SEVERAL MEMBERS OF THE HEROIC LEGION HAVE JOURNEYED FROM THE FUTURE TO AID **SUPERGIRL**!

CONGRATULATIONS, SUPERMEN! WE'VE BEEN WATCHING YOU ON OUR MONITOR SCREENS! WHEN WE HEARD OF **SUPERGIRL'S** PROBLEMS, WE BROUGHT THIS SPACE-ARK HERE FROM THE FUTURE FOR HER!

NOW I AND THE OTHERS CAN JOURNEY SAFELY TO **NEW KRYPTON**, **SATURN GIRL**! HOW CAN I EVER THANK YOU?

EVEN THOUGH YOU'LL NO LONGER BE SUPER, YOU'LL ALWAYS BE AN HONORARY MEMBER OF THE LEGION! WE'LL NEVER FORGET YOU, **SUPERGIRL**!

CHOKE! IT'S HARD TO SAY GOODBYE, BUT WE MUST EMBARK NOW! HERE'S A PARTING KISS!

AND AS THE MIGHTY SPACE-ARK SPEEDS OFF ON ITS EPIC JOURNEY...

WE'LL MISS HER, **BLUE**! **SUPERGIRL** ACCOMPLISHED SOME OF THE GREATEST SUPER-DEEDS ON RECORD!

EARTH WILL NEVER SEEM THE SAME WITHOUT **SUPERGIRL**!

AFTER THE LEGION RETURNS TO THE FUTURE, THE TWIN SUPERMEN RECEIVE AN EMERGENCY CALL ON THE FORTRESS MONITOR...

ATTENTION, SUPERMEN! **LUTHOR** CALLING! I'VE JUST SPOTTED YOUR ENEMY, **MXYZPTLK**, OVER **METROPOLIS**! HE PROBABLY SLIPPED IN FROM THE 5TH DIMENSION FOR SOME OF HIS MISCHIEF!

THANKS, **LUTHOR**! WE'LL CHECK INTO IT AT ONCE!

2

AS THE SUPER-DUO STREAKS TO *METROPOLIS*...

LURE THAT IMP OVER THIS WAY! MY FIVE-DIMENSIONAL CANNON WILL HURL HIM BACK INTO THE FIFTH DIMENSION WHERE HE BELONGS!

RELAX, *LUTHOR!* I'VE JUST SPOTTED *MR. MXYZPTLK* WITH MY TELESCOPIC VISION! HE'S NOT UP TO HIS USUAL TRICKS!

CHECKING ON *MR. MXYZPTLK*, THE SUPER-TWINS FOLLOW HIM TO A NEARBY MOUNTAIN, WHERE...

OH-OH! WE COULD BE MAKING A MISTAKE! HE SEEMS TO BE PUTTING SOME KIND OF MAGIC SPELL ON THAT HUGE ROCKY CLIFF!

I WONDER WHAT KIND OF DEVILMENT HE'S UP TO NOW!

VOOOOMMMM!

BUT AS THE SMOKE CLEARS...

THERE YOU ARE, GENTLEMEN! THIS MONUMENT IS DEDICATED TO ALL SUPER-BEINGS! IT'S THE LEAST I COULD DO TO MAKE UP FOR ALL THE MISCHIEF I'VE DONE IN THE PAST!

GOOD GRIEF! THIS IS SO UNLIKE HIM! BUT I THINK I UNDERSTAND! *MXYZPTLK* HAS *ALSO* BEEN AFFECTED BY OUR ANTI-EVIL RAY!

AND NOW, AS A TOKEN OF MY ESTEEM, I WILL RETURN TO MY OWN DIMENSION BY RECITING MY NAME BACKWARD! *KLTPZYXM!*

ASTOUNDING! THAT'S THE FIRST TIME HE RETURNED TO HIS OWN DIMENSION WILLINGLY! NO TRICK WAS NECESSARY!

POOF!

PRESENTLY...

OUR HYPNO-BEAM IS WORKING PERFECTLY! NOW THAT ALL CRIME AND EVIL ARE ABOLISHED, WE CAN FULLFILL ANOTHER AMBITION! WE CAN GET MARRIED!

YOU'RE RIGHT! THE WOMAN WE LOVE IS NO LONGER IN DANGER FROM THE EVIL PLOTS ON THE CRIMINAL WORLD!

HOLD EVERYTHING, *RED!* THERE HAVE ALWAYS BEEN TWO GIRLS WHO WERE RIVALS FOR OUR LOVE! LOIS LANE AND LANA LANG! WHICH WILL IT BE?

WELL, NOW THAT THERE ARE TWO OF US, WE CAN EACH MARRY ONE OF THE GIRLS! BUT WHO WILL MARRY WHOM? ...WAIT, I HAVE AN IDEA!

3

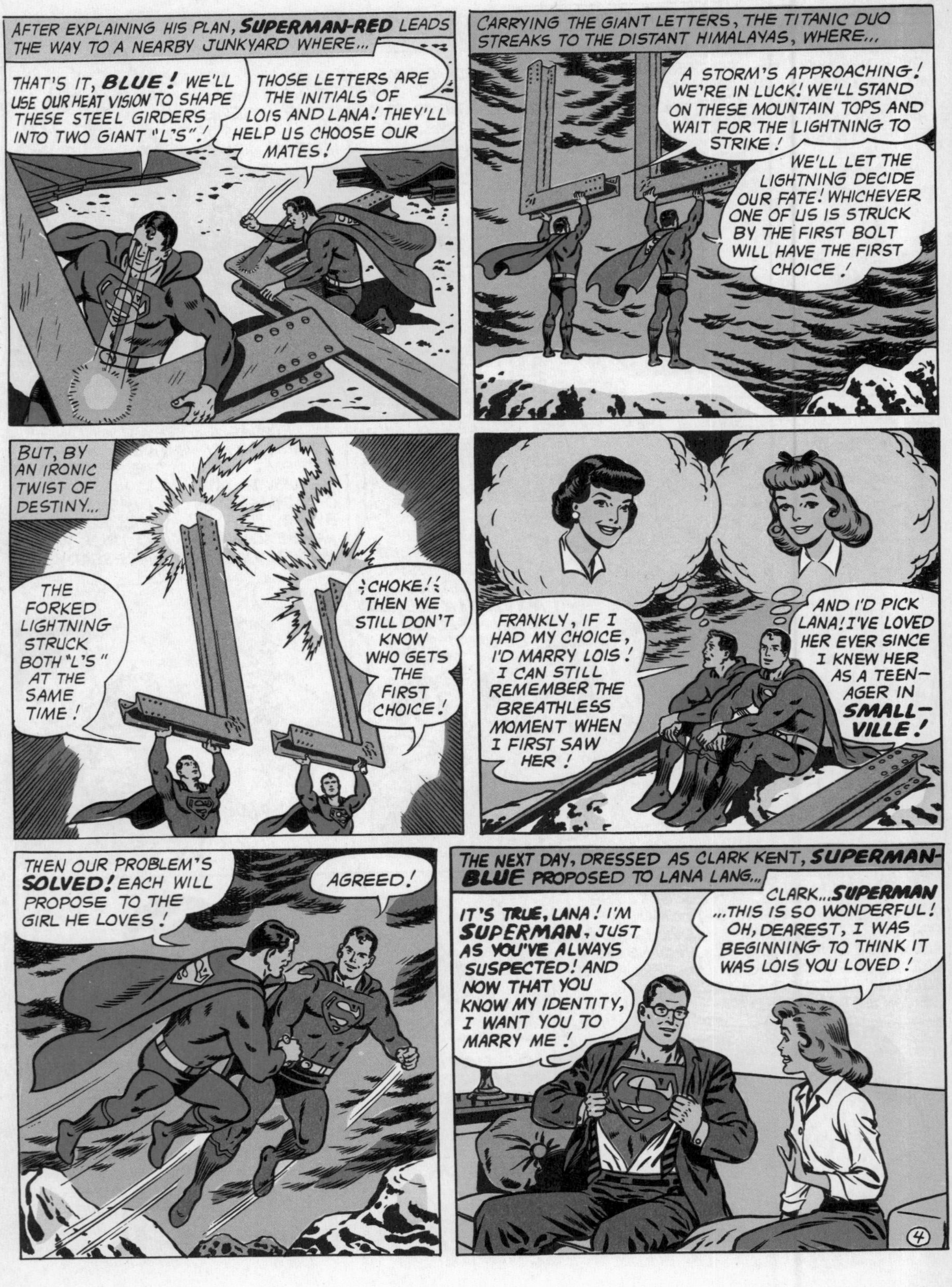

AFTER EXPLAINING HIS PLAN, SUPERMAN-RED LEADS THE WAY TO A NEARBY JUNKYARD WHERE...
THAT'S IT, BLUE! WE'LL USE OUR HEAT VISION TO SHAPE THESE STEEL GIRDERS INTO TWO GIANT "L'S"!
THOSE LETTERS ARE THE INITIALS OF LOIS AND LANA! THEY'LL HELP US CHOOSE OUR MATES!
CARRYING THE GIANT LETTERS, THE TITANIC DUO STREAKS TO THE DISTANT HIMALAYAS, WHERE...
A STORM'S APPROACHING! WE'RE IN LUCK! WE'LL STAND ON THESE MOUNTAIN TOPS AND WAIT FOR THE LIGHTNING TO STRIKE!
WE'LL LET THE LIGHTNING DECIDE OUR FATE! WHICHEVER ONE OF US IS STRUCK BY THE FIRST BOLT WILL HAVE THE FIRST CHOICE!
BUT, BY AN IRONIC TWIST OF DESTINY...
THE FORKED LIGHTNING STRUCK BOTH "L'S" AT THE SAME TIME!
-CHOKE!- THEN WE STILL DON'T KNOW WHO GETS THE FIRST CHOICE!
FRANKLY, IF I HAD MY CHOICE, I'D MARRY LOIS! I CAN STILL REMEMBER THE BREATHLESS MOMENT WHEN I FIRST SAW HER!
AND I'D PICK LANA! I'VE LOVED HER EVER SINCE I KNEW HER AS A TEEN-AGER IN SMALLVILLE!
THEN OUR PROBLEM'S SOLVED! EACH WILL PROPOSE TO THE GIRL HE LOVES!
AGREED!
THE NEXT DAY, DRESSED AS CLARK KENT, SUPERMAN-BLUE PROPOSED TO LANA LANG...
IT'S TRUE, LANA! I'M SUPERMAN, JUST AS YOU'VE ALWAYS SUSPECTED! AND NOW THAT YOU KNOW MY IDENTITY, I WANT YOU TO MARRY ME!
CLARK...SUPERMAN ...THIS IS SO WONDERFUL! OH, DEAREST, I WAS BEGINNING TO THINK IT WAS LOIS YOU LOVED!
4

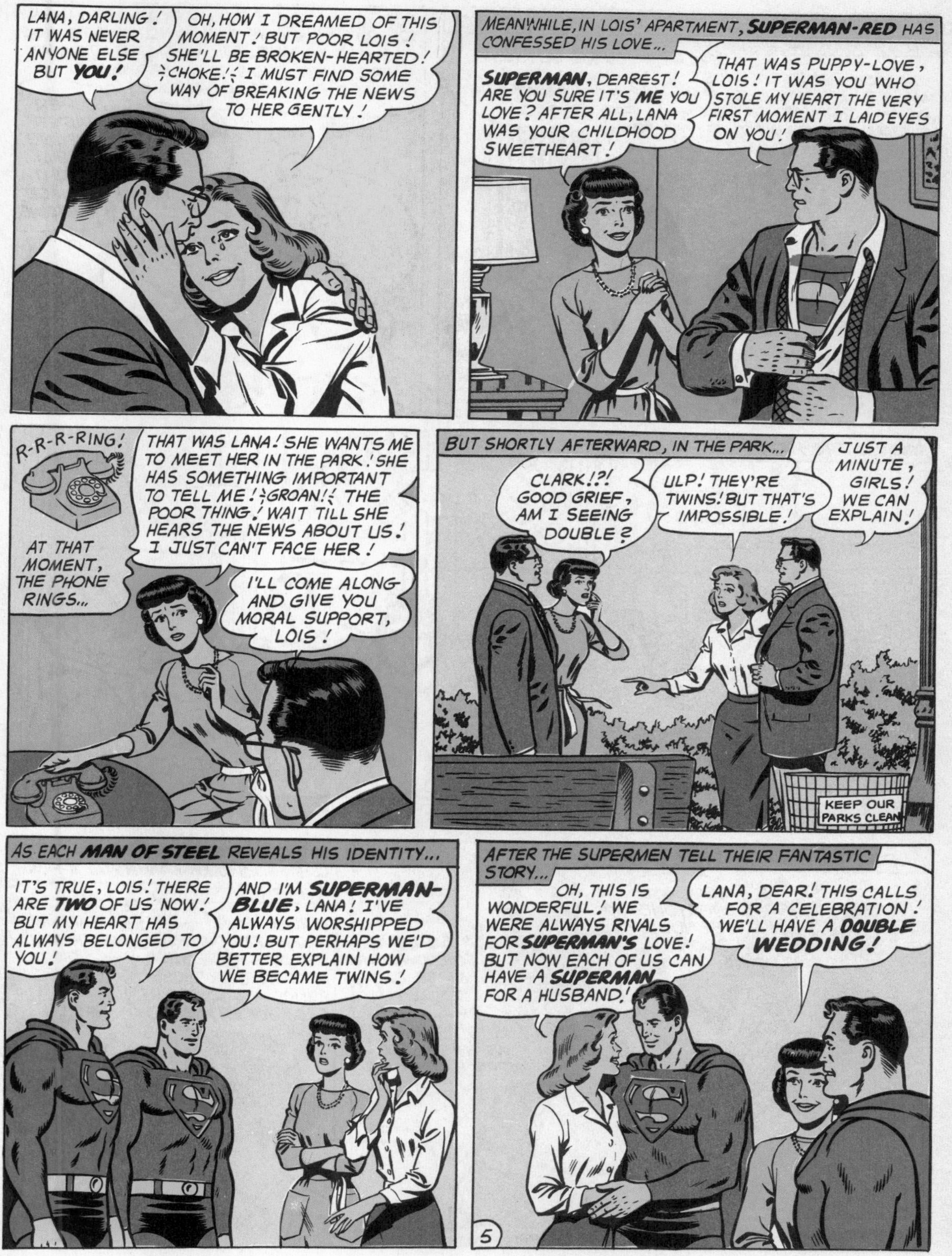
LANA, DARLING! IT WAS NEVER ANYONE ELSE BUT YOU!
OH, HOW I DREAMED OF THIS MOMENT! BUT POOR LOIS! SHE'LL BE BROKEN-HEARTED! ≈CHOKE!≈ I MUST FIND SOME WAY OF BREAKING THE NEWS TO HER GENTLY!
MEANWHILE, IN LOIS' APARTMENT, SUPERMAN-RED HAS CONFESSED HIS LOVE...
SUPERMAN, DEAREST! ARE YOU SURE IT'S ME YOU LOVE? AFTER ALL, LANA WAS YOUR CHILDHOOD SWEETHEART!
THAT WAS PUPPY-LOVE, LOIS! IT WAS YOU WHO STOLE MY HEART THE VERY FIRST MOMENT I LAID EYES ON YOU!
R-R-R-RING!
AT THAT MOMENT, THE PHONE RINGS...
THAT WAS LANA! SHE WANTS ME TO MEET HER IN THE PARK! SHE HAS SOMETHING IMPORTANT TO TELL ME! ≈GROAN!≈ THE POOR THING! WAIT TILL SHE HEARS THE NEWS ABOUT US! I JUST CAN'T FACE HER!
I'LL COME ALONG AND GIVE YOU MORAL SUPPORT, LOIS!
BUT SHORTLY AFTERWARD, IN THE PARK...
CLARK!?! GOOD GRIEF, AM I SEEING DOUBLE?
ULP! THEY'RE TWINS! BUT THAT'S IMPOSSIBLE!
JUST A MINUTE, GIRLS! WE CAN EXPLAIN!
KEEP OUR PARKS CLEAN
AS EACH MAN OF STEEL REVEALS HIS IDENTITY...
IT'S TRUE, LOIS! THERE ARE TWO OF US NOW! BUT MY HEART HAS ALWAYS BELONGED TO YOU!
AND I'M SUPERMAN-BLUE, LANA! I'VE ALWAYS WORSHIPPED YOU! BUT PERHAPS WE'D BETTER EXPLAIN HOW WE BECAME TWINS!
AFTER THE SUPERMEN TELL THEIR FANTASTIC STORY...
OH, THIS IS WONDERFUL! WE WERE ALWAYS RIVALS FOR SUPERMAN'S LOVE! BUT NOW EACH OF US CAN HAVE A SUPERMAN FOR A HUSBAND!
LANA, DEAR! THIS CALLS FOR A CELEBRATION! WE'LL HAVE A DOUBLE WEDDING!
5

AFTER WEEKS OF EXCITED PREPARATION, THE WEDDING DAY COMES AT LAST...

LUCY LANE, YOU LOOK BEAUTIFUL! JUST IMAGINE...ME, THE BEST MAN, AND YOU, THE MAID OF HONOR AT *SUPERMAN*'S WEDDING! IT SURE IS A GREAT DAY!

YOU'RE SO RIGHT, JIMMY! AND IT'S GOING TO BE A GREAT DAY FOR US, TOO!

FOR YEARS YOU'VE BEEN ASKING ME TO MARRY YOU, BUT I'VE ALWAYS TURNED YOU DOWN BECAUSE I WANTED TO WAIT UNTIL MY SISTER LOIS WAS MARRIED! WELL NOW, IT'S HAPPENED AT LAST! SO IF YOU STILL WANT ME!

SUPER-DUPER! DARLING, WE'LL MAKE IT A *TRIPLE WEDDING*.

AND SO THE HAPPY COUPLES TAKE THEIR VOWS...

I DO!

I DO!

I DO!

AND AS THE HONEYMOONS BEGIN...

GOODBYE EVERYONE! SEE YOU SOON!

SO LONG FOR NOW, FOLKS, WE'RE ON OUR WAY!

LOIS!... LANA... WE WISH YOU EVERY HAPPINESS!

BUT HAPPINESS PROVES A MIRAGE FOR LOIS AND *SUPERMAN-RED*...A FEW WEEKS LATER...

DARLING! SOMETHING'S WRONG! FOR THE PAST FEW DAYS YOU'VE BEEN MOONING OVER THOSE RELICS AND SOUVENIRS FROM *KRYPTON*!

ER...I WAS JUST... ER...REARRANG-ING THEM, LOIS!

6

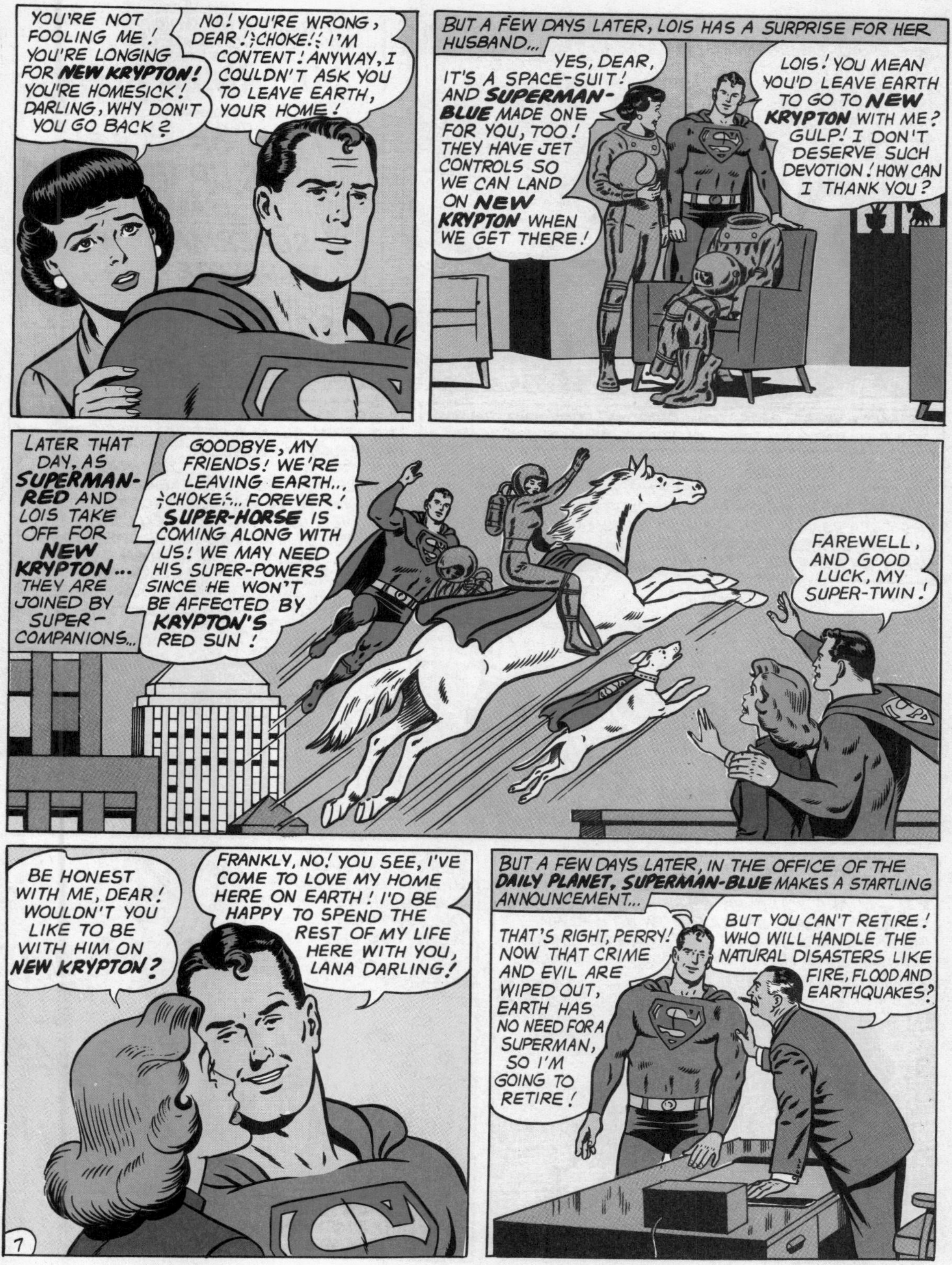
YOU'RE NOT FOOLING ME! YOU'RE LONGING FOR NEW KRYPTON! YOU'RE HOMESICK! DARLING, WHY DON'T YOU GO BACK?
NO! YOU'RE WRONG, DEAR! -CHOKE!- I'M CONTENT! ANYWAY, I COULDN'T ASK YOU TO LEAVE EARTH, YOUR HOME!
BUT A FEW DAYS LATER, LOIS HAS A SURPRISE FOR HER HUSBAND...
YES, DEAR, IT'S A SPACE-SUIT! AND SUPERMAN-BLUE MADE ONE FOR YOU, TOO! THEY HAVE JET CONTROLS SO WE CAN LAND ON NEW KRYPTON WHEN WE GET THERE!
LOIS! YOU MEAN YOU'D LEAVE EARTH TO GO TO NEW KRYPTON WITH ME? GULP! I DON'T DESERVE SUCH DEVOTION! HOW CAN I THANK YOU?
LATER THAT DAY, AS SUPERMAN-RED AND LOIS TAKE OFF FOR NEW KRYPTON... THEY ARE JOINED BY SUPER-COMPANIONS...
GOODBYE, MY FRIENDS! WE'RE LEAVING EARTH... -CHOKE-... FOREVER! SUPER-HORSE IS COMING ALONG WITH US! WE MAY NEED HIS SUPER-POWERS SINCE HE WON'T BE AFFECTED BY KRYPTON'S RED SUN!
FAREWELL, AND GOOD LUCK, MY SUPER-TWIN!
BE HONEST WITH ME, DEAR! WOULDN'T YOU LIKE TO BE WITH HIM ON NEW KRYPTON?
FRANKLY, NO! YOU SEE, I'VE COME TO LOVE MY HOME HERE ON EARTH! I'D BE HAPPY TO SPEND THE REST OF MY LIFE HERE WITH YOU, LANA DARLING!
7
BUT A FEW DAYS LATER, IN THE OFFICE OF THE DAILY PLANET, SUPERMAN-BLUE MAKES A STARTLING ANNOUNCEMENT...
THAT'S RIGHT, PERRY! NOW THAT CRIME AND EVIL ARE WIPED OUT, EARTH HAS NO NEED FOR A SUPERMAN, SO I'M GOING TO RETIRE!
BUT YOU CAN'T RETIRE! WHO WILL HANDLE THE NATURAL DISASTERS LIKE FIRE, FLOOD AND EARTHQUAKES?

MY ROBOTS CAN TAKE CARE OF ALL EMERGENCIES! LOOK THERE! THEY'VE SAVED A SINKING TANKER AND NOW THEY'RE TAKING IT TO THE SHIPYARD FOR REPAIR!

YOU'RE RIGHT! THE EARTH IS SAFE IN THEIR HANDS! AND YOU'RE ENTITLED TO RETIRE AFTER ALL YOU'VE DONE FOR THE WORLD!

AND SOON, THE WORLD READS THE ASTOUNDING HEADLINES...

SUPERMAN RETIRES

NEWS JOURNAL

MAN OF STEEL HANGS UP UNIFORM

DAILY PLAN

SUPERMAN TO DEVOTE LIFE TO SCIENCE

THE HAPPY YEARS PASS. THEN, ONE DAY, LUCY AND JIMMY VISIT THE KENTS ON THEIR FOURTH WEDDING ANNIVERSARY...

LANA AND CLARK SEEM TO BE DIVINELY HAPPY, DON'T THEY, JIMMY? HE'S WEARING HIS SUPERMAN-BLUE COSTUME IN HONOR OF THIS OCCASION! I WONDER IF MY SISTER LOIS AND SUPERMAN-RED ARE AS HAPPY ON NEW KRYPTON!

WE'LL CHECK ON IT WHEN WE GET HOME!

LATER, AS LUCY AND JIMMY TUNE IN ON NEW KRYPTON, USING A MONITOR SCREEN BUILT BY SUPERMAN-BLUE...

THERE THEY ARE NOW, LOIS AND SUPERMAN-RED! ONLY HE'S USING HIS OLD KRYPTONIAN NAME KAL-EL, NOW!

LOOK, KAL-EL IS READING A SCRAP-BOOK ABOUT HIS EXPLOITS WHEN HE WAS SUPERMAN ON EARTH! I WONDER IF HE HAS ANY REGRETS?

BUT AS THE SCENE SHIFTS...

KAL-EL, ARE YOU EVER SORRY YOU GAVE UP YOUR SUPER-POWERS TO LIVE HERE ON NEW KRYPTON?

I'VE NO REGRETS, DARLING! I'M HAPPY TO SEE OUR TWINS GROWING UP HERE ON MY NATIVE WORLD!

8

THERE'S YOUR ANSWER, LUCY! I GUESS BOTH COUPLES HAVE FOUND THE HAPPINESS THEY WERE LOOKING FOR!

HM! I WONDER!

WHAT'S YOUR OPINION, READERS? SUPPOSE THIS IMAGINARY STORY REALLY HAPPENED! WHICH COUPLE DO YOU THINK WOULD BE HAPPIEST?

The End

SUPERMAN'S GIRL FRIEND LOIS LANE

AN IMAGINARY NOVEL

"The THREE WIVES of SUPERMAN!"

SUPERMAN HAS OFTEN SAID THAT HE WOULD NOT MARRY FOR FEAR HIS ENEMIES WOULD TAKE VENGEANCE ON HIM BY STRIKING AT HIS WIFE. IN THIS *IMAGINARY* TALE, THE MAN OF STEEL CHANGES HIS MIND AND TAKES A BRIDE -- NOT ONCE, BUT *THREE* TIMES -- AS TRAGEDY STRIKES AT THE VERY HEART OF HIS HAPPINESS, AGAIN AND AGAIN!

PART 1. "The TERRIBLE SECRET of MRS. LOIS SUPERMAN!"

PART 2. "The TRAGIC TORMENT of MRS. LANA SUPERMAN!"

PART 3. "The SHOCKING FATE of MRS. LORI SUPERMAN!"

OUR IMAGINARY TALE, WHICH MAY OR MAY NOT EVER HAPPEN, BEGINS ONE DAY AT THE DAILY PLANET OFFICE...

MAY I INTERRUPT YOUR CONVERSATION WITH PERRY LONG ENOUGH, SUPERMAN, TO ASK YOU ONE QUESTION?--WILL YOU MARRY ME?!!

LOIS! YOU CAN'T BE SERIOUS!! HAVE YOU NO PRIDE, PROPOSING TO ME?

SUPERMAN, I'VE LOVED YOU FOR YEARS, BUT YOU WOULDN'T PROPOSE! BUT NOW THAT IT'S LEAP YEAR, I'VE THE RIGHT TO ASK! JUST ANSWER YES OR NO! WILL YOU, OR WON'T YOU, MARRY ME?

AND DON'T TELL ME HOW THE LIFE OF YOUR WIFE WOULD BE IN CONSTANT DANGER FROM YOUR FOES, BECAUSE I'D RATHER BE HAPPY WITH YOU A SHORT WHILE AS YOUR WIFE, AND DIE-- THAN SPEND MY WHOLE LIFE YEARNING HOPELESSLY FOR YOU!

MY ANSWER IS... YES!

Y-YOU MEAN IT? YOU AREN'T JOKING?

OF COURSE NOT! I'VE LOVED YOU SECRETLY FOR YEARS! SINCE YOU'RE BRAVE ENOUGH TO FACE THE RISKS, I'D BE PROUD TO HAVE YOU FOR MY BRIDE! AND IF I CAN SUCCESSFULLY COMPLETE A CERTAIN EXPERIMENT, I'LL BE ABLE TO GIVE YOU SUPER-POWERS FOR LIFE!

SOON, AS THE ENTIRE WORLD WATCHES VIA TELSTAR RELAY TV...

I NOW PRONOUNCE YOU MAN AND WIFE...

AT LAST... THE MAN I LOVE IS MINE...

POOR LANA MUST BE HEARTSICK BECAUSE SUPERMAN HAS MARRIED LOIS INSTEAD OF HER!

JIMMY LOOKS A LITTLE SAD! MAYBE HE THINKS HIS FRIENDSHIP WITH SUPERMAN WILL WANE NOW THAT HIS SUPER-PAL IS MARRYING MY SISTER! HMM... IF I MARRIED JIMMY, HE AND SUPERMAN WOULD BECOME BROTHERS-IN-LAW!

LATER, IN THE NEWLYWEDS' ARCTIC **FORTRESS OF SOLITUDE** HOME...

NOW THAT I'VE FLOWN YOU ACROSS THE THRESHOLD, WOULD YOU LIKE TO SEE MY PRIVATE SPACE ZOO, AND TROPHIES OF MINE THAT NO ONE ELSE HAS EVER SEEN?

SILLY! DON'T YOU KNOW MY ENTIRE UNIVERSE IS--**YOU**?

THOUGH HE'S THE MIGHTIEST MAN IN ALL CREATION, HIS KISS IS SOFT AND...TENDER! I'M THE LUCKIEST WOMAN ALIVE! **SUPERMAN** IS THE MOST BELOVED HERO OF ALL TIME...YET ALL HIS LOVE BELONGS TO...ME...

DEAR...ADORABLE LOIS! WE'LL BE HAPPY FOREVER!

EACH DAY BRINGS NEW BLISS...

I HATE TO LEAVE YOU FOR EVEN A MOMENT, BUT I MUST MAKE MY PATROL! I'LL BE THINKING OF YOU!

YOU'LL BE IN MY THOUGHTS, TOO!

ALONE, LOIS MAKES AN ENTRY IN A DIARY, WHOSE RARE ALLOY COVERS ARE JEWEL-STUDDED, A GIFT FROM ONE OF **SUPERMAN'S** ALIEN FRIENDS...

DIARY

Another glorious day! Superman is so sweet and attentive to me! He's the best husband any girl ever had! I love him so...

BUT EVERYTHING ISN'T JOY AND BLISS, FOR WHEN LOIS VENTURES INTO **METROPOLIS**...

¿GASP!¿... A BOMB...TOSSED AT ME BY A MOBSTER FROM A SPEEDING CAR! IF I HADN'T DUCKED BEHIND THIS ARMORED BANK TRUCK IN TIME, I'D BE DEAD!

BAROOM!

AND DURING A SHOPPING TRIP...

A SNIPER'S BULLET... B-BARELY MISSED ME!

KRACK!

UPSET BY THE ATTEMPTS ON LOIS' LIFE, **SUPERMAN** LABORS UNCEASINGLY IN HIS LAB, AND A FEW DAYS LATER...

LOIS, DEAR, I'M POSITIVE THIS SERUM I'VE CREATED WILL GIVE YOU SUPER-POWERS LIKE MINE FOR MANY MONTHS! DRINK!

I HOPE FOR HIS SAKE, AS WELL AS MINE, THAT THE SERUM WILL BE A SUCCESS!

JOR-EL   LARA

MOMENTS AFTERWARD...

OH, MY GOODNESS! THIS MONUMENT OF YOUR KRYPTONIAN PARENTS! I C-CAN LIFT IT *EASILY!*

JOR-EL   LARA

THAT'S BECAUSE YOU'VE GAINED *SUPER-STRENGTH!*...HMM... THIS *SPECTRO-VIEWER* REVEALS YOU'LL BE SUPER FOR SEVERAL MONTHS! LET'S STEP OUTSIDE, NOW, AND OBSERVE YOUR INVULNERABILITY TO THE SUB-ZERO TEMPERATURE!

PRESENTLY... I FEEL WARM AS TOAST, DESPITE THE BITTER COLD! BUT I CAN'T SEE A CLOSE VIEW OF THOSE MOVING FORMS FAR BELOW! I GUESS THE SERUM FAILED TO GIVE ME SUPER-VISION LIKE YOURS!

TOO BAD! BUT I'LL DESCRIBE WHAT I SEE!

A PACK OF WOLVES IS CLOSING IN TO ATTACK A COUPLE OF ESKIMOS! EXCUSE ME, HONEY, WHILE I GO AND RESCUE THOSE MEN!

STAY PUT! LET *ME* HANDLE THIS! FIRST I'LL SNAP OFF THIS GIGANTIC ICICLE...

AND NOW I'LL TOSS IT TOWARD THE WOLF PACK! KEEP WATCHING WITH YOUR TELESCOPIC VISION AND TELL ME IF MY STRATEGY WORKS!

QUICK THINKING... AND GOOD TOSSING, LOIS! THE ICICLE IS SCARING THE WOLVES OFF! YOU'VE SAVED THE ESKIMOS...

I'M SO GLAD!

KR-RUMPP!

4

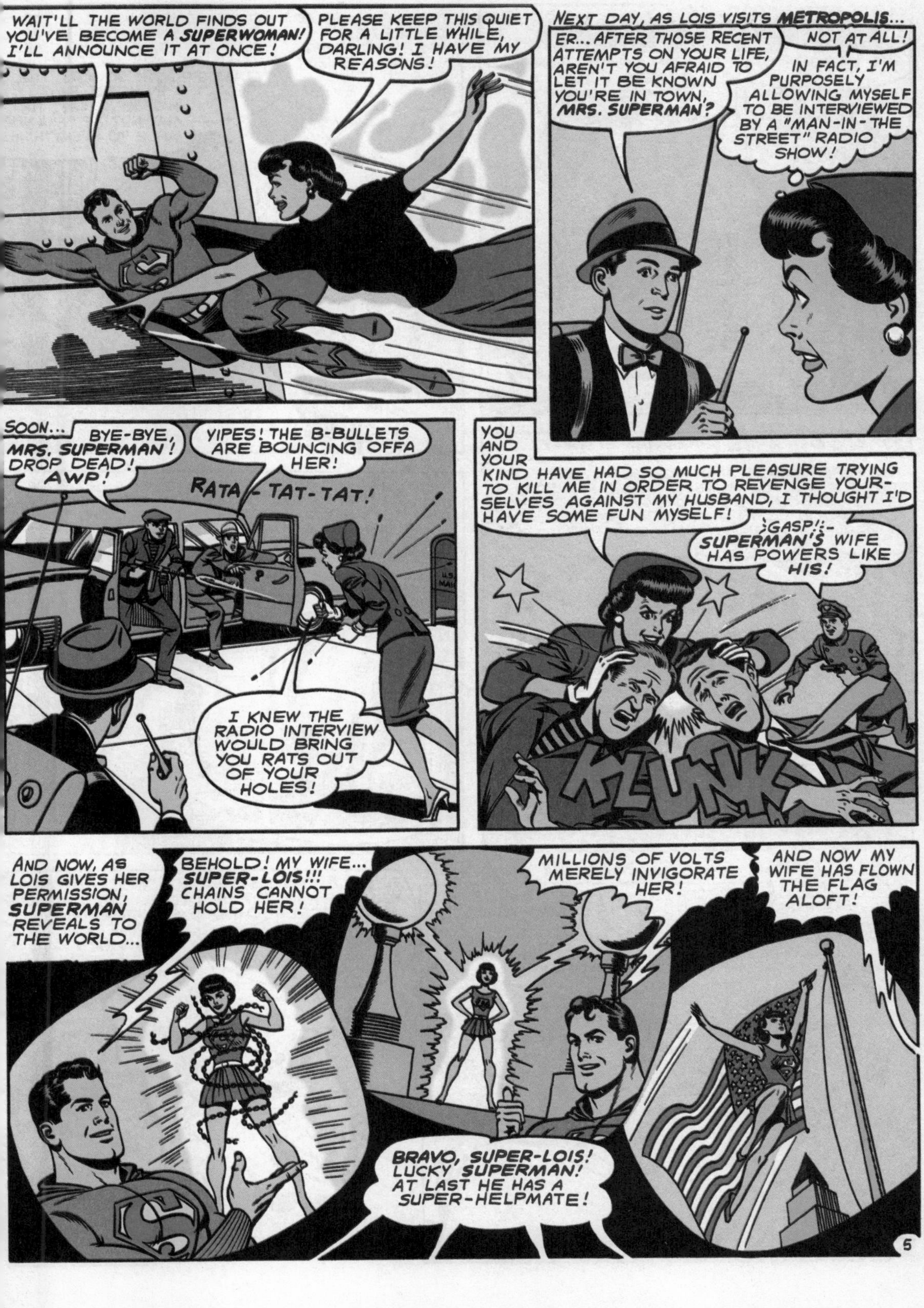
WAIT'LL THE WORLD FINDS OUT YOU'VE BECOME A SUPERWOMAN! I'LL ANNOUNCE IT AT ONCE!
PLEASE KEEP THIS QUIET FOR A LITTLE WHILE, DARLING! I HAVE MY REASONS!
NEXT DAY, AS LOIS VISITS METROPOLIS...
ER... AFTER THOSE RECENT ATTEMPTS ON YOUR LIFE, AREN'T YOU AFRAID TO LET IT BE KNOWN YOU'RE IN TOWN, MRS. SUPERMAN?
NOT AT ALL!
IN FACT, I'M PURPOSELY ALLOWING MYSELF TO BE INTERVIEWED BY A "MAN-IN-THE STREET" RADIO SHOW!
SOON...
BYE-BYE, MRS. SUPERMAN! DROP DEAD! AWP!
YIPES! THE B-BULLETS ARE BOUNCING OFFA HER!
RATA-TAT-TAT!
I KNEW THE RADIO INTERVIEW WOULD BRING YOU RATS OUT OF YOUR HOLES!
YOU AND YOUR KIND HAVE HAD SO MUCH PLEASURE TRYING TO KILL ME IN ORDER TO REVENGE YOURSELVES AGAINST MY HUSBAND, I THOUGHT I'D HAVE SOME FUN MYSELF!
-GASP!- SUPERMAN'S WIFE HAS POWERS LIKE HIS!
KLUNK
AND NOW, AS LOIS GIVES HER PERMISSION, SUPERMAN REVEALS TO THE WORLD...
BEHOLD! MY WIFE... SUPER-LOIS!!! CHAINS CANNOT HOLD HER!
MILLIONS OF VOLTS MERELY INVIGORATE HER!
AND NOW MY WIFE HAS FLOWN THE FLAG ALOFT!
BRAVO, SUPER-LOIS! LUCKY SUPERMAN! AT LAST HE HAS A SUPER-HELPMATE!
5

LATER, AT THE **FORTRESS**...

LOIS, WHY ARE YOU EXPERIMENTING IN THE LABORATORY?

I'VE STUDIED YOUR RESEARCH NOTES...! I HOPE TO DISCOVER A WAY I CAN GAIN SUPER-VISION, TOO!

KEEP OUT

I WANT TO BE AS COMPLETELY SUPER-POWERFUL AS YOU, HONEY! I FEEL IT'LL BRING US EVEN CLOSER!

LOIS, I FORBID YOU TO EXPERIMENT HERE! SOME OF THE ELEMENTS YOU'RE HANDLING ARE EXTREMELY DANGEROUS! SO ARE THE DEVICES IN HERE THAT I'M WORKING ON! YOU MAY NOT BE INVULNER-ABLE TO EVERYTHING!

EARTHQUAKE MACHINE

LIMBORANG

TRANS-MUTA GUN

BUT ONE DAY, WHILE **SUPERMAN** IS AWAY...

THE SUPER-SERUM HAS WORN OFF, AND I...I FEEL SUCH AWFUL PAINS! I SENSE IT'S SOMETHING SERIOUS! I DON'T WANT WORD OF THIS TO LEAK OUT ON EARTH, AND SO I'LL CONSULT A KANDORIAN DOCTOR!

THE **TRANSFER-RAY** IS REDUCING ME IN SIZE AND TRANSPORTING ME INTO THE CITY OF **KANDOR**! LONG AGO, **BRAINIAC** REDUCED **KANDOR** TO MINIATURE SIZE AND PUT IT IN THIS BOTTLE! KANDORIAN SCIENCE IS FAR ADVANCED BEYOND THE KNOWLEDGE OF EARTH SCIENTISTS!

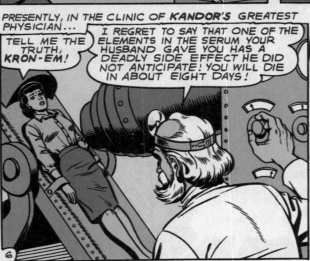

PRESENTLY, IN THE CLINIC OF **KANDOR'S** GREATEST PHYSICIAN...

TELL ME THE TRUTH, KRON-EM!

I REGRET TO SAY THAT ONE OF THE ELEMENTS IN THE SERUM YOUR HUSBAND GAVE YOU HAS A DEADLY SIDE EFFECT HE DID NOT ANTICIPATE! YOU WILL DIE IN ABOUT EIGHT DAYS!

SCIENCE CAN'T SAVE YOU! EVEN IF **SUPERMAN** SEARCHED THE ENTIRE UNIVERSE FOR HELP, IT WOULD BE IN VAIN! I'M SORRY...

¡CHOKE!¡ -- SWEAR YOU'LL TELL NO ONE! IF **SUPERMAN** LEARNED HIS BLUNDER KILLED ME, HE WOULD NEVER FORGIVE HIMSELF! HE MUST **NEVER** FIND OUT!!

6

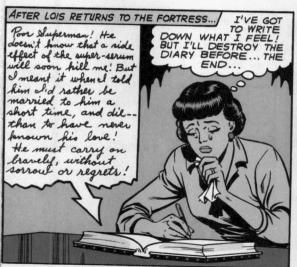

AFTER LOIS RETURNS TO THE FORTRESS...

Poor Superman! He doesn't know that a side effect of the super-serum will soon kill me! But I meant it when I told him I'd rather be married to him a short time, and die-- than to have never known his love! He must carry on bravely, without sorrow or regrets!

I'VE GOT TO WRITE DOWN WHAT I FEEL! BUT I'LL DESTROY THE DIARY BEFORE... THE END...

SHORTLY...

HURRY AND FINISH DRINKING THAT SECOND DOSE OF SERUM SO THAT YOU'LL BE SUPER AGAIN! I'VE DREAMED UP A TERRIFIC PROJECT WE CAN TACKLE TOGETHER!

I'M ALREADY DOOMED, AND SO THIS C-CAN'T HARM ME FURTHER!... :CHOKE! G-GOT TO KEEP SMILING ... HE MUSTN'T SUSPECT MY HEART IS B-BREAKING! :SOB!:

PRESENTLY, AS A MAMMOTH STRUCTURE NEARS COMPLETION AT SUPER-SPEED...

LOIS AND I ARE BUILDING A COLOSSAL BRIDGE ACROSS THE ATLANTIC OCEAN, BETWEEN AMERICA AND EUROPE! FOOD AND FUEL STATIONS, AS WELL AS MOTELS, ARE ON IT! MOTORISTS WILL LOVE IT!

:SOB, SOB!: - MUST... FIGHT BACK TEARS! MUST MAKE MY S-SMILE LOOK GENUINE... OR HIS SUPER-VISION WILL DISCOVER I'M ONLY PRETENDING TO BE CAREFREE!

THEN...

WE DID IT! THE PROJECT'S FINISHED! HA, HA! THEY'LL PROBABLY NAME IT "THE SUPER HIGHWAY", IN OUR HONOR! - THAT'S A JOKE, LOIS! - HAPPY?

SUBLIMELY!

SOON, I'LL NEVER FEEL HIS TOUCH AGAIN... HEAR HIS LAUGHTER... THRILL TO HIS DYNAMIC PRESENCE!... :CHOKE!:

BUT THERE ARE LIMITS TO EVEN A SUPER-WOMAN'S ENDURANCE...

WHY, YOU'RE... CRYING! IS SOMETHING WRONG, LOIS?

OF COURSE NOT! THOSE ARE TEARS OF HAPPINESS! - I LOVE BEING HELPFUL TO YOU!

CAN'T LET HIM KNOW THE TRUTH...

7

AND ON THE MORNING OF THE FATEFUL EIGHTH DAY...

THIS IS MY LAST DAY... I'LL AWAKEN MY DARLING WITH A KISS, THEN SEND HIM OFF TO A DISTANT GALAXY FOR SOME BAUBLE I'LL PRETEND I WANT. WHILE HE'S GONE, I'LL DO WHAT I MUST DO... TO LESSEN THE TORMENT THAT'LL BE HIS OTHERWISE...

WHEN *SUPERMAN* LEAVES...

MY SUPER-POWERS WORE OFF SOONER THAN USUAL! I FEEL SO...VERY, VERY W-WEAK AND DIZZY! THE END IS ONLY MINUTES AWAY! I'LL THROW THE DIARY INTO THE INCINERATOR! THE FLAMES WILL SOON COME ON AUTOMATICALLY AND DESTROY IT!

MINUTES LATER, IN THE LAB...

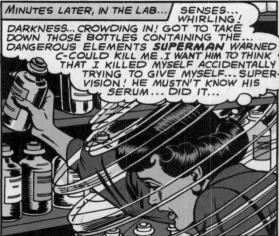

SENSES... WHIRLING! DARKNESS... CROWDING IN! GOT TO TAKE DOWN THOSE BOTTLES CONTAINING THE... DANGEROUS ELEMENTS *SUPERMAN* WARNED C-COULD KILL ME. I WANT HIM TO THINK THAT I KILLED MYSELF ACCIDENTALLY TRYING TO GIVE MYSELF... SUPER-VISION! HE MUSTN'T KNOW HIS SERUM... DID IT...

AS DEATH CLOSES IN, AND LOIS' BODY COLLAPSES, BY CHANCE ONE OF HER ARMS STRIKES THE LEVER ON AN *EARTHQUAKE-MACHINE*, ACTIVATING IT! INSTANTLY, THE FORTRESS IS WRACKED BY MIGHTY TREMORS...

RUMBLE!

EARTHQUAKE MACHINE

A SPLIT SECOND BEFORE DEATH CLAIMS LOIS FOREVER, A FINAL THOUGHT ENGULFS HER CONSCIOUSNESS...

THANK YOU FOR LOVING ME, DARLING! THOSE FEW MONTHS AS YOUR WIFE MEANT MORE TO ME THAN TEN LIFETIMES WOULD'VE MEANT SPENT WITH-OUT YOU...! GOODBYE... HAVE NO REGRETS... NO REGRETS... NO REGR...

MEANWHILE, FREED FROM ITS STONE CAVE IN THE SPACE ZO BY THE EARTHQUAKE, A *METAL-EATER BEAST* FROM *KRYPTON* BLUNDERS INTO LOIS' ROOM AND ATTACKS THE METAL INCINERATOR VORACIOUSLY...

CRUNCH!

CARRYING OFF THE **METAL**-BOUND DIARY, THE CREATURE RETURNS TO ITS ZOO CAVE WITH THE "SNACK" TO BE SAVED FOR A FUTURE TASTY TREAT...

SHORTLY, **SUPERMAN** RETURNS TO THE FORTRESS...

SHE'S **DEAD!** WHY DIDN'T LOIS OBEY MY WARNING NOT TO EXPERIMENT WITH THE DANGEROUS ELEMENTS? SH-SHE WANTED SUPER VISION TO BRING HER **CLOSER** TO ME! NOW WE'RE APART ...FOREVER! ¡SOB, SOB!¿ OH, LOIS...¡CHOKE!¿ ...LOIS...

EVERYONE ON EARTH, AND ELSEWHERE, IS SHOCKED AT THE TRAGEDY WHICH HAS BEFALLEN THE **MAN OF STEEL**...

I LOVED HER... LIKE A DAUGHTER!

MY HEART GOES OUT TO **SUPERMAN** IN HIS GRIEF! THOUGH I WANTED TO MARRY HIM MYSELF, I SINCERELY WISHED HAPPINESS FOR HIM AND LOIS!

THE WHOLE UNIVERSE ADORED HER WIT AND KINDNESS!

AND THEN COMES AN EVEN GREATER SHOCK, AS **SUPERMAN** ANNOUNCES...

NOW THAT THE WOMAN I LOVED IS GONE, NOTHING MATTERS TO ME ANY MORE. I AM QUITTING EARTH. MY SUPER-CRUSADING HERE HAS COME TO AN END. **SUPERGIRL** WILL CARRY ON FOR ME. GOODBYE!

END OF **PART 1**

A LOOK AT OTHER GREAT IMAGINARY STORIES

LOIS LANE #46, 1964
art by Kurt Schaffenberger

LOIS LANE #47, 1964
art by Kurt Schaffenberger

SUPERMAN'S GIRL FRIEND LOIS LANE

IN THE SECOND PART OF OUR *IMAGINARY STORY*, *SUPERMAN* PUTS HIS SORROW BEHIND HIM AND RETURNS TO LIFE...AND LOVE! FOR NOW LANA LANG BECOMES THE MAN OF STEEL'S BRIDE. BUT STRANGE DOUBTS ENTER HER HEART TO MAR HER HAPPINESS AND BRING ABOUT... "*The TRAGIC TORMENT of MRS. LANA SUPERMAN!*"

PART II OF AN IMAGINARY STORY

GASP!? – LOIS IS STILL ALIVE! HOW COULD SUPERMAN DO THIS TO ME...FIRST MARRY ME AND THEN BRING ME TO *KANDOR*, WHERE HE HAS HIS FIRST WIFE HIDDEN?!!

OUR *IMAGINARY TALE* RESUMES ALMOST A YEAR LATER, ON THE "HEARTBREAK ASTEROID" TO WHICH *SUPERMAN* HAS EXILED HIMSELF...

I FEEL MORE BLUE THAN EVER. PERHAPS...IF I VISIT THE *FORTRESS OF SOLITUDE* AGAIN – WHERE LOIS AND I WERE HAPPY... IT WILL CHEER ME UP!

PRESENTLY, ON EARTH... THERE...IN OUR SECRET SANCTUM ...LOIS AND I LIVED AND LAUGHED AND LOVED...EVERY DAY SEEMED AN ETERNITY OF HAPPINESS...WE'D HAVE SWORN THAT *NOTHING* COULD PART US, EVER...

ENTERING, **SUPERMAN** TURNS ON A TAPE-PROJECTOR AND WATCHES YESTERDAYS RECREATED BEFORE HIM...

I'LL NEVER FORGET THE BEGINNING OF OUR MARRIAGE...WHEN I CARRIED LOIS ACROSS THE THRESHOLD...

GOT TO...TURN THE MACHINE OFF! CAN'T WATCH...ANY LONGER...

SHORTLY, WHILE ROAMING THROUGH THE FORTRESS, HE DISCOVERS LOIS' DIARY IN THE METAL-EATER'S ZOO CAVE...

¡GASP!...THEN IT WAS A **SIDE EFFECT** OF THE SUPER-SERUM THAT KILLED HER! SHE MUST HAVE **PRETENDED** HER OWN EXPERIMENT DESTROYED HER, BECAUSE SHE WANTED TO SPARE ME ANY FEELING OF GUILT!

THEN, ON THE ANNIVERSARY OF LOIS' DEATH, AS **SUPERMAN** VISITS HER TOMB NEAR **METROPOLIS**...

SUPERMAN! I DIDN'T KNOW YOU WERE VISITING EARTH! I THOUGHT...

YOU, JIMMY! I'VE DECIDED TO RESUME MY CAREER. I KNOW NOW THAT LOIS WOULD HAVE WANTED ME TO CARRY ON!

LOIS SUPERMAN

ONES

SHORTLY, THE **DAILY PLANET** ISSUES AN EXTRA CONTAINING **TWO** BIG STORIES WHICH APPEAR UNRELATED, BUT WILL SOON BE ANYTHING BUT THAT...

DAILY PLANET — EXTRA ★★★

SUPERMAN WILL RESUME HIS CAREER ON EARTH

SCIENTIFIC CRIMINAL, LEX LUTHOR, ANNOUNCES HE'S QUITTING CRIME

GIVES MEDICAL WORLD ASTOUNDING CURE FOR HEART DISEASE

LATER, AS LANA LANG INTERVIEWS **SUPERMAN** ON HER TV NEWS PROGRAM...

IN ANSWER TO YOUR QUESTION: NO, I DON'T THINK I'LL EVER MARRY AGAIN! MY CAREER COMES FIRST!

YOUR FEMALE FANS WILL BE DISAPPOINTED!

INCLUDING...ME!

AFTERWARD, WHEN SHE INTERVIEWS LEX LUTHOR...

WHAT DO I WANT MOST OF ALL, NOW THAT I'VE GONE STRAIGHT? A WIFE AND KIDS!

HOW HE'S CHANGED! NOW THAT HE'S NO LONGER EVIL, THERE'S A CERTAIN ATTRACTIVENESS ABOUT HIM!

METV

Lana Lang presents

②

THE REFORMED LUTHOR DATES LANA OFTEN. THEN, ONE DAY...

MARRY ME, AND I'LL TREAT YOU LIKE A QUEEN! PLEASE SAY "YES"!

I... ACCEPT! NOW THAT I KNOW *SUPERMAN* WILL NEVER MARRY ME, I'LL WED LUTHOR. IT'S BETTER THAN BEING AN *OLD MAID!*

SEVERAL WEEKS LATER, IN A CHAPEL ROOM MINUTES BEFORE THE CEREMONY IS TO START...

MUST WIPE THESE TEARS AWAY AND GET *SUPERMAN* OUT OF MY MIND FOREVER!... I'LL BE A GOOD WIFE TO LEX!

BUT AS THE CEREMONY BEGINS...

IF ANYONE PRESENT KNOWS WHY THESE TWO SHOULD NOT BE MARRIED, LET HIM SPEAK *NOW*, OR FOREVER HOLD HIS PEACE!

GREAT SCOTT! SUDDENLY, I REALIZE...! *STOP THE WEDDING!*

PLEASE DON'T MARRY LUTHOR, LANA! UNTIL NOW, I DIDN'T KNOW HOW MUCH I LOVE YOU! MARRY *ME*, INSTEAD!

TELL HIM TO GET LOST, LANA! IF I HAVE ANY PRIDE, I'LL REFUSE *SUPERMAN!*

BUT WHO CARES ABOUT PRIDE? ALL I KNOW IS, *SUPERMAN* IS STILL NO. 1 IN MY HEART! I'M SORRY, LEX! I'M GOING TO ACCEPT *SUPERMAN'S* PROPOSAL!

WONDERFUL!!!

AND SO THE WEDDING CONTINUES, BUT SOMEWHAT DIFFERENTLY THAN PLANNED ORIGINALLY...

I NOW PRONOUNCE YOU, *SUPERMAN*, AND YOU, LANA, MAN AND WIFE!

YIPPEE! I'M SO GLAD MY PAL *SUPERMAN* WILL FIND HAPPINESS AGAIN!

CONGRATU.... OOOOLP!

IF THIS IS MY "REWARD" FOR GOING STRAIGHT, I'D RATHER BE A CROOK AGAIN! FROM NOW ON, I'LL LIVE **ONLY** FOR THE DAY WHEN I'LL BE REVENGED AGAINST BOTH OF YOU!

LATER, IN THE NEWLYWEDS' FORTRESS OF SOLITUDE HOME...

OH, DARLING, I CAN'T BELIEVE YOU'RE REALLY MINE! I-I'M STILL CONFUSED AND SURPRISED!

YOU'VE AN EVEN BIGGER SURPRISE COMING! I'M GOING TO SWITCH TO MY SECRET IDENTITY AT SUPER-SPEED!

A SPLIT-INSTANT AFTERWARD...

OH, NO! YOU **ARE** REALLY **CLARK KENT!** AND WHEN I THINK HOW OFTEN I SUSPECTED IT AND TRIED TO PROVE IT, LONG AGO, WHEN YOU WERE **SUPERBOY...**

₤CHUCKLE₤... YES, LANA! YOU ALMOST EXPOSED ME MANY TIMES...

"LIKE THAT TIME, YEARS AGO, IN GEOLOGY CLASS IN SMALLVILLE, WHEN..."

LOOK, CLARK... **KRYPTONITE,** THE ONE SUBSTANCE THAT CAN HARM **SUPERBOY!** WHY, YOU'RE NOT AFFECTED! THEN **YOU** CAN'T BE **SUPERBOY!**

"BUT WHAT YOU **DIDN'T** KNOW, LANA, WAS WHAT HAD HAPPENED THE NIGHT BEFORE..."

I SPOTTED A PIECE OF **KRYPTONITE** AMONG THE GEOLOGY TEACHER'S NEW SPECIMENS, WITH MY TELESCOPIC VISION. I'LL HAVE ONE OF MY ROBOTS REPLACE IT WITH THIS ROCK I'M COVERING WITH LUMINOUS GREEN PAINT. THEN, IF LANA TRIES TO TRAP ME...

HA, HA! BUT THERE'S NO NEED TO HIDE ANYTHING FROM ME **NOW!** YOU KNOW, DEAR, WHEN YOU WORKED AT THE **PLANET,** I USED TO WORRY THAT YOU CARED MORE FOR LOIS THAN YOU DID FOR ME. DID YOU?

THERE'S ONLY ONE WAY TO ANSWER A QUESTION LIKE THAT! I ADORE **YOU!**

"WHEN *SUPERMAN* TAKES ME IN HIS ARMS... AND KISSES ME... LIKE THIS... I FORGET EVERYTHING! I'M SURE HE'S FORGOTTEN LOIS!"

BUT, A FEW NIGHTS LATER...

"DARLING... YOU'VE MADE ME SO HAPPY... (MUMBLE, MUMBLE)..."

"HE'S TALKING IN HIS SLEEP! IS HE DREAMING ABOUT LOIS, OR ME? – THIS IS RIDICULOUS! I SHOULD HAVE ENOUGH *CONFIDENCE* IN MYSELF NOT TO WORRY ABOUT SUCH A THING! BUT – I DO..."

ALL THROUGH THE DAY, LANA TORMENTS HERSELF...

"WHOM DOES HE LOVE MOST? HIS FIRST WIFE, LOIS... OR ME?"

"HAVE A SNACK, DEAR!"

"THANKS, LANA. I WON'T STOP EXPERIMENTING UNTIL I PERFECT A SUPER-SERUM THAT HAS **NO** BAD SIDE EFFECTS!"

ONE MORNING...

"WHATEVER HAPPENED TO LUTHOR?"

"HE'S BECOME A SPACE PIRATE, RAIDING OTHER WORLDS! SOME DAY I'LL CATCH UP WITH HIM, AND HIS NEW CAREER WILL COME TO AN END! BUT FORGET ABOUT HIM, AND PUT ON THESE ANTI-GRAVITY SHOES!"

"I WANT YOU TO MEET SOME OF MY FRIENDS IN *KANDOR!* SINCE *KANDOR'S* ARTIFICIAL GRAVITY IS THE SAME AS THAT WHICH EXISTED ON THE HUGE PLANET *KRYPTON,* YOU'LL NEED THE SPECIAL SHOES TO ESCAPE BEING CRUSHED BY THE GREATER GRAVITY!"

PRESENTLY, AS THEY MATERIALIZE IN THE MINIATURE SIZED CITY...

"¡GASP!¡... IT'S *LOIS! ALIVE!!* B–BUT I THOUGHT SHE WAS *DEAD!* I KNEW MY HAPPINESS WAS TOO GOOD TO BE TRUE!"

"*SUPERMAN!*"

:CHUCKLE:...THIS ISN'T LOIS... IT'S SYLVIA, A DOUBLE OF LOIS! MEET HER HUSBAND, VAN-ZEE, WHO, AMAZINGLY, IS A DOUBLE OF ME! THESE TWINS ARE THEIR CHILDREN!

WHAT A STRIKING RESEMBLANCE!

SEE LOIS LANE NO.15, FEB., 1960 ISSUE, FOR THE FULL STORY! EDITOR

SHORTLY, AS THEY TOUR KANDOR...

DID SUPERMAN KISS SYLVIA SO EAGERLY BECAUSE SHE REMINDS HIM OF HIS GREAT LOVE FOR LOIS? THE TRIP IS SPOILED FOR ME... IF YOU DON'T MIND, I'D LIKE TO GO HOME NOW!

ALL RIGHT! IF YOU WISH!

A FEW DAYS LATER, BACK ON EARTH, AS LANA CURIOUSLY EXPLORES THE FORTRESS WHILE SUPERMAN IS ON PATROL...

I WONDER WHAT OTHER LITTLE SECRETS SUPERMAN KEEPS FROM ME? I'LL LOOK INTO THIS LAB-SAFE OF HIS! I'VE GOT THE RIGHT! AFTER ALL, I AM HIS WIFE!

MOMENTS AFTERWARD...

:GASP!: PICTURES OF HIS FIRST WIFE, LOIS...!!! THE SKUNK! WHILE PRETENDING TO LOVE ME MORE THAN ANYTHING IN THE UNIVERSE, HE SNEAKS IN HERE AND MOONS OVER THESE PHOTOGRAPHS OF HER! THAT PROVES HE LOVES HER MORE THAN ME!... :CHOKE!:

I WON'T PLAY SECOND FIDDLE TO A DEAD WOMAN! I'LL DAMAGE HIS DIRECTIONAL-TRACER DEVICE SO HE WON'T BE ABLE TO FIND ME WITH IT WHEN I RUN AWAY! THEN I'LL WRITE A GOODBYE NOTE! WE'RE THROUGH!

KRASH!

AFTER WRITING HER FAREWELL MESSAGE, LANA STREAKS OFF INTO THE UNIVERSE IN A TINY SPACE CRAFT...

:SOB!:... HOW IRONIC! SUPERMAN GAVE ME THIS SPACE SHIP AS A WEDDING PRESENT, AND I'M USING IT TO FLEE HIM. I'LL SPEND THE REST OF MY DAYS ON ANOTHER PLANET, WHERE HE'LL NEVER FIND ME!

⑥

BUT AS HER VEHICLE FLASHES PAST ONE SOLAR SYSTEM AFTER ANOTHER, ABRUPTLY...

AWP! MY SHIP IS BEING DRAWN DOWN TO THAT NEARBY WORLD BY SOME SORT OF AN *ATTRACTION RAY!*

AS HER VESSEL LANDS...

COME OUT, OR BE DE-ATOMIZED! WELCOME, LANA! I RECOGNIZED YOUR CRAFT BY THE EMBLEM ON IT! THAT'S WHY I DREW IT DOWN WITH MY RAY!

DON'T SHOOT! OH, DEAR! *LUTHOR* VOWED VENGEANCE AGAINST *SUPERMAN* AND *ME...*

SOON, IN *LUTHOR'S* LAB...

SEE MY *ASTRO-CANNON?* I CAN FIRE THIS *GOLD KRYPTONITE* METEOR IN IT TO *ANY* POINT IN THE UNIVERSE! THAT WORRIES YOU, EH?

GOLD KRYPTONITE CAN REMOVE *SUPERMAN'S* SUPER-POWERS *PERMANENTLY!*

MEANWHILE, RETURNING TO HIS FORTRESS, AND FINDING LANA'S LETTER, *SUPERMAN* HURTLES TOWARD OUTER SPACE...

I'VE GOT TO FIND LANA AND ASK HER TO COME BACK!

...I won't be a second fiddle! I never want to see you again! Goodbye! Lana.

SHORTLY... HA, HA, HA! I ZEROED IN ON THAT SUPER-RAT WHO STOLE YOU FROM ME! HE'LL PAY DEARLY FOR THAT! — WATCH MY VENGEANCE ON THE MONITOR! DON'T INTERFERE, OR ONE OF MY HIDDEN BOOBY TRAPS WILL DESTROY YOU!

DEEP DOWN, I LOVE *SUPERMAN* AS MUCH AS EVER, THOUGH HE CARES MORE FOR THE MEMORY OF HIS FIRST WIFE THAN HE DOES FOR ME! I'VE GOT TO TRY TO SAVE HIM, EVEN IF IT MEANS LOSING MY LIFE...

GET BACK, YOU FOOL!

BOOOM

MAYBE PULLING THESE CONTROL-LEVERS WILL...

OWW!...TH-THAT BEAM OF LIGHT...

IDIOT! BY STEPPING ON A CONCEALED PUSH-BUTTON ON THE FLOOR, YOU ACTIVATED A *DEATH RAY* WHOSE EFFECT WILL SOON *KILL* YOU!

THE G-GOLDEN METEOR'S COURSE...IT'S ALTERED! IT'S...FALLING INTO A SUN, INSTEAD OF INTERCEPTING *SUPERMAN!*

BLAST YOU! I HAD ONLY *ONE* OF THOSE RARE METEORS!

MOMENTS AFTERWARD...

MY SUPER VISION SAW WHAT HAPPENED TO THAT *GOLD K* METEOR! TRACING ITS TRAJECTORY, I WITNESSED HOW LANA SACRIFICED HERSELF TO SAVE ME! HMM...THAT *COSMIC POLICE* CRAFT MUST HAVE COME TO INVESTIGATE THE ATTEMPT AGAINST ME...

POLICE

SHORTLY, IN THE LAB OF *SUPERMAN'S* ARCH-FOE...

HA, HA! I DON'T CARE WHAT YOU SPACE COPS DO TO ME NOW! I'M *AVENGED!* *NOTHING* CAN SAVE *SUPERMAN'S* WIFE! SHE'LL SOON BE DEAD FROM MY DEATH RAY...!

SHUT UP, MURDERER!

PLACING LANA IN THE SPACE CRAFT, *SUPERMAN* STREAKS EARTHWARD...

MUST TRY TO SAVE HER SOME WAY! PERHAPS THERE'S SOMETHING IN MY FORTRESS THAT WILL ACCOMPLISH IT!

SHORTLY, IN THE FORTRESS...

¡CHOKE!... IT'S HOPELESS! NOT A THING HERE CAN SAVE HER! SHE HAS ONLY MOMENTS TO LIVE! BUT THERE'S SOMETHING I *MUST* KNOW!

WHY DID YOU LEAVE ME, LANA?

WHEN I DISCOVERED THE...PICTURES OF LOIS IN YOUR SAFE... I KNEW THEN YOU LOVED HER *MORE* THAN ME...

8

BUT THIS **ISN'T** A SAFE! IT'S A PROCESSING MACHINE WHICH CREATES **BUSTS** FROM PHOTO-IMAGES! SEE? AND THIS IS **SYLVIA, NOT** LOIS! I WAS FASHIONING THESE BUSTS OF **SYLVIA** AND **VAN-ZEE** AS GIFTS FOR THEIR WEDDING ANNIVERSARY!

≷CHOKE≷— OH, N-NO!

PLEASE...FORGIVE ME...FOR DOUBTING YOUR LOVE! AFTER I'M DEAD...CARRY ON YOUR CAREER ...FIND HAPPINESS WITH ANOTHER WOMAN...

WAIT! MAYBE MY **SUPER-SERUM** CAN SAVE YOU!

EVEN IF ITS SIDE EFFECTS PROVE FATAL LATER, AT LEAST IT MAY PROLONG HER LIFE A WHILE!

BUT WHEN **SUPERMAN** SPEEDS BACK TO LANA...

TOO LATE! ≷CHOKE≷ MY SECOND WIFE-LANA-IS DEAD! SHE SACRIFICED HER LIFE SO I COULD CONTINUE MY CAREER! – I WON'T LET HER DOWN...

BUT AS FOR MY EVER FALLING IN LOVE AGAIN, I DON'T EVEN WANT TO THINK ABOUT IT! ALL I KNOW IS THAT I'LL ALWAYS REMEMBER...AND LOVE...LANA...

END OF PART II

A LOOK AT OTHER GREAT IMAGINARY STORIES

LOIS LANE #39, 1963
art by Kurt Schaffenberger

WORLD'S FINEST COMICS #154, 1965
art by Curt Swan and George Klein

SUPERMAN'S GIRL FRIEND LOIS LANE

AND NOW WE COME TO THE CONCLUSION OF OUR *IMAGINARY NOVEL!* LOIS LANE LOVED AND MARRIED *SUPERMAN,* BUT SUFFERED AN UNTIMELY DEATH! THEN LANA LANG WED *SUPERMAN...* AND SACRIFICED *HER* LIFE SO THAT HE WOULD SURVIVE! NOW *SUPERMAN* MARRIES FOR A THIRD TIME, AND HIS MERMAID BRIDE IS *LORI LEMARIS,* OF *ATLANTIS!* THOUGH *SUPERMAN* IS THE MIGHTIEST MAN IN THE COSMOS, WILL HE BE ABLE TO AVERT....

"The SHOCKING FATE OF MRS. LORI SUPERMAN!"

YOU LOOK SO BEAUTIFUL, *LORI!...* I NEVER THOUGHT I'D MARRY AGAIN! I WAS SO AFRAID THAT THE "CURSE" WHICH DESTROYED MY FIRST TWO WIVES WOULD STRIKE AGAIN! BUT I'M NOT WORRIED *NOW!*

AFTER ALL THE GOOD YOU'VE DONE FOR OTHERS, DARLING, FATE COULDN'T DESTROY YOUR HAPPINESS AGAIN! DESTINY COULDN'T BE *THAT* CRUEL!

AFTER LANA IS LAID TO REST, *SUPERMAN* RESUMES HIS CAREER...

THOUGH LANA TOLD ME TO GET MARRIED AGAIN, I NEVER WILL! I'LL BE CONTENT WITH MY MEMORIES OF HER AND LOIS!

MEANWHILE, A TRAGEDY OCCURS AT SEA OVER ATLANTIS AS *LORI* THE MERMAID AND HER HUSBAND, *RONAL,* SEEK TO SAVE SOME WHALES FROM HUNTERS...

HIDE WITHIN THAT FOGGY AREA!

OW-WW! A HARPOON INTENDED FOR THE WHALES HAS S-STRUCK *ME!*

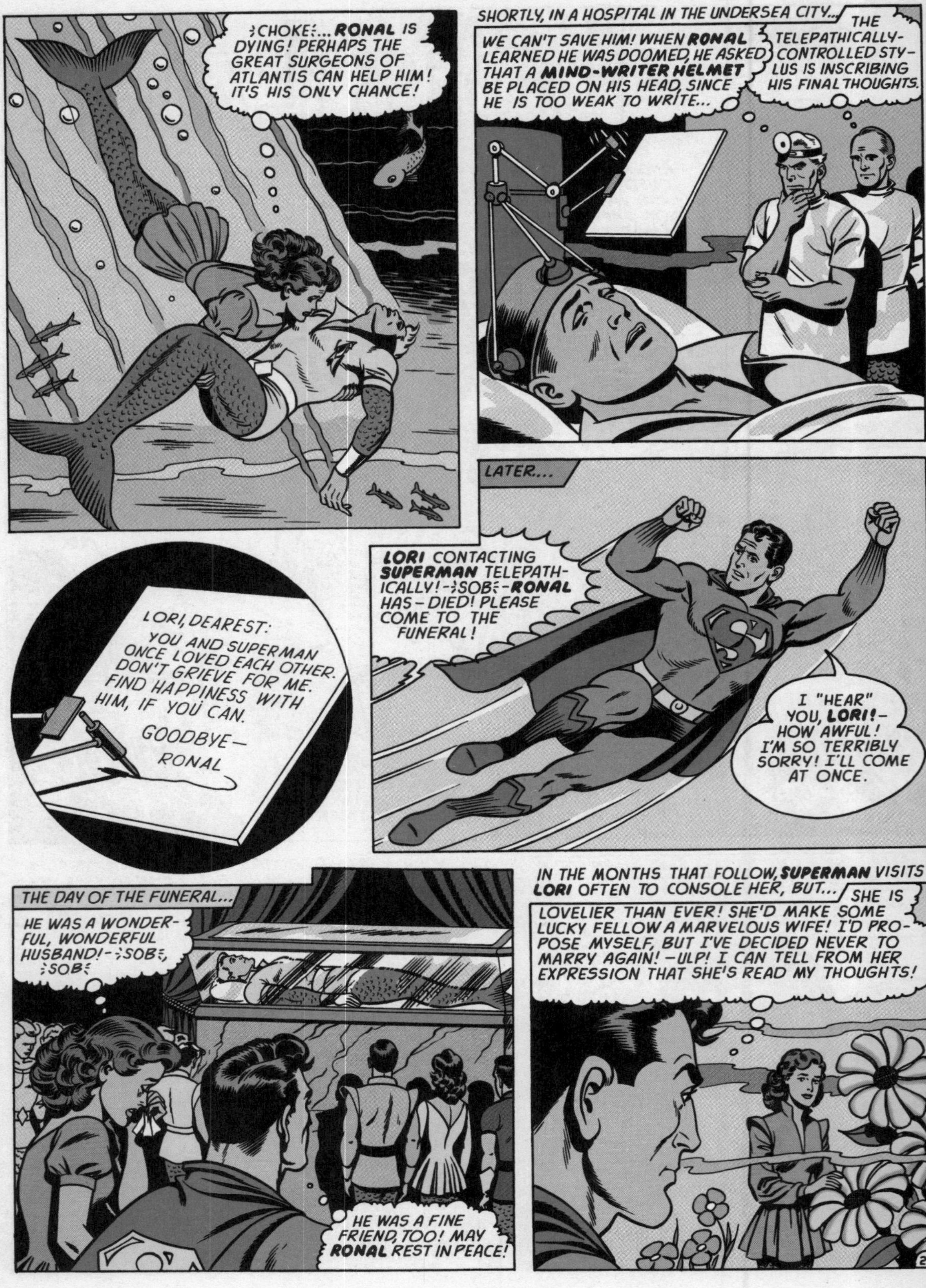

⁑CHOKE⁑... RONAL IS DYING! PERHAPS THE GREAT SURGEONS OF ATLANTIS CAN HELP HIM! IT'S HIS ONLY CHANCE!
SHORTLY, IN A HOSPITAL IN THE UNDERSEA CITY...
WE CAN'T SAVE HIM! WHEN RONAL LEARNED HE WAS DOOMED, HE ASKED THAT A MIND-WRITER HELMET BE PLACED ON HIS HEAD, SINCE HE IS TOO WEAK TO WRITE...
THE TELEPATHICALLY-CONTROLLED STYLUS IS INSCRIBING HIS FINAL THOUGHTS.
LORI, DEAREST: YOU AND SUPERMAN ONCE LOVED EACH OTHER. DON'T GRIEVE FOR ME. FIND HAPPINESS WITH HIM, IF YOU CAN. GOODBYE— RONAL
LATER...
LORI CONTACTING SUPERMAN TELEPATHICALLY! -⁑SOB⁑- RONAL HAS—DIED! PLEASE COME TO THE FUNERAL!
I "HEAR" YOU, LORI! — HOW AWFUL! I'M SO TERRIBLY SORRY! I'LL COME AT ONCE.
THE DAY OF THE FUNERAL...
HE WAS A WONDERFUL, WONDERFUL HUSBAND! -⁑SOB⁑, ⁑SOB⁑
HE WAS A FINE FRIEND, TOO! MAY RONAL REST IN PEACE!
IN THE MONTHS THAT FOLLOW, SUPERMAN VISITS LORI OFTEN TO CONSOLE HER, BUT...
SHE IS LOVELIER THAN EVER! SHE'D MAKE SOME LUCKY FELLOW A MARVELOUS WIFE! I'D PROPOSE MYSELF, BUT I'VE DECIDED NEVER TO MARRY AGAIN! —ULP! I CAN TELL FROM HER EXPRESSION THAT SHE'S READ MY THOUGHTS!
2.

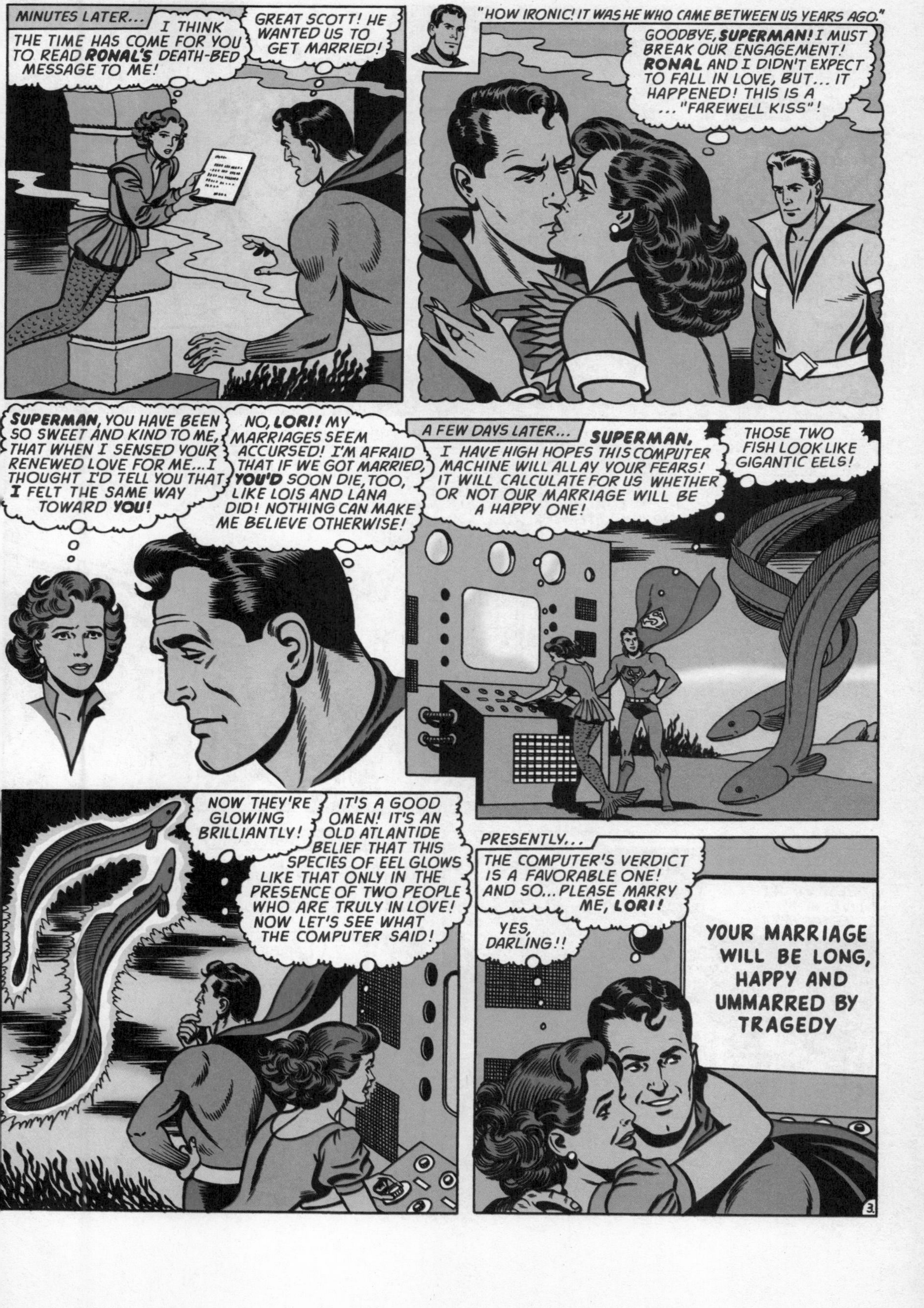
MINUTES LATER...
I THINK THE TIME HAS COME FOR YOU TO READ RONAL'S DEATH-BED MESSAGE TO ME!
GREAT SCOTT! HE WANTED US TO GET MARRIED!
"HOW IRONIC! IT WAS HE WHO CAME BETWEEN US YEARS AGO."
GOODBYE, SUPERMAN! I MUST BREAK OUR ENGAGEMENT! RONAL AND I DIDN'T EXPECT TO FALL IN LOVE, BUT... IT HAPPENED! THIS IS A ..."FAREWELL KISS"!
SUPERMAN, YOU HAVE BEEN SO SWEET AND KIND TO ME, THAT WHEN I SENSED YOUR RENEWED LOVE FOR ME...I THOUGHT I'D TELL YOU THAT I FELT THE SAME WAY TOWARD YOU!
NO, LORI! MY MARRIAGES SEEM ACCURSED! I'M AFRAID THAT IF WE GOT MARRIED, YOU'D SOON DIE, TOO, LIKE LOIS AND LANA DID! NOTHING CAN MAKE ME BELIEVE OTHERWISE!
A FEW DAYS LATER...
SUPERMAN, I HAVE HIGH HOPES THIS COMPUTER MACHINE WILL ALLAY YOUR FEARS! IT WILL CALCULATE FOR US WHETHER OR NOT OUR MARRIAGE WILL BE A HAPPY ONE!
THOSE TWO FISH LOOK LIKE GIGANTIC EELS!
NOW THEY'RE GLOWING BRILLIANTLY!
IT'S A GOOD OMEN! IT'S AN OLD ATLANTIDE BELIEF THAT THIS SPECIES OF EEL GLOWS LIKE THAT ONLY IN THE PRESENCE OF TWO PEOPLE WHO ARE TRULY IN LOVE! NOW LET'S SEE WHAT THE COMPUTER SAID!
PRESENTLY...
THE COMPUTER'S VERDICT IS A FAVORABLE ONE! AND SO...PLEASE MARRY ME, LORI!
YES, DARLING!!
YOUR MARRIAGE WILL BE LONG, HAPPY AND UMMARRED BY TRAGEDY
3.

SOON, ALL ATLANTIS REJOICES AS THE **MAN OF STEEL** AND **LORI** ARE JOINED IN MATRIMONY...

YOU ARE NOW... MAN AND WIFE!

WHAT A HANDSOME COUPLE!

MAY THEY KNOW **ONLY** HAPPINESS!

AFTER THE CEREMONY...

NOW TO FLASH THROUGH THE TIME-BARRIER, ACROSS MORE THAN TEN THOUSAND YEARS, TO AN ERA THAT PRECEDED OUR CIVILIZATION! **LORI** AND I WILL HONEYMOON IN **ANCIENT ATLANTIS**, BEFORE IT SANK BENEATH THE WAVES!

PRESENTLY, ON THE FABULOUS ISLE OF ATLANTIS...

THIS DEVICE ON MY WRIST, WHICH I CREATED, HAS PLACED AN **INVISIBILITY AURA** ABOUT US, SO WE'RE **UNSEEN**!

I'M... SO HAPPY! TOO BAD WE CAN'T WARN MY ANCESTORS OF THEIR DOOM, BUT FATE CAN'T BE CHANGED!

WHEN THE HONEYMOON IS OVER...

NOW THAT WE'VE RETURNED TO THE PRESENT, WE'LL LIVE IN MY ARCTIC **FORTRESS**!

LATER, IN THE SANCTUM...

I'VE INSTALLED SEVERAL TANKS IN THE **FORTRESS**, SINCE YOU MUST SPEND 8 HOURS A DAY IN SALT WATER! I HOPE THAT WATCHING ME TRYING TO CREATE A PERMANENT SUPER-SERUM ISN'T BORING YOU!

I **LOVE** BEING NEAR YOU!

ONE DAY, AFTER **SUPERMAN** LEAVES HIS FORTRESS TO GO ON PATROL, THE KRYPTONIAN CRIMINALS WHO WERE EXILED YEARS AGO INTO THE **PHANTOM ZONE** PREPARE TO STRIKE...

SHE'S ABOUT TO ENTER THE TANK!

IN HER WEAKENED STATE, SHE'LL BE EASY PREY!

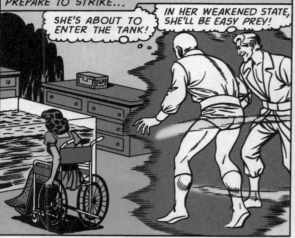

CONCENTRATING MIGHTILY, THE PHANTOM VILLAINS BRIDGE THE GULF BETWEEN THEIR TWILIGHT REALM AND THE EARTH'S DIMENSION WITH A MIGHTY TELEPATHIC COMMAND...

OPEN THAT BOX!!

OPEN THAT BOX!!!

I... HEAR VOICES! CAN'T— RESIST! **MUST OBEY!**

ÃÃÃÃÃÃÃÃ- AAGHHHH!!

HA, HA! **SUPERMAN** HOPED THAT A TINY AMOUNT OF THAT UNKNOWN SPACE ELEMENT IN THE LEAD BOX WOULD HELP HIM PERFECT THE PERMANENT SUPER-SERUM HE HAS BEEN SEEKING...!

THE MASSIVE RADIATION DOSAGE IS KILLING HIS WIFE! HA, HA!

MINUTES LATER, AS **SUPERMAN** ROBOTS INVESTIGATE **LORI'S** MOANS...

SHE IS DYING!

I WILL SUMMON OUR MASTER WITH AN ULTRA-SONIC SIGNAL!

AS THE **MAN OF STEEL** RESPONDS TO THE SUPER-SUMMONS...

SHE'S DOOMED!

¦CHOKE¦-LORI, DEAREST, **WHY** DID YOU OPEN THAT LEAD BOX? YOU KNOW I WORK WITH DANGEROUS MATERIALS!

VOICES... MADE... ME DO IT...

HER PULSE HAS STOPPED! HER HEART ISN'T BEATING ANY MORE! SHE'S DEAD... AND NOTHING CAN BRING HER BACK! "VOICES"! SHE HEARD EVIL, COMMANDING "VOICES"! I... I THINK I KNOW WHO **KILLED** HER!!

5

DAZEDLY, **SUPERMAN** TURNS ON THE **PHANTOM ZONE** MONITOR...

YOU DID THIS AWFUL THING, DIDN'T YOU? HOW COULD YOU HARM **LORI**, WHO NEVER HURT **ANY-ONE?**

HA, HA, HA! BY DESTROYING YOUR THIRD WIFE, WE HAVE ACHIEVED **VENGEANCE SUPREME!!!**

AND SOON A GRIEVING HUSBAND MOURNS HIS TRAGIC LOSS...

MUST FIND OUT WHY THAT ATLANTIDE COMPUTER MACHINE PREDICTED WRONGLY THAT NO HARM WOULD COME TO **LORI** IF WE MARRIED! I'LL TEST IT AGAIN...

LORI

PRESENTLY, IN ATLANTIS, AS **SUPERMAN** FEEDS THE SAME DATA INTO THE COMPUTER...

?!..NOW THE VERDICT IS EXACTLY THE **OPPOSITE!** - WAIT! THAT EEL SWIMMING BY...! I'VE GOT IT! I KNOW WHAT WENT WRONG!

IF YOU TWO MARRY, LORI WILL SOON DIE

TWO GIGANTIC EELS APPROACHED WHILE **LORI** WAS OPERATING THE COMPUTER! THE ELECTRICAL ENERGY FROM THE GLOWING EELS AFFECTED THE MACHINE, CAUSING IT TO MALFUNCTION AND GIVE AN INCORRECT PREDICTION!

WHAT AN UNFORTUNATE TWIST OF FATE! **LORI** WOULD BE ALIVE NOW IF THE COMPUTER HADN'T GONE AWRY. :CHOKE: WHAT'S DONE IS DONE! I'LL RESUME MY CAREER! I KNOW **LORI** WOULD WANT ME TO.

TO DIVERT HIS MIND WHEN HE ISN'T PATROLLING, **SUPERMAN** CONTINUES HIS SEARCH FOR A PERMA-NENT SUPER-SERUM, UNTIL ONE DAY...

THIS NEW CHEMICAL "X" I'VE ADDED TO THE SERUM MAY BE SAFE FOR A MORTAL TO TAKE-BUT I DON'T DARE EXPERIMENT ON ANY HUMANS, LEST IT BE FATAL AS IT WAS WITH **LOIS!**

BUT THE NEXT MORNING, AS **SUPERMAN** ENTERS HIS LAB...

*GREAT KRYPTON! THE **METAL-EATER BEAST** ESCAPED FROM THE FORTRESS ZOO, AGAIN! IT'S SEIZING THE METAL BOX WHICH CONTAINS THE EXPERIMENTAL SUPER-SERUM!*

BWAMM!

*THE KRYPTONIAN CREATURE HAS SUPER-POWERS LIKE MINE! THERE IT GOES, CRASHING UP THROUGH THE FORTRESS WALL! I'LL REPAIR THE WALL AT ONCE! I'VE A HUNCH THE BEAST'S INSTINCT WILL LEAD IT TO A WORLD SIMILAR TO **KRYPTON!***

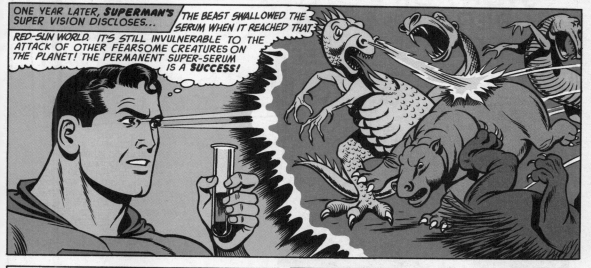

ONE YEAR LATER, **SUPERMAN'S** SUPER VISION DISCLOSES...

THE BEAST SWALLOWED THE SERUM WHEN IT REACHED THAT *RED-SUN WORLD. IT'S STILL INVULNERABLE TO THE ATTACK OF OTHER FEARSOME CREATURES ON THE PLANET! THE PERMANENT SUPER-SERUM IS A **SUCCESS!***

*"SUCCESS"?... IF I'D DISCOVERED THIS FORMULA EARLIER, THE LIVES OF MY WIVES COULD'VE BEEN SAVED! HMM...THERE'S ONLY ENOUGH OF THIS RARE SERUM HERE TO MAKE ONE DOSE. IF IT HAD BEEN WITHIN MY POWER TO RESCUE ONLY **ONE** OF MY WIVES, **WHICH ONE** WOULD I HAVE SAVED???*

*LOIS?... LANA?... LORI?... WHICH ONE, I WONDER? **WHICH ONE! WHICH ONE?!!!***

AND SO ENDS OUR *IMAGINARY* NOVEL, WHICH **MAY** OR **MAY NOT** EVER HAPPEN. READERS—WHICH OF HIS THREE WIVES DO YOU THINK **SUPERMAN** WOULD HAVE SAVED IF HE COULD ONLY SAVE ONE?

SUPERMAN
REG. U.S. PAT. OFF.

AN IMAGINARY NOVEL

"The FANTASTIC STORY OF SUPERMAN'S SONS!"

HERE IS THE STRANGE STORY OF SUPERMAN'S TWO SONS, IN A DAY YET TO COME! IT IS THE SAGA OF A MIGHTY MENACE OUT OF SPACE AND TIME, AND OF THE STRUGGLE AGAINST IT THAT RANGES FROM THE GREAT WORLD OF KRYPTON IN THE PAST, TO GLAMOROUS KANDOR AND EARTH OF THE NEAR FUTURE... A STRUGGLE THAT CENTERS UPON JOR-EL II AND KAL-EL II, THE TWO UNLIKE BROTHERS!

Part I
"JOR-EL II and KAL-EL II!"
Part II
"The NEW NIGHTWING and FLAMEBIRD!"
Part III
"KAL-EL'S MISSION TO KRYPTON!"

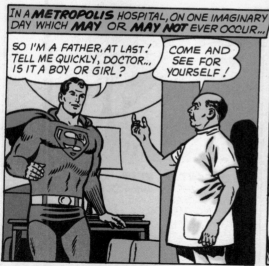

IN A **METROPOLIS** HOSPITAL, ON ONE IMAGINARY DAY WHICH **MAY** OR **MAY NOT** EVER OCCUR...

SO I'M A FATHER, AT LAST! TELL ME QUICKLY, DOCTOR... IS IT A BOY OR GIRL?

COME AND SEE FOR YOURSELF!

TWIN BOYS! THEY'RE NOT IDENTICAL TWINS... THEY'LL LOOK DIFFERENT. BUT BOTH ARE FINE BABIES!

TWO SONS! THIS... THIS IS THE GREATEST THING THAT EVER HAPPENED TO ME!

AND ONE OF THE MOST **TRAGIC** THINGS, AS **SUPERMAN** WILL LEARN IN TIME!

SOON, AT **SUPERMAN'S** SUBURBAN HOME OUTSIDE **METROPOLIS**, THE TWIN BABIES ARE GIVEN HISTORIC NAMES!

JOR-EL II, WHOM WE NAMED AFTER YOUR FATHER, IS TRYING OUT HIS SUPER-STRENGTH!

AND **KAL-EL II** IS TRYING TO IMITATE HIS BROTHER, BUT HE HASN'T LEARNED HOW TO USE HIS SUPER-STRENGTH YET!

BUT LATER, ON THE GROUNDS OF **SUPERMAN'S** PRIVATE ESTATE...

ME SEE BALL... ME GET IT!

IT'S FUNNY THAT **KAL-EL II** DIDN'T ALSO SEE THE BALL, WITH HIS X-RAY VISION! MAYBE I'D BETTER HAVE A SPECIALIST LOOK HIM OVER TO MAKE SURE HIS SUPER-POWERS ARE DEVELOPING PROPERLY!

THE NEXT DAY, A GREAT SCIENTIFIC SPECIALIST GIVES THE **MAN OF STEEL** A STUNNING SHOCK!

I'VE EXAMINED **KAL-EL II** THOROUGHLY, AND IT GRIEVES ME TO TELL YOU... **HE HAS NO SUPER-POWERS!**

BUT THAT CAN'T BE! **JOR-EL II** INHERITED ALL MY SUPER-POWERS! SO WHY WOULDN'T **KAL-EL II** ALSO INHERIT THEM?

BY THE GENETIC LAWS OF INHERITANCE, ONE CHILD CAN INHERIT CHARACTERISTICS FROM THE FATHER, ANOTHER FROM THE MOTHER! **KAL-EL II** IS PHYSICALLY HIS MOTHER'S SON... HE HAS NO SUPER-POWERS, AND KRYPTONITE DOESN'T AFFECT HIM!

THIS WILL BE A TERRIBLE SHOCK TO MY WIFE! AND HOW WILL **KAL-EL II** FEEL ABOUT IT WHEN HE'S OLDER?

AS THE NEXT FEW YEARS PASS...

HOW CAN I CATCH THE BALL WHEN YOU THROW IT AT SUPER-SPEED? I CAN'T EVEN SEE IT!

HA, HA... I WAS ONLY JOKING! I'LL GO AFTER THE BALL!

HE *CAUGHT* THE *VERY* BALL HE THREW! JOR-EL'S ALWAYS TEASING ME, MAKING ME LOOK SLOW AND WEAK!

AND WHEN THE TWO BROTHERS GO "CAMPING"...

ARE YOU STILL RUBBING THOSE STICKS TOGETHER TO MAKE FIRE? I'LL DO IT IN AN INSTANT, WITH MY HEAT-VISION!

BUT I ALMOST HAD A FIRE STARTED... OH, ALL RIGHT...

VALIANTLY, THE NON-SUPER-TWIN TRIES TO KEEP UP WITH HIS SUPER-BROTHER!

ARE YOU GOING TO TAKE ALL DAY TO GET UP HERE? TOO BAD YOU CAN'T FLY UP LIKE ME!

I'LL CLIMB IT, YOU'LL SEE... OOPS, I SLIPPED!

YOU DIDN'T GET HURT, DID YOU?

NO... I... I'M ALL RIGHT...

I WON'T CRY, NOT WHEN HE'S LOOKING AT ME! I WON'T!

BUT THAT NIGHT, WHEN *JOR EL II* IS ASLEEP...

KAL-EL, IS THAT YOU CRYING? WHAT'S WRONG, DEAR?

I... SOB... CAN'T HELP IT! OTHER KIDS ALL LAUGH AT ME BECAUSE I CAN'T DO SUPER-THINGS LIKE *JOR-EL!* WHY COULDN'T I HAVE SUPER-POWERS, TOO?

③

IT'S NOTHING TO CRY ABOUT, DEAR! I DON'T HAVE ANY SUPER-POWERS EITHER, REMEMBER! AND YOUR GRANDFATHER, JOR-EL I OF KRYPTON, HAD NO SUPER-POWERS, BUT HE WAS A GREAT MAN! THERE... GO TO SLEEP...

NEXT DAY... JOR-EL, YOUR TEASING OF KAL-EL MUST STOP OR I'LL HAVE TO PUNISH YOU, SUPER THOUGH YOU ARE! YOU'RE GIVING HIM A COMPLEX!

GEE, DAD, I WASN'T THINKING ...I'M SORRY!

I'LL NEVER TEASE KAL AGAIN! WITH MY SUPER-POWERS, I GUESS IT'S UP TO ME TO PROTECT HIM, JUST THE WAY YOU PROTECT MOTHER!

I KNEW YOU'D FEEL THAT WAY IF YOU THOUGHT ABOUT IT... YOU'RE GROWING UP!

BUT GOOD INTENTIONS DON'T ALWAYS WORK OUT!

COME ON, KAL... WE'RE ALL GOING BOATING! I'M FLYING THE BOAT OVER TO METROPOLIS LAKE!

YOU GO AHEAD ...I...ER... WANT TO READ A BOOK!

AND LATER... BUT I WANT TO TAKE YOU OUT IN SPACE WITH ME, KAL! I MADE THIS SPACE-SUIT SO IT'D BE SAFE FOR YOU!

NO, I'D JUST BE IN YOUR WAY... YOU GO AHEAD, JOR!

FINALLY, SUPERMAN REACHES A DECISION...

KAL-EL IS GROWING UP WITH A TERRIBLE INFERIORITY COMPLEX! I'VE GOT TO GIVE HIM SUPER-POWERS, SOME-HOW, FOR AT LEAST A TEMPORARY PERIOD, OR HIS LIFE MAY BE RUINED!

I'M AFRAID YOU'RE RIGHT... HE'S BECOMING BROODING, SHY, AND ANTI-SOCIAL!

4

AFTER A SUPER-SWIFT SEARCH, THE *MAN OF STEEL* FINDS A POSSIBLE ANSWER ON A DISTANT WORLD...

THE MIXED RADIATIONS FROM THOSE TWO SUNS IS UNIQUE IN THE UNIVERSE --IT'S CAUSED METAL LIFE TO EVOLVE HERE! BY MY DEDUCTIONS, THESE SAME RADIATIONS SHOULD GIVE AN ORDINARY EARTH PERSON SUPER-POWERS, EVEN THOUGH THEY HAVE NO EFFECT ON ME!

SOON, RETURNING TO EARTH...

WOULD YOU LIKE TO STAY FOR A WHILE ON THAT DISTANT PLANET, *KAL?* YOU'D HAVE SUPER-POWERS, THERE!

THAT WOULD BE TERRIFIC! I'VE ALWAYS DREAMED OF HAVING SUPER-POWERS LIKE *JOR!*

KAL NEEDN'T LIVE HIS WHOLE LIFE ON THIS WORLD, BUT JUST BEING SUPER-POWERED THERE FOR A TIME SHOULD HELP RID HIM OF HIS INFERIORITY COMPLEX!

I CAN *FLY* HERE, JUST AS *JOR-EL* DOES ON EARTH!

MY THEORY WAS RIGHT... THE MIXED RADIATIONS OF THE TWO SUNS HAS THE EFFECT OF GIVING HIM SUPER-POWERS!

AND NOW I HAVE X-RAY, HEAT AND TELESCOPIC VISION, INVULNERABILITY, AND *SUPER-STRENGTH!* I CAN DO MANY THINGS FOR THESE FRIENDLY PEOPLE, LIKE MOVING THIS BRIDGE FOR THEM!

FINE, *KAL!* SINCE YOU'RE IMMUNE TO ALL HARM, I'LL LEAVE YOU HERE FOR A WHILE WITH THESE PEOPLE!

BUT LATER, DESPITE HIS NEW SUPER-POWERS, KAL'S FEELINGS CHANGE!

THERE, THAT NEW BUILDING THEY NEEDED IS FINISHED! THEY'RE NICE FOLKS... BUT I CAN'T HELP THINKING ABOUT EARTH! I WONDER WHAT THEY'RE DOING AT HOME NOW?

5

USING SUPER-TELESCOPIC VISION TO LOOK ACROSS SPACE, KAL-EL II SEES!

IT'S CHRISTMAS, AT HOME! GEE, I WISH I WERE THERE... WITH MOTHER AND DAD AND JOR-EL... I WANT TO GO HOME!

A DESPERATE KAL-EL MAKES A COSMIC SIGNAL!

THE HUGE ROCK I THREW OUT HIT THAT LITTLE ASTEROID AND IS CREATING A BIG FLASH! DAD WILL SEE IT, AND COME!

AND WHEN THE WATCHFUL MAN OF STEEL SEES, AND HURRIES TO THAT FAR WORLD...

I DON'T KNOW WHY, BUT WHEN I THOUGHT OF YOU AND MOTHER AND JOR, I FELT SO BLUE THAT EVEN MY NEW SUPER-POWERS DIDN'T MAKE UP FOR IT!

I'LL TAKE YOU BACK HOME FOR A WHILE, KAL!

HE WAS HOMESICK, THAT'S ALL! HE CAN'T STAND BEING AWAY SO FAR FROM US!

BUT AFTER COMING HOME, THE SAME PROBLEM FACES SUPERMAN!

KAL-EL IS STILL OVERSHADOWED BY HIS SUPER-BROTHER... IF ONLY HE HAD SUPER-POWERS HERE ON EARTH!

THERE OUGHT TO BE SOME WAY! I'LL TRY TO MAKE HIM SUPER-POWERED, BY SCIENTIFIC TREATMENT!

USING THE UNIQUE EFFECT OF THE TWO SUNS' MIXED RADIATIONS AS A CLUE, I'VE DEVISED THIS ELIXIR!

"DRINK IT, KAL... I'M HOPING IT WILL MAKE YOU SUPER ON EARTH!

I WILL!

IT WORKED, DAD! LOOK, I HAVE SUPER-STRENGTH... RIGHT HERE ON EARTH!

BUT THE ELIXIR HAS A SIDE EFFECT I DIDN'T FORESEE! YOU'RE BECOMING...

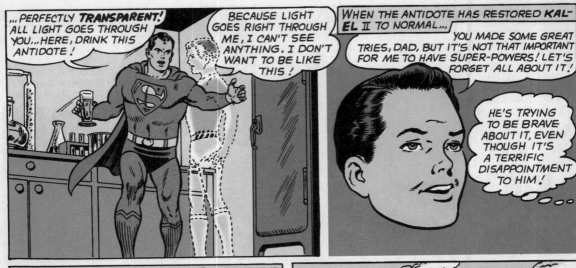

...PERFECTLY **TRANSPARENT!** ALL LIGHT GOES THROUGH YOU...HERE, DRINK THIS ANTIDOTE!

BECAUSE LIGHT GOES RIGHT THROUGH ME, I CAN'T SEE ANYTHING. I DON'T WANT TO BE LIKE THIS!

WHEN THE ANTIDOTE HAS RESTORED **KAL-EL II** TO NORMAL...

YOU MADE SOME GREAT TRIES, DAD, BUT IT'S NOT THAT IMPORTANT FOR ME TO HAVE SUPER-POWERS! LET'S FORGET ALL ABOUT IT!

HE'S TRYING TO BE BRAVE ABOUT IT, EVEN THOUGH IT'S A TERRIFIC DISAPPOINTMENT TO HIM!

AND NEXT MORNING, BEFORE LEAVING ON AN URGENT MISSION...

I HAVE TO ROUND UP THOSE SCIENTIFIC RACKETEERS WHO HAVE BEEN PREYING ON **METROPOLIS**, ONCE AND FOR ALL! **JOR'S** GOING WITH ME, BUT I'M LEAVING THIS ROBOT TO GUARD YOU!

I'M NOT AFRAID!

JOR CAN GO WITH DAD AND HELP HIM, BUT I'LL NEVER BE ABLE TO! OH, WELL, I'D BETTER JUST FORGET IT, AS I PROMISED I WOULD!

BUT, A LITTLE LATER... THIS IS THE BROTHER THAT'S NON-SUPER! WE'LL HOLD HIM FOR A HOSTAGE, AND **SUPERMAN** WON'T DARE BREAK UP OUR RACKET!

MMMF!

IT'S A SWELL IDEA...BUT LOOK, WHAT'S THAT COMING?

IT'S A **ROBOT!** **SUPERMAN** MUST HAVE LEFT IT TO GUARD THE KID! I CAN'T BREAK ITS HOLD!

IT'S GOT US... AND IT MUST HAVE SENT SOME KIND OF SIGNAL, FOR THERE COMES **SUPERMAN!** WE'RE SUNK!

THAT NIGHT, AFTER THE CAPTURED RACKETEERS HAVE BEEN JAILED...

THEY DIDN'T KNOW I'D LEFT *TWO* ROBOTS ON GUARD HERE... ONE TO GUARD YOU, AND ONE TO GUARD *KAL-EL!*

SINCE HE'S THE WEAKER ONE OF OUR TWO SONS, YOU MUST ALWAYS GUARD *KAL-EL* AGAINST SUCH PERILS!

BUT ACCIDENTALLY, OUTSIDE THE WINDOW, *KAL-EL* HAS OVERHEARD!

"THE WEAKER ONE"! THAT'S WHAT I AM! I'M NOT ONLY NO HELP TO MY DAD, I'M ACTUALLY A *DANGER* TO HIM! I... I CAN'T STAY HERE ANY MORE...

I'LL RUN AWAY! I LOVE THEM, BUT I'LL ALWAYS BE A BURDEN TO THEM BECAUSE I'M NON-SUPER! THEY'LL NEVER SEE ME AGAIN!

LATER, NIGHT AND STORM CLOSE DOWN ON THE WEARY RUNAWAY.

I'LL SLEEP IN THAT BARN TONIGHT AND START ON AGAIN EARLY IN THE MORNING! I MUST NEVER LET THEM KNOW WHERE I'VE GONE!

BUT WHEN HE AWAKES AT DAWN...

DAD! YOU FOUND ME ...ALREADY!

IT WASN'T HARD WITH SUPER-VISION! COME ON, *KAL*...WE'RE GOING BACK HOME! YOU LEFT BEFORE YOU HEARD MY PLANS FOR YOU BOYS!

SOON...

MY SONS, I ONCE TOLD YOU HOW YOU'RE DESCENDED FROM KRYPTONIAN ANCESTORS AS WELL AS EARTH ONES! NOW I WANT BOTH OF YOU TO HAVE A *KRYPTONIAN* EDUCATION AS WELL AS AN EARTHLY ONE!

BUT HOW CAN WE, DAD? *KRYPTON* PERISHED YEARS AGO!

8

THE **MAN OF STEEL** HAS THE ANSWER FOR THAT...

YOU'LL FIND OUT HERE, IN MY **FORTRESS OF SOLITUDE!**

THIS IS **KANDOR**, THE LAST CITY OF **KRYPTON**... STOLEN BY THE SPACE VILLAIN **BRAINIAC**, YEARS AGO, AND SHRUNK BY HIM TO TINY SIZE! IN **KANDOR**, YOU'LL LEARN KANDORIAN LORE, BUT YOU'LL HAVE NO SUPER-POWERS THERE, **JOR-EL!**

I DON'T CARE, IF I GET TO LIVE IN A REAL KRYPTONIAN CITY FOR A WHILE! WOW!

THE SHRINKING-RAY PROJECTOR MAKES **SUPERMAN** AND HIS TWO SONS TINY, AND THEN...

WE'LL FLOAT DOWN INTO **KANDOR** ON PARACHUTES... THEY KNOW BY THEIR MONITORS THAT WE'RE COMING! AS THERE'S NO CRIME IN **KANDOR**, NEITHER OF YOU WILL BE IN ANY DANGER!

WE'LL BE ALL RIGHT!

BUT AS THEY DESCEND TOWARD THE KRYPTONIAN CITY...

IN **KANDOR**, WHERE NEITHER OF THEM HAS SUPER-POWERS, **KAL-EL** WILL GET OVER HIS INFERIORITY COMPLEX!

DAD DOESN'T REALIZE THAT I UNDERSTAND **WHY** HE'S DOING THIS! I CAN'T LET ON I KNOW...BUT THIS WON'T REALLY CHANGE ME!

BUT **KAL-EL** IS WRONG, FOR HIS FATEFUL VISIT TO **KANDOR** WILL CHANGE HIS LIFE AND OTHER LIVES FOREVER!

A LOOK AT OTHER GREAT IMAGINARY STORIES

WORLD'S FINEST COMICS #157, 1966 art by Cuert Swan and George Klein

BATMAN #145, 1962 art by Sheldon Moldoff

SUPERMAN

REG. U.S PAT. OFF.

PART II

IN SHRUNKEN **KANDOR**, THE ONLY SURVIVING CITY OF **KRYPTON**, **JOR-EL II** HAS NO SUPER-POWERS, AND HIS BROTHER **KAL-EL II** IS AT LAST ON EVEN TERMS WITH HIM AND NEED NOT FEEL INFERIOR! THAT IS THE WAY **SUPERMAN** PLANNED IT... BUT FATE STEPS IN TO CHANGE THOSE PLANS WHEN, TO COMBAT A MYSTERIOUS AND DEADLY MENACE, THE TWO SONS OF **SUPERMAN** REVIVE THE LEGEND OF AN HEROIC DUO AND BECOME—

The NEW
NIGHTWING
and
FLAMEBIRD!

LOOK OUT, **FLAMEBIRD**... THAT KRYPTONIAN SQUID IS GOING TO GRAB YOU!

EVEN HERE IN **KANDOR**, WHERE MY BROTHER **JOR-EL** HAS NO SUPER-POWERS, HE HAS TO PROTECT ME!

AS THE TWO BROTHERS OF KRYPTONIAN DESCENT LOOK ON THE LAST CITY OF **KRYPTON**...

FOR THE FIRST TIME IN MY LIFE, I REALIZE WHAT IT'S LIKE TO HAVE NO SUPER-POWERS, FOR I HAVE NONE HERE!

IT'S LIKE BEING ON **KRYPTON** ITSELF BEFORE IT EXPLODED! I WANT TO LEARN ALL THE HISTORY OF OUR ANCESTRAL WORLD!

WE WELCOME YOUR TWO SONS, **SUPERMAN**! THEY CAN ENTER **KANDOR UNIVERSITY**!

THANKS..., AND NOW I MUST RETURN TO MY OWN WORK ON EARTH! MY SONS, YOU'LL FIND LIFE ON **KANDOR** A NEW EXPERIENCE!

BUT **SUPERMAN** DOESN'T DREAM HOW FANTASTIC THAT EXPERIENCE WILL BE!

AT **KANDOR** UNIVERSITY, ALL THE LORE AND WISDOM OF OLD **KRYPTON** IS GATHERED!

I WONDER WHAT KIND OF ATHLETICS THEY GO IN FOR HERE?

LOOK, **JOR**... THESE STATUES ARE OF THE GREATEST AND WISEST MEN IN **KRYPTON**'S HISTORY!

THE PLAQUE SAYS THIS IS **ZAN ZARN**, THE KRYPTONIAN WHO FIRST DISCOVERED ATOMIC POWER!

AND IN THE STATUE'S HAND IS A SMALL RADIATING ATOMIC GENERATOR... AN ETERNAL POWER-LIGHT IN HIS HONOR!

THIS WAS **MURN ABBAS**, WHOSE "REPULSION-HALO" INVENTION DEFEATED AN ALIEN INVASION OF **KRYPTON**, WITHOUT TAKING A LIFE!

WHAT A GREAT HONOR... TO BE REMEMBERED LIKE THIS, EVEN THOUGH **KRYPTON** IS GONE!

BUT THE NEXT STATUE IS THE MOST IMPRESSIVE OF ALL!

LOOK, **KAL**, IT'S A STATUE OF **JOR-EL I**, MY NAMESAKE AND OUR GRANDFATHER! THE PLAQUE SAYS HE'S HONORED FOR HIS MANY MIGHTY DEEDS FOR **KRYPTON**!

IF ONLY HE COULD HAVE SAVED THE PEOPLE OF **KRYPTON**, AS HE TRIED TO DO! I...I FEEL UNWORTHY BESIDE SUCH A GREAT ANCESTOR!

JOR-EL II, ALWAYS ACTION-LOVING, CAN'T LONG REMAIN AWED! A LITTLE FARTHER...

THEY RIDE ROCKET-POWERED MOUNTS AND PLAY WITH A BALLOON-LIKE BALL...IT'S A SORT OF **SKY-POLO** GAME!

WOW! THAT LOOKS LIKE FUN! LET'S TRY TO GET INTO ALL THESE KRYPTONIAN ATHLETICS, **KAL**!

WHEN THEY DO SO LATER, **KAL-EL II** FINDS HIMSELF AGAIN OVERSHADOWED BY HIS BROTHER!

I COULDN'T EVEN MAKE THE TEAM, BUT **JOR-EL II** IS ALREADY A STAR AT THE GAME! I'M GLAD, FOR HIS SAKE...

2

AND IN OTHER SPORTS, LIKE THE KANDORIAN WEIGHT-LIFTING CONTESTS...

THE WEIGHT IS OF AN ELEMENT THAT DRAWS ATOMS FROM THE AIR AND GETS *HEAVIER* BY THE MINUTE! YOUR BROTHER HAS HELD UP HIS WEIGHT THE LONGEST, AND HE WINS!

EVEN WITHOUT HIS SUPER-POWERS, *JOR-EL* ALWAYS EXCELS ME! I...I GUESS I'D BETTER STICK TO MY BOOKS AND NOT TRY TO COMPETE WITH HIM!

AND FAR INTO THE NIGHTS, IN THE GREAT UNIVERSITY LIBRARY, A LONELY, INFERIORITY-RIDDEN *KAL-EL II* READS THE LORE OF *KRYPTON!*

THIS "HISTORY OF THE *PHANTOM ZONE,*" TO WHICH KRYPTONIAN CRIMINALS WERE SENTENCED, IS FASCINATING! AND I WANT TO READ ALL ABOUT MY GRANDFATHER'S ACHIEVEMENTS IN THESE OTHER BOOKS!

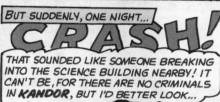

BUT SUDDENLY, ONE NIGHT...

CRASH!

THAT SOUNDED LIKE SOMEONE BREAKING INTO THE SCIENCE BUILDING NEARBY! IT CAN'T BE, FOR THERE ARE NO CRIMINALS IN *KANDOR,* BUT I'D BETTER LOOK...

KAL-EL II IS IN TIME TO GLIMPSE A SINISTER VISITANT...

THAT MASKED THIEF... HE'S FLYING AWAY CARRYING A SCIENTIFIC APPARATUS HE'S STOLEN!

CRIME IN *KANDOR?* IT SEEMS IMPOSSIBLE, BUT THE NEXT NIGHT, IN THE GREAT KANDORIAN MUSEUM...

IT'S THAT *MYSTERY RAIDER* THEY TALKED OF... HE'S STOLEN THE ONLY KNOWN SPECIMEN OF THE RARE KRYPTONIAN MINERAL *VOLIUM!*

AND AS THE CITY SEETHES WITH EXCITEMENT AND ALARM...

THIS MYSTERY RAIDER FLIES, THEY SAY... BUT HOW COULD THAT BE? AND WHO IS HE?

JOR, THAT THIEF WORE A FLYING-BELT LIKE THE ONES IN OUR FATHER'S TROPHIES, IN THE *FORTRESS OF SOLITUDE!* MAYBE HE'S SOMEONE FROM EARTH... BUT HOW COULD HE HAVE FOUND AND ENTERED THE FORTRESS?

3

IF ONLY **NIGHTWING** AND **FLAMEBIRD**, WHO CONQUERED CRIMINALS IN **KANDOR** YEARS AGO, WOULD COME BACK TO DEAL WITH THIS ONE!

JOR, COME WITH ME QUICKLY... I'VE GOT AN IDEA!

OUR FATHER, **SUPERMAN**, AND HIS PAL, JIMMY OLSEN, WERE SECRETLY **NIGHTWING** AND **FLAMEBIRD**, YEARS AGO! WHY CAN'T WE BECOME THE **DUO OF KANDOR** IN THIS EMERGENCY?

WE'LL DO IT! DAD TOLD US WHERE THEIR SECRET BASE, THE **NIGHT-CAVE**, WAS HIDDEN... LET'S GO THERE!

SOON, IN THE LONG-HIDDEN **NIGHT-CAVE**...

ALTERING THE COSTUMES MAKES THEM FIT PERFECTLY, **FLAMEBIRD**!

AND EACH OF US WEARS ONE OF THE JET-POWERED FLYING HARNESSES THAT DAD AND JIMMY WORE YEARS AGO! WE'LL USE THE **NIGHTMOBILE** TO SEARCH FOR THE RAIDER!

SOON, WORD RUNS THROUGH **KANDOR** THAT TWO HEROES HAVE RETURNED!

LOOK.., **NIGHTWING** AND **FLAMEBIRD** ARE BACK! THEY'LL SOON CATCH THE MYSTERIOUS RAIDER!

JOR... I MEAN, **NIGHTWING**... I FEEL SOMEHOW THAT DAD AND JIMMY OLSEN ARE RIDING WITH US ON THIS MISSION!

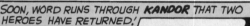

LOOK, THERE'S THE RAIDER NOW, ZOOMING DOWN TOWARD THE AQUARIUM!

WHAT COULD HE WANT THERE? NO MATTER, IT'S OUR CHANCE TO GRAB HIM!

AQUARIUM OF KRYPTONIAN SEA-LIFE

IN THE GREAT AQUARIUM WHICH CONTAINS THE LAST LIVING SPECIMENS OF **KRYPTON'S** OCEAN-CREATURES...

I CAN HEAR HIM RANSACKING THE ROOM AHEAD, WHERE THE RARE CHEMICALS THAT DUPLICATE **KRYPTON'S** SEA-WATER ARE KEPT!

ANOTHER SCIENTIFIC ROBBERY, FOR SOME MYSTERIOUS PURPOSE! AFTER HIM!

4

BUT THE THIEF TAKES ALARM AND FLEES...

I'VE GOT TO STOP THEIR PURSUIT, AND THERE'S ONE WAY TO DO IT...

THAT SHOULD KEEP THEM BUSY!

USE YOUR JET-POWER, FLAMEBIRD...OVER THE SQUID, BEFORE IT GRABS US!

JUST IN TIME!

BUT THE RAIDER'S GETTING OUT THROUGH A SKYLIGHT! WE MUSTN'T LET HIM GET AWAY!

AS THE NEW DUO OF KANDOR EMERGES FROM THE ROOF IN PURSUIT...

FLAMEBIRD, LOOK OUT! HIS REPELLOR-HALO KNOCKED YOU AROUND AND YOU'RE PLUNGING TOWARD THE GROUND!

ABANDONING PURSUIT, JOR-EL II DIVES TO HIS BROTHER'S SIDE!

GOT YOU!

THANKS, JOR... I MEAN, NIGHTWING, BUT THE RAIDER GOT AWAY!

5

WHY IS HE LOOTING ALL THESE SCIENTIFIC MATERIALS... EVERY ONE OF WHICH ORIGINATED ON OLD *KRYPTON?*

EVEN MORE BAFFLING... HE USED A REPELLOR-HALO WHICH WAS USED ONLY ON *KRYPTON* YEARS AGO! NO KANDORIAN WOULD KNOW HOW TO USE IT SINCE CRIME IS UNKNOWN HERE!

AND AS THEY RETURN, BAFFLED, TO THE *NIGHT-CAVE*...

SOMEHOW, ALL THIS MYSTERY SEEMS TO BE LINKED TO PERISHED *KRYPTON*... IT'S STRANGE, EERIE!

WHO-EVER IS BEHIND IT, HE STRIKES AT NIGHT ONLY! SO WE'LL BE ON THE WATCH FOR HIM TOMORROW NIGHT!

AT *KANDOR* UNIVERSITY NEXT DAY, AFTER CLASSES...

JOR, I THINK I HAVE A CLUE FROM STUDYING THE HISTORY OF *KRYPTON!* I FOUND IT IN A STRANGE CASE, FAR IN THE PAST...

IT'S THE *PRESENT* WE HAVE TO WORRY ABOUT! WE MUST GET TO THE *NIGHT-CAVE* AND SWITCH TO OUR SECRET IDENTITIES! THAT RAIDER MUSTN'T ESCAPE AGAIN!

AS NIGHT FALLS, WHEN *KANDOR'S* ARTIFICIAL SUN IS TURNED OFF...

BUT I THINK THE CLUE THAT POINTS BACK TO OLD *KRYPTON* MAY BE IMPORTANT!

YOU'VE GOT TO FORGET YOUR OBSESSION WITH KRYPTONIAN HISTORY UNTIL WE GRAB THIS RAIDER! WE'LL BE READY TONIGHT IN THE AIR IF HE TRIES ANOTHER RAID!

LOOK, A REAL FLYING *NIGHTWING* AND *FLAMEBIRD*...THE TWO BIRDS AFTER WHOM DAD AND JIMMY MODELED THEIR COSTUMES!

THE BIRDS AREN'T IMPORTANT... BUT THE FLASH OF LIGHT I SAW DOWN THERE IN THE JUNGLE IS! NOBODY LIVES IN THE JUNGLE, BUT THE RAIDER COULD HAVE HIS BASE THERE!

PRESENTLY...

WE'VE FOUND HIM, *FLAMEBIRD!* HE'LL MAKE NO MORE RAIDS!

YOU'RE RIGHT... BUT ONLY BECAUSE THE OBJECT OF MY RAIDS IS FINALLY ACCOMPLISHED WITH THOSE MATERIALS I STOLE, I'VE BUILT A WEAPON WHICH I'LL DEMONSTRATE FOR YOU... HA, HA!

6

UNEXPECTEDLY, THE CRYPTIC WEAPON IS DIRECTED AT THE TWO HARMLESS *BIRDS*!

SINCE YOU CALL YOURSELVES *NIGHTWING* AND *FLAMEBIRD*, YOU'LL ENJOY THIS! MY MACHINE'S POWER WILL TURN THAT REAL *NIGHTWING* AND *FLAMEBIRD* INTO *PETS* FOR YOU!

IN SECONDS, A TERRIBLE TRANSFORMATION OCCURS!

LOOK OUT, *FLAMEBIRD*... HIS MACHINE SOMEHOW CHANGED THOSE TWO BIRDS INTO HUGE, WINGED MONSTERS!

THEY'LL KEEP YOU BUSY WHILE I TAKE MY WEAPON UP TO USE ON ALL EARTH!

GET AWAY, *JOR*... YOU CAN'T SAVE ME!

I CAN TRY, BROTHER! DON'T PANIC!

MY POWER-JETS FLASHING IN ITS FACE STARTLED IT... IT'S DROPPED *KAL*!

YOU SAVED MY LIFE, *JOR*!

EVEN HERE, WHERE *JOR* HAS NO SUPER-POWERS, HE'S PROVED THAT *I'M* THE "WEAKER SON"... AND WILL *ALWAYS* BE!

THESE TWO MONSTROUS BIRDS ARE FLYING TOWARD *KANDOR*! HAVE TO STOP THEM!

7

THESE NETS USED BY LAKE FISHERMEN ARE OUR ONLY CHANCE!

HURRY...THOSE TWO MONSTERS ARE SWOOPING ON *KANDOR*!

THE TERRIFIED PEOPLE OF *KANDOR* SEE A LAST-MINUTE EFFORT!

WE'VE GOT THEM TANGLED IN THE NETS...THE PEOPLE OF *KANDOR* CAN CONFINE THEM SAFELY NOW!

THERE'S NOT A SECOND TO LOSE! YOU HEARD THAT DEADLY RAIDER ...HE'S TAKING HIS MACHINE UP TO USE ON EARTH!

SWIFTLY, *NIGHTWING* AND *FLAMEBIRD* SWITCH BACK TO BECOME *JOR-EL II* AND *KAL-EL II*, AND...

I TOLD YOU I HAD A CLUE FROM HISTORY TO THAT RAIDER, AND NOW I KNOW I'M RIGHT...A TERRIBLE MENACE HAS COME OUT OF *KRYPTON* TO THREATEN EARTH!

BUT *KRYPTON* PERISHED A LIFETIME AGO...HOW COULD ANY DANGER COME FROM THERE?

FASTER, FASTER! WE HAVE TO WARN THE WORLD OF DANGER!

A DANGER THAT IS UNLOOSED BECAUSE *JOR-EL* HAD TO SAVE *ME*! MY WEAKNESS MAY BRING TERRIBLE DOOM ON EARTH!

END PART II

8

A LOOK AT OTHER GREAT IMAGINARY STORIES

ACTION COMICS #279, 1961
art by Curt Swan
and Stan Kaye

ACTION COMICS #327, 1965
art by Curt Swan
and George Klein

SUPERMAN

REG. U.S. PAT. OFF.

PART III

A MENACE THAT HAD ITS ORIGIN ON **KRYPTON**, LONG AGO, LEADS **KAL-EL II**, THE NON-SUPER SON OF **SUPERMAN**, BACK TO THAT LOST WORLD! HERE'S THE DRAMATIC STORY OF AN ODYSSEY INTO THE PAST, IN WHICH NOT ONLY THE FATE OF EARTH, BUT THE LIFE OF **SUPERMAN** HIMSELF AND HIS SUPER-SON DEPEND UPON--

KAL-EL II'S MISSION TO KRYPTON!

OUR RELENTLESS ENEMY HAS PARALYZED BOTH **JOR-EL II** AND ME... WE'RE DYING! **KAL-EL II** IS COMING TO HELP US, BUT WITHOUT ANY SUPER-POWERS, HE'LL FAIL!

UP OUT OF THE BOTTLE CITY OF **KANDOR** COME TWO TINY, HURRYING FIGURES!

I DON'T SEE THAT MYSTERIOUS RAIDER ANYWHERE HERE!

QUICK! PUT THE STOPPER BACK IN THE BOTTLE AND THEN WE'LL USE THE ENLARGING RAY TO MAKE OURSELVES NORMAL-SIZED AGAIN!

BUT WHEN **JOR-EL II** AND **KAL-EL II** HAVE DONE SO...

THE RAIDER MADE HIMSELF NORMAL-SIZED AND IS **GONE**...TO USE HIS STRANGE WEAPON AGAINST EARTH, AS HE THREATENED!

WE'VE GOT TO WARN DAD AT ONCE!

TIME-BUBBLE GIVEN SUPERMAN BY THE LEGION OF SUPER-HEROES.

I HAVE MY SUPER-POWERS BACK NOW... I'LL CARRY YOU AND WE'LL REACH HOME SUPER-FAST!

WITHOUT JOR'S SUPER-POWERS, I'D BE HELPLESS.. BUT I HAVE TO RESIGN MYSELF TO BEING SECOND-BEST! WITH EARTH IN DANGER, IT'S NOT IMPORTANT!

MINUTES LATER, AT SUPERMAN'S SUBURBAN ESTATE...

WE DON'T KNOW THIS RAIDER'S IDENTITY, BUT WE DO KNOW HIS WEAPON HAS TERRIFIC POWERS! I SUSPECT THAT...

WAIT, KAL... A NEWSFLASH!

A STRANGE CATASTROPHE HAS HIT METROPOLIS. FIRST REPORTS ARE CONFUSED, BUT SOMETHING BIG IS HAPPENING THERE!

A NIGHTMARE HAS INDEED BURST UPON THE GREAT CITY, BEGINNING WITH...

THAT STRANGE FORCE FROM THE SKY... IT HIT THE LIZARD CAGE!

LOOK, THE LIZARDS ARE BEGINNING TO CHANGE...

IT TURNED THEM INTO GIANT DINOSAURS LIKE THEIR EVOLUTIONARY ANCESTORS!

RUN... NO ONE CAN STOP THOSE MONSTERS!

BUT ONE MAN... AND HIS SUPER-SON CAN!

I GOT THIS ONE, DAD, BUT WHAT DO WE DO WITH THEM?

WE'LL ISOLATE THEM IN THE DEEP QUARRY PIT NEAR METROPOLIS! BUT THIS THING IS WORLD-WIDE... I HEARD A RADIO-BULLETIN SAYING THAT LONDON AND CAIRO HAVE BEEN STRICKEN, TOO!

2

OUT OF THE THAMES RIVER, A NIGHTMARE CREATURE OF EARTH'S PAST HAS ARISEN!

A FORCE LIKE STRANGE LIGHTNING HIT A SMALL WATER-SNAKE... AND IT CHANGED INTO THAT TERRIBLE SEA-SERPENT!

IT'S A FORM OF LIFE NOT SEEN ON EARTH FOR AGES!

BUT, FLASHING ACROSS THE ATLANTIC IN SECONDS, HELP ARRIVES!

THIS PUNCH IN THE NOSE WILL DISCOURAGE THE CREATURE SO IT WILL SWIM BACK TO MID-OCEAN! BUT I WONDER HOW *JOR* IS DOING WITH THE MONSTER REPORTED IN CAIRO?

JOR-EL II HAS PROVED HIMSELF A WORTHY SON OF THE *MAN OF STEEL!*

THE WEIRD FORCE FROM THE SKY CHANGED A MONKEY INTO THAT HUGE *APE!* BUT LOOK... THAT BOY IS SUBDUING IT!

GET CHAINS TO BIND THE CREATURE! I'LL HOLD IT FOR YOU!

AS THE WORLD ROCKS WITH THE MONSTROUS INVASION, **SUPERMAN** AND **JOR-EL** II RETURN FOR A TENSE CONFERENCE!

THAT FORCE IN EACH CASE ACTED AS A *REVERSE EVOLUTIONARY RAY*, MAKING EACH ANIMAL RESEMBLE ONE OF ITS ANCESTORS OF THOUSANDS OF YEARS AGO! THE RAIDER YOU FOUGHT IN *KANDOR* IS LOOSING THESE RAYS FROM SOME HIDDEN PLACE!

I'M SURE THIS MENACE ORIGINALLY CAME FROM *KRYPTON*, AND...

LISTEN, ANOTHER FLASH!

THIS BROADCAST IS AN ULTIMATUM!

PEOPLE OF THE WORLD, I HAVE GIVEN YOU A SAMPLE OF MY POWERS! ACCEPT ME AS WORLD RULER IN 24 HOURS, OR I'LL TURN LOOSE MONSTERS IN EVERY CITY ON EARTH!

SO THAT'S HIS PURPOSE! WE'VE GOT TO FIND HIM, FAST!

DAD, I WANT TO HELP...

3

I'M SORRY, KAL, BUT WITHOUT SUPER-POWERS, YOU COULDN'T HELP! THE SEARCH FOR THE RAIDER WILL BE DANGEROUS!

I ONLY MEANT I WANTED TO HELP WITH WHAT I LEARNED FROM THE HISTORY OF KRYPTON! BUT THEY WERE IN TOO GREAT A HURRY TO LISTEN!

I WILL HELP, EVEN THOUGH I'M "THE WEAK ONE"! THE SECRET OF HOW TO MEET THIS MONSTROUS ATTACK LIES BACK IN THE PAST... BACK ON THE WORLD OF KRYPTON, BEFORE IT PERISHED!

AND WITH A DESPERATE RESOLVE, KAL-EL II IS SOON ARROWING NORTHWARD!

THIS SUPER-FAST SPEED PLANE DAD GOT ME SO I WOULDN'T FEEL BAD ABOUT NOT HAVING THE POWER OF FLIGHT COMES IN HANDY NOW! BUT IT'S LUCKY JOR WAS IN SUCH A HURRY THAT HE DIDN'T CLOSE THE FORTRESS DOOR!

INSIDE, KAL-EL STUDIES A DANGEROUS DEVICE...

THIS TIME-BUBBLE MACHINE WAS GIVEN DAD BY THE LEGION OF SUPER-HEROES! ITS BLUE-PRINT PLANS TELL HOW IT WAS BUILT AND HOW IT WORKS! I'LL USE IT TO TAKE ME BACK TO KRYPTON BEFORE IT BLEW UP!

PRESENTLY, AS THE TIME-BUBBLE BEGINS ITS AWESOME JOURNEY...

I CAN SEE NOTHING BUT A GRAY BLUR, BUT THE DIALS SHOW THAT I'M SPEEDING INTO THE PAST! I MUST MANEUVER THE TIME-BUBBLE IN TIME AND SPACE, SO IT STOPS AT A CERTAIN DATE IN KRYPTON'S PAST!

WHEN THAT DATE IS REACHED, AND THE TIME-BUBBLE STOPS...

I'M ON KRYPTON, THE LOST WORLD OF MY FATHER'S PEOPLE!

4

EVERYTHING IS STRANGE, DIFFERENT FROM EARTH! I COULDN'T EVEN WALK IN THE GRAVITY HERE IF I HADN'T PUT ON "ANTI-GRAVITY SHOES" FROM DAD'S RELICS IN THE FORTRESS!

IN THE GREATEST OF **KRYPTON'S** CITIES...

YOU ASKED THE LOCATION OF THE HOME OF **JOR-EL**, THE SCIENTIST! THIS MAP SHOWS YOU HOW TO GET THERE!

INFORMATION **MACHINES** LIKE THIS ONE WILL HELP A LOT... I'M GLAD DAD TOLD ME ABOUT THEM, AND TAUGHT US TO SPEAK KRYPTONESE!

WITH DEEP EMOTION, **KAL-EL** II SOON LOOKS UPON THE MAN WHO WILL BE HIS GRANDFATHER...

SORRY I CAN'T MAKE THE PARTY, **LARA**, BUT I'M DUE SOON AT AN IMPORTANT SCIENTIFIC MEETING!

ALL RIGHT, **JOR-EL**, BUT WHEN WE'RE MARRIED, YOU'LL HAVE TO GO OUT A LITTLE MORE!

GEE, THE WOMAN WHO IS TO BE MY GRAND-MOTHER SURE IS PRETTY!

MINUTES LATER...

I'VE COME A GREAT DISTANCE IN HOPES YOU'LL LET ME STUDY SCIENCE WITH YOU! MY NAME IS **KALEL KENT!**

STAY WITH ME A FEW DAYS TILL I SEE WHAT YOUR ABILITIES ARE... BUT I CAN PROMISE NOTHING!

SINCE KENT WAS MY DAD'S ADOPTED EARTH NAME, IT'S THE TRUTH!

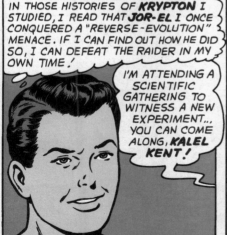

IN THOSE HISTORIES OF **KRYPTON** I STUDIED, I READ THAT **JOR-EL** I ONCE CONQUERED A "REVERSE-EVOLUTION" MENACE. IF I CAN FIND OUT HOW HE DID SO, I CAN DEFEAT THE RAIDER IN MY OWN TIME!

I'M ATTENDING A SCIENTIFIC GATHERING TO WITNESS A NEW EXPERIMENT... YOU CAN COME ALONG, **KALEL KENT!**

5

SOON, IN THE LABORATORY OF A BRILLIANT KRYPTONIAN BIOLOGIST...

WHAT IS THE GREAT DISCOVERY YOU PROMISED TO SHOW US, **GANN ARTAR?**

YOU SEE THAT ANIMAL... AN ORDINARY LITTLE PET **QUALAT?** WATCH IT WHEN I TURN MY NEWLY-DISCOVERED FORCES ON IT!

169

MY **DE-EVOLUTIONARY RAY** HAS THROWN IT BACK BY INDUCED ATAVISM INTO A PRIMEVAL, ANCESTRAL FORM!

IT'S TERRIBLE, TAMPERING WITH EVOLUTION TO PRODUCE SUCH MONSTERS! WE OF THE **SCIENCE COUNCIL** FORBID ANY MORE SUCH EXPERIMENTS!

FOOLS! YOU'RE ONLY JEALOUS OF ME... BUT I'LL MAKE YOU ALL REGRET THIS!

THEN THIS WAS THE ORIGIN OF THE RAIDER'S **DE-EVOLUTION RAY** THAT'S WREAKING HAVOC ON EARTH! BUT HOW DID THE RAIDER LEARN THIS TERRIBLE SCIENTIFIC SECRET OF THE PAST?

LATER, AT THE HOME OF **JOR-EL I**...

JOR-EL I'S DOG... IT MUST'VE BEEN **KRYPTO'S** FATHER! HOW STRANGE IT SEEMS!

SOMETHING ABOUT YOU HAS PUZZLED ME, **KALEL KENT!** I WANT YOU TO COME WITH ME!..

THIS FAMILY CRYPT CONTAINS THE STATUES OF MY ANCESTORS... AND IT'S STRANGE, BUT YOU LOOK LIKE THEM!

NOT SO STRANGE, SINCE THEY'RE **MY** ANCESTORS, TOO!

NATURE DOES PRODUCE ODD RESEMBLANCES, DOESN'T IT?

VAL-EL   SUL-EL   TALA-EL   HATU...

HIS LIFE WILL BE CUT SHORT WHEN **KRYPTON** EXPLODES... BUT I WON'T **LET** IT BE CUT SHORT! I'M GOING TO RESCUE HIM, AND **LARA**, AND AS MANY OTHERS AS POSSIBLE, FROM THIS DOOMED WORLD!

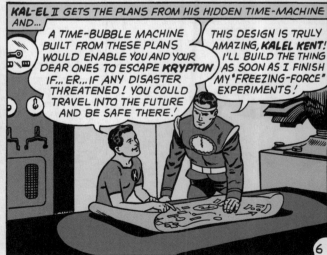

KAL-EL II GETS THE PLANS FROM HIS HIDDEN TIME-MACHINE AND...

A TIME-BUBBLE MACHINE BUILT FROM THESE PLANS WOULD ENABLE YOU AND YOUR DEAR ONES TO ESCAPE **KRYPTON** IF... ER... IF ANY DISASTER THREATENED! YOU COULD TRAVEL INTO THE FUTURE AND BE SAFE THERE!

THIS DESIGN IS TRULY AMAZING, **KALEL KENT!** I'LL BUILD THE THING AS SOON AS I FINISH MY "FREEZING-FORCE" EXPERIMENTS!

6

BUT ONLY A FEW NIGHTS LATER...

OBSERVE! MY "FREEZING FORCE" SUSPENDS ANIMATION WITHOUT HARMING THE SUBJECT... IT WILL REPLACE ANAESTHETICS IN SURGERY!

THAT RAY FROM OUTSIDE ...IT'S GANN ARTAR'S DE-EVOLUTIONARY RAY, AND IT'S HITTING YOUR DOG!

THE FAITHFUL DOG OF JOR-EL I IS TRANSFORMED BY ARTIFICIAL ATAVISM INTO A TERRIBLE MONSTER OF KRYTON'S PAST!

THIS IS GANN ARTAR'S REVENGE! RUN FOR YOUR LIFE!

NO, I'VE GOT AN IDEA! YOUR FREEZING FORCE MIGHT STOP THE THING...

IT WORKED!

YOU SAVED MY LIFE, KALEL KENT! THIS GIVES US A CHANCE TO FIGHT GANN ARTAR! I'M SURE THAT IF I STUDY THE PHYSICAL CHANGES IN THIS ANCESTRAL STATE, I MAY FIND AN ANTIDOTE FOR HIS TERRIBLE RAY!

HOURS LATER, AFTER FEVERISH EXPERIMENTS...

IF MY THEORY IS CORRECT, THE CHEMICALS IN THIS GAS SHOULD BE AN ANTIDOTE TO THE ARTIFICIALLY-INDUCED ATAVISM!

IF IT ONLY WORKS! AS LONG AS GANN ARTAR IS AT LARGE, HIS RAY IS A TERRIBLE MENACE!

7

NEXT MOMENT...

THERE'S NO TIME TO LOSE...

SUCCESS! THE GAS REVERSED THE ARTIFICIAL ATAVISM! NOW WE CAN RESTORE TO NORMAL THE OTHER MONSTERS GANN ARTAR HAS CREATED!

MONSTERS OF **KRYPTON'S** PAST, DRIVEN INTO A GREAT STOCKADE, ARE RETURNED TO NORMAL!

IT'S WORKING ON THESE CREATURES, TOO!

GANN ARTAR HAS BEEN CAPTURED... AND IS ABOUT TO BE SENTENCED FOR HIS CRIME OF CREATING THESE DANGEROUS MONSTERS!

A SOLEMN JUDGMENT IS GIVEN!

I'LL HAVE VENGEANCE YET... YOU'LL SEE!

YOU ARE SENTENCED TO THE **PHANTOM ZONE** FOR 50 **KRYPTON** TIME-CYCLES FOR YOUR CRIME!

NOW THAT I KNOW THAT THE FORMULA FOR UNDOING THE ATAVISM EFFECT, I MUST RETURN TO MY OWN TIME AND EARTH!

BUT WHEN **KAL-EL II** BIDS **JOR-EL I** FAREWELL...

I'M SORRY YOU MUST LEAVE, **KAL-EL**-KENT, FOR I FEEL SOMEHOW DRAWN TO YOU! YOU'LL BE A GREAT SCIENTIST SOMEDAY,... I PREDICT IT!

THANKS, GRANDF... I MEAN, **JOR-EL!**

I...÷CHOKE÷... I HATE TO LEAVE, BUT THE TIME-BUBBLE PLANS I LEFT SHOULD SAVE HIM AND **LARA** FROM DOOM!

BUT WHEN **KAL-EL** II RETURNS TO EARTH AND HIS OWN TIME IN THE TIME-BUBBLE,...

THE PLANS I LEFT WITH **JOR-EL**...THEY WERE AFFECTED BY THE ENERGY FORCE OF MY TIME-BUBBLE, BECAUSE THEY WENT BACK INTO THE PAST WITH ME, SO, WHEN I LEFT **KRYPTON**, THEY WERE DRAWN **BACK** WITH ME! I...÷CHOKE÷... SEE NOW THAT **JOR-EL I** CAN'T ESCAPE...AND THAT HISTORY CAN'T BE CHANGED!

IN THE FORTRESS, **KAL-EL** USES THE ZONE-O-PHONE TO VERIFY A TERRIBLE SUSPICION!

GANN ARTAR SHOULD STILL BE A PRISONER IN THE **PHANTOM ZONE**, BUT HE ISN'T THERE!

HA...**GANN ARTAR** ESCAPED WHEN A SPACE-WARP TEMPORARILY OPENED THE ZONE! HE USED YOUR FATHER'S INSTRUMENTS TO GO DOWN INTO **KANDOR** AND GET KRYPTONIAN MATERIALS FOR A NEW GENERATOR OF **DE-EVOLUTIONARY RAYS!** HE IS THE RAIDER, AND HE'S CONQUERED YOUR FATHER AND BROTHER!

8

AND WHEN **KAL-EL** SPEEDS TO HIS HOME...

SUPERMAN AND **JOR-EL** THOUGHT THEY'D LOCATED **GANN ARTAR'S** BASE ON THE **WILD MOUNTAINS**! THEY WENT THERE, BUT HAVEN'T RETURNED!

I'M GOING AFTER THEM, MOTHER! I BROUGHT SOMETHING FROM THE FORTRESS THAT MAY HELP!

SHORTLY, AS **KAL-EL** REACHES THE **WILD MOUNTAINS**...

GANN ARTAR RINGED HIS BASE WITH CAMOUFLAGED **GREEN KRYPTONITE** ...AND WE FELL INTO HIS TRAP! WE'RE PARALYZED... SLOWLY DYING... GET AWAY, **KAL**, FOR WITHOUT SUPER-POWERS... YOU CAN'T FACE HIM!

I'M GOING TO TRY!

AND ACROSS THE HIDDEN **GREEN KRYPTONITE** WHICH DOESN'T AFFECT HIM...

SUPERMAN'S WEAKLING SON WILL SOON JOIN HIM AND HIS OTHER SON IN DEATH! FOR **I** HAVE SUPER-STRENGTH, AS YOU'LL SOON FIND OUT!

SOMETIMES SCIENCE CAN BEAT SUPER-POWERS, **GANN ARTAR**!

I KEPT THIS WRAPPED IN LEAD TILL NOW SO YOU COULDN'T SEE WHAT IT IS! IT'S THE **PHANTOM ZONE** PROJECTOR FROM THE FORTRESS!

IT'S HURLING ME BACK INTO THE **PHANTOM ZONE**! MY GREAT PLAN TO DOMINATE EARTH IS RUINED!

MINUTES LATER... ...SO **GANN ARTAR** IS SAFELY BACK IN THE **ZONE**! AND WHEN I'VE CARRIED YOU AND THEN **JOR-EL II** OUT OF THE INFLUENCE OF THE HIDDEN KRYPTONITE, WE CAN USE THE DISCOVERY OF MY GRANDFATHER TO RETURN THE MONSTERS HE CREATED TO NORMAL!

WHEN THAT HAS BEEN DONE...

IT'S WONDERFUL HOW **KAL-EL II** HAS CHANGED, HE'S STILL NON-SUPER, BUT HE NO LONGER HAS AN INFERIORITY COMPLEX!

HE SHOULDN'T HAVE, FOR HE SAVED US ALL! IF HIS GRANDFATHER, **JOR-EL I**, WERE ALIVE TODAY, HE WOULD BE PROUD INDEED OF HIS GRANDSON, **KAL-EL II**!

AND SO ENDS OUR IMAGINARY NOVEL, WHICH **MAY** OR **MAY NOT** HAPPEN ONE DAY!

The End

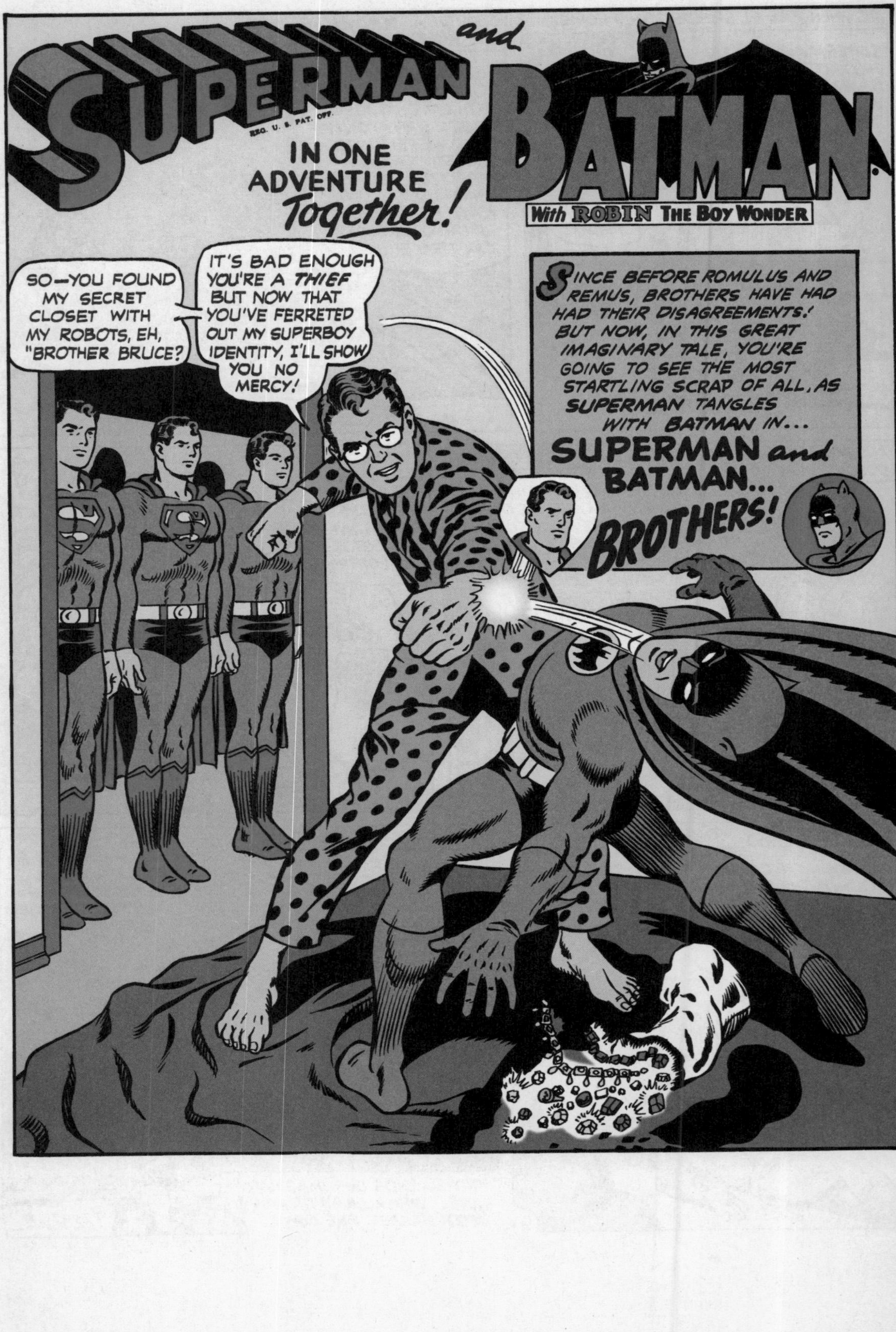
SUPERMAN and BATMAN
REG. U. S. PAT. OFF.
IN ONE ADVENTURE Together!
With ROBIN THE BOY WONDER
SO—YOU FOUND MY SECRET CLOSET WITH MY ROBOTS, EH, "BROTHER BRUCE?
IT'S BAD ENOUGH YOU'RE A THIEF BUT NOW THAT YOU'VE FERRETED OUT MY SUPERBOY IDENTITY, I'LL SHOW YOU NO MERCY!
SINCE BEFORE ROMULUS AND REMUS, BROTHERS HAVE HAD HAD THEIR DISAGREEMENTS! BUT NOW, IN THIS GREAT IMAGINARY TALE, YOU'RE GOING TO SEE THE MOST STARTLING SCRAP OF ALL, AS SUPERMAN TANGLES WITH BATMAN IN...
SUPERMAN and BATMAN... BROTHERS!

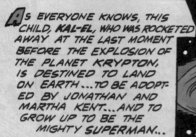

As everyone knows, this child, **KAL-EL**, who was rocketed away at the last moment before the explosion of the planet Krypton, is destined to land on Earth...to be adopted by Jonathan and Martha Kent...and to grow up to be the mighty Superman...

But do you know that this child, walking home with his parents from a movie one night, years later is **also** destined to be adopted by the Kents? (At least...such is the case in this imaginary tale...)

I'M GLAD WE DECIDED TO WALK ...IT'S SUCH A NICE NIGHT!

LAST CHA ONE WEEK

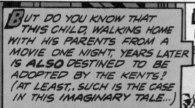

Suddenly, from the darkness...

I'LL TAKE THAT NECKLACE, LADY...AND YOUR WALLET, MISTER!

EEEEEK! HELP

A HOLDUP, EH? YOU'LL GET **NOTHING** FROM US!

NO FUNNY STUFF, MISTER... AN'...HEY! SHUT UP, LADY...I'M WARNING YOU!

ALL RIGHT, YOU ASKED FOR IT!

NO... MOTHER ...DAD... NO!

BLAM! BLAM!

And so, in one, brief, maniacal moment, young Bruce Wayne is orphaned...left alone...victim of a cruel fate!

But now let us switch our scene from this site of tragedy to Smallville, days later, where Superboy performs at a charity show...

SUPERBOY'S BATTLING THAT GIANT ROBOT HE BUILT! DID IT GO HAYWIRE?

OF COURSE NOT ...IT'S JUST AN EXHIBITION! WOW! LOOK AT IT GO!

2

HOLY TOLEDO! *SUPERBOY'S* SUPER-SPEED GOT THE ROBOT SO CONFUSED, HE HIT *HIMSELF!* HA!

YOO-HOO! ROBOT! I'M BACK *HERE!*

MAN! I'D HATE TO BE A *BAD GUY* WHEN SUPIE GETS *MAD!*

NOW FOR THE FINALE... A SUPER-BLOW THAT WILL SHATTER THE EXHIBITION ROBOT INTO A *THOUSAND PIECES,* TO BE AUCTIONED OFF AS SOUVENIRS!

MEANWHILE, ACROSS TOWN, AT THE HOME OF THE KENTS...

MRS. KENT, I'M MRS. SWAN FROM THE SMALLVILLE ORPHANAGE! MAY I COME IN?

OF COURSE!

IS THIS SOMETHING ABOUT CLARK? IS SOMETHING WRONG?

NO, MRS. KENT, NOTHING LIKE THAT... AS A MATTER OF FACT, I'M HERE TO SEE YOU BECAUSE EVERYTHING'S *RIGHT!*

YOU SEE, EVER SINCE YOU ADOPTED CLARK, WE'VE BEEN KEEPING AN EYE ON HIM! AND HE'S DONE *QUITE WELL!*

SO WE'D LIKE YOU TO ADOPT *ANOTHER* BOY!

ANOTHER BOY... OH, MRS. SWAN, I DON'T THINK...

WAIT! BEFORE YOU SPEAK, LET ME *EXPLAIN* ABOUT THIS BOY...

HIS PARENTS WERE BOTH KILLED BY A GUNMAN BEFORE THE CHILD'S EYES! IT HAD QUITE A TRAUMATIC EFFECT ON HIM!

WE FEEL IT IS NECESSARY TO GET HIM INTO THE WARM SUR-ROUNDINGS OF HOME AND FAMILY AS QUICKLY AS POS-SIBLE...AT LEAST, TEMPORARILY, TILL THE SHOCK WEARS OFF!

HMM? CLARK *HAS* ALWAYS BEEN *LONELY*...IT MIGHT BE GOOD FOR HIM TO HAVE COMPANY...AT LEAST FOR A WHILE! AND I'M *SURE* HE COULD MANAGE TO KEEP HIS *SUPERBOY* IDENTITY SAFE!

I'LL HAVE TO SPEAK TO JONATHAN, BUT I'M CERTAIN HE'LL AGREE!

WONDERFUL! I HAVE THE PAPERS HERE AND BRUCE CAN COME THIS AFTERNOON!

LATER, AS SUPERBOY RETURNS...

DAD! I'M HOME...HUH?

SHH! QUICKLY, SON, CHANGE TO YOUR *CLARK* CLOTHES!

NO TIME TO EXPLAIN NOW ...HURRY... BUT YOU MUST *NEVER* COME IN *THAT* WAY AGAIN!

IN SECONDS...

CLARK, I WANT YOU TO MEET YOUR NEW BROTHER, BRUCE!

WHA...NEW BROTHER?

WE ADOPTED BRUCE TODAY, CLARK...I'M SURE YOU'LL MAKE HIM FEEL AT HOME!

BUT THEN, AS MRS. KENT EXPLAINS TO CLARK PRIVATELY...

I KNOW YOU'LL LIKE HIM, CLARK! I'VE ALWAYS WORRIED ABOUT YOU BEING LONELY! NOW YOU'LL HAVE A BROTHER...A PAL TO DO THINGS WITH!

I SEE, MOM! WELL, I HOPE YOU'RE RIGHT!

BUT IN THE WEEKS THAT FOLLOW...

VERY GOOD, BRUCE!

$Y = \dfrac{FL}{AAL}$

ELASTIC MODULU

WHY WOULD MOM AND DAD DO THIS? THEY KNOW IT WILL HAMPER MY SUPERBOY ACTIVITIES!

WHILE I HAVE TO RESTRAIN MYSELF AND GET ONLY GOOD GRADES TO KEEP FROM BEING SUSPECTED AS SUPERBOY, BRUCE GRABS TOP HONORS IN EVERY CLASS!

4

AND TALK ABOUT WORKERS...PEOPLE THINK OF CLARK KENT AS A BOOKWORM BUT BRUCE READS TWICE AS MUCH AS I DO! HE NEVER STOPS...NEVER LETS UP...NEVER HAS ANY FUN!

COMPLEX ORGANIC COMPOUNDS COLLEGE TEXT

ONE DAY, AS THE TWO WALK HOME FROM SCHOOL...

HEY, BRUCE KENT! YEAH, YOU, BRIGHT BOY!

OH-OH! THE SCHOOL BULLY...PICKING ON BRUCE!

LISTEN, SHRIMP! I'M GETTING SICK OF THE WAY YOU ALWAYS KNOW IT ALL IN CLASS! WE DON'T LIKE TEACHER'S PETS AROUND HERE AND THIS IS JUST A REMINDER!

BUT...

HEY... YOU CAN'T DO THAT... UHHN!

≥GASP≤ YOU CAN'T BE AS STRONG AS ME...I'M BIGGER THAN YOU!

CAN'T I?

WHAM!

URK!

WOW! NICE GOING, BRUCE!

BRUCE BEAT UP BIG BENNY! YAHOO!

THERE'S ANOTHER DIFFERENCE BETWEEN BRUCE AND ME! TIMID CLARK COULD NEVER PULL A STUNT LIKE THAT!

BUT MORE IMPORTANT IS HIS ATTITUDE... HE'S ENTIRELY SELF-ABSORBED! HE DIDN'T EVEN NOTICE THE KIDS CHEERING HIM! AND THE WAY HE CLOBBERED BENNY...WITH A SORT OF VENGEANCE!

5

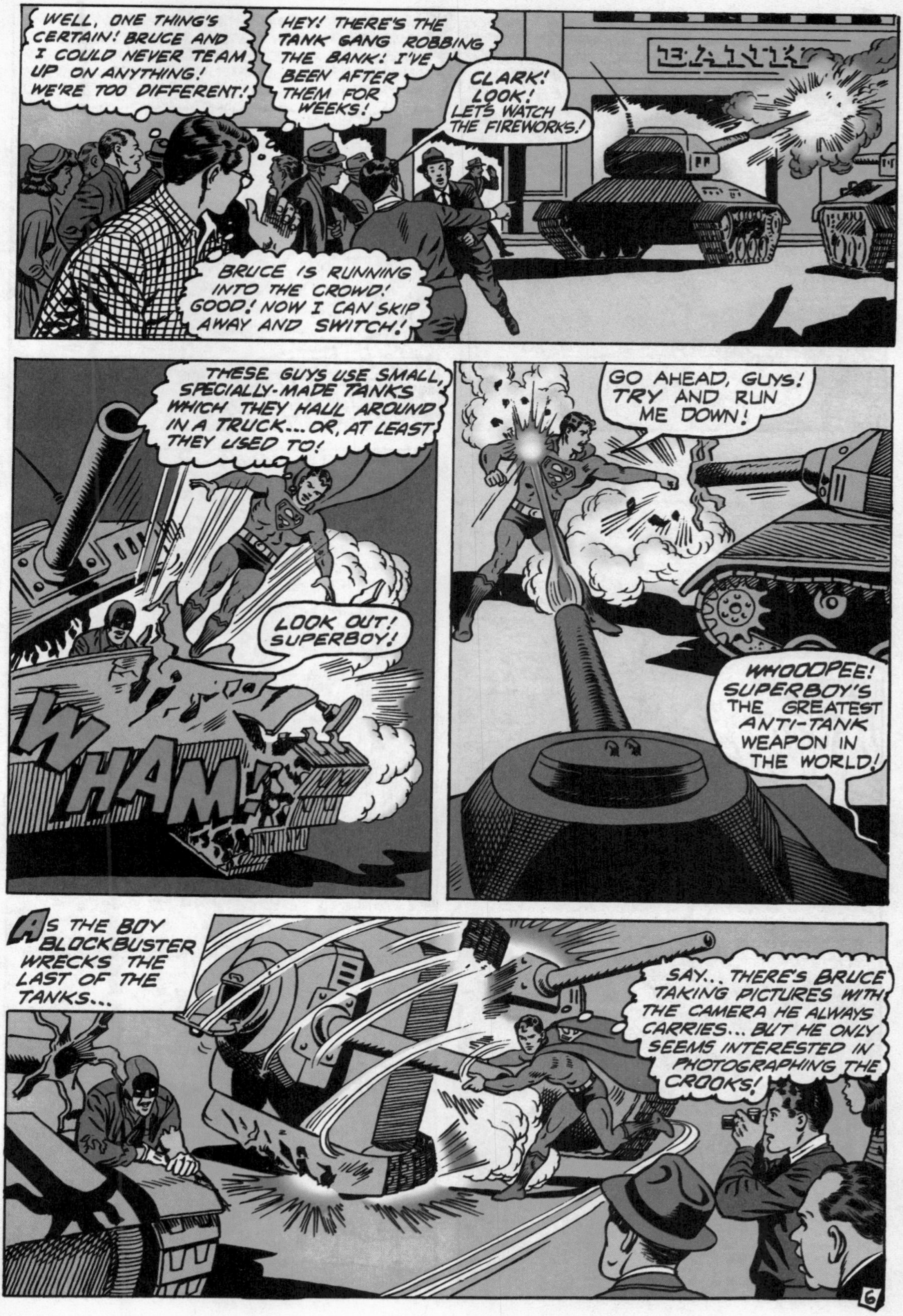
WELL, ONE THING'S CERTAIN! BRUCE AND I COULD NEVER TEAM UP ON ANYTHING! WE'RE TOO DIFFERENT!
HEY! THERE'S THE TANK GANG ROBBING THE BANK! I'VE BEEN AFTER THEM FOR WEEKS!
CLARK! LOOK! LETS WATCH THE FIREWORKS!
BANK
BRUCE IS RUNNING INTO THE CROWD! GOOD! NOW I CAN SKIP AWAY AND SWITCH!
THESE GUYS USE SMALL, SPECIALLY-MADE TANKS WHICH THEY HAUL AROUND IN A TRUCK... OR, AT LEAST THEY USED TO!
LOOK OUT! SUPERBOY!
WHAM!
GO AHEAD, GUYS! TRY AND RUN ME DOWN!
WHOOOPEE! SUPERBOY'S THE GREATEST ANTI-TANK WEAPON IN THE WORLD!
AS THE BOY BLOCKBUSTER WRECKS THE LAST OF THE TANKS...
SAY... THERE'S BRUCE TAKING PICTURES WITH THE CAMERA HE ALWAYS CARRIES... BUT HE ONLY SEEMS INTERESTED IN PHOTOGRAPHING THE CROOKS!
6

LATER, AT HOME... I WAS RIGHT! BRUCE ONLY SNAPPED PICS OF THE CRIMINALS IN ACTION... AND HE EVEN TOOK NOTES ON THEIR TECHNIQUES! BUT...

HEY! WHAT'S IN THIS DRAWER?

DOZENS OF BOOKS...ALL ABOUT CRIME AND CRIMINALS! POLICE FILES...BIOGRAPHIES OF FAMOUS OUTLAWS...PHOTOS OF MURDERERS...BANK ROBBERS...COPIES OF THE PLANS OF FAMOUS THEFTS!

WHAT WOULD BRUCE WANT WITH THIS STUFF? COULD HE BE IDOLIZING THESE RATS?

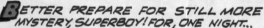

BETTER PREPARE FOR STILL MORE MYSTERY, SUPERBOY! FOR, ONE NIGHT...

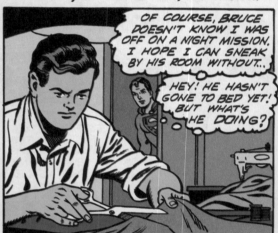

OF COURSE, BRUCE DOESN'T KNOW I WAS OFF ON A NIGHT MISSION. I HOPE I CAN SNEAK BY HIS ROOM WITHOUT...

HEY! HE HASN'T GONE TO BED YET! BUT WHAT'S HE DOING?

≡GASP≡ HE'S MAKING A COSTUME FOR HIMSELF ...AND A DARK HOOD TO COVER HIS FACE! BUT WHY? HMM... I'VE SEEN SUCH A HOOD BEFORE SOMEWHERE...

OF COURSE....! IT'S THE SAME TYPE OF HOOD THE TANK BANDITS WORE!

BUT...WHAT DOES IT MEAN? IS MY BROTHER BECOMING A CRIMINAL?

WHAT ELSE CAN IT MEAN? NOW HE'S PREPARING WEAPONS FOR HIMSELF!

I CAN'T CONFRONT HIM YET WITHOUT REVEALING MY IDENTITY... BUT FROM NOW ON, I'LL KEEP AN EYE ON BRUCE!

DAYS LATER... IN A WAY, I'M GLAD BRUCE HAS TO SHARE MY ROOM WHILE HIS IS BEING PAINTED!

I'LL HAVE TO BE CAREFUL TO GUARD MY SUPERBOY IDENTITY... BUT BRUCE WON'T WORK ON HIS MYSTERIOUS "HOBBY" NOW WHEN HE KNOWS I CAN SEE IT!

7

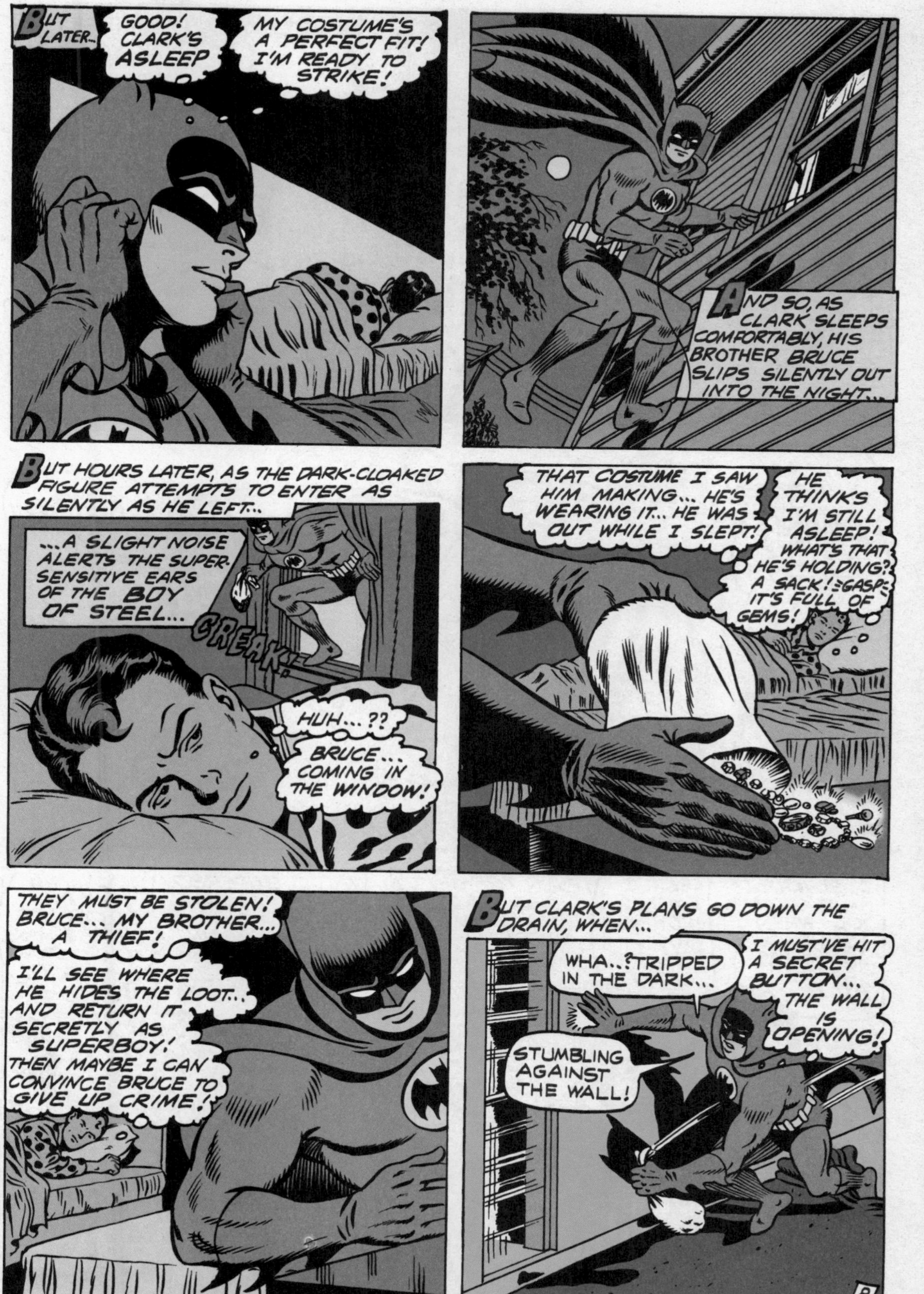
BUT LATER...
GOOD! CLARK'S ASLEEP
MY COSTUME'S A PERFECT FIT! I'M READY TO STRIKE!
AND SO, AS CLARK SLEEPS COMFORTABLY, HIS BROTHER BRUCE SLIPS SILENTLY OUT INTO THE NIGHT...
BUT HOURS LATER, AS THE DARK-CLOAKED FIGURE ATTEMPTS TO ENTER AS SILENTLY AS HE LEFT...
...A SLIGHT NOISE ALERTS THE SUPER-SENSITIVE EARS OF THE BOY OF STEEL...
CREAK!
HUH...??
BRUCE... COMING IN THE WINDOW!
THAT COSTUME I SAW HIM MAKING... HE'S WEARING IT... HE WAS OUT WHILE I SLEPT!
HE THINKS I'M STILL ASLEEP! WHAT'S THAT HE'S HOLDING? A SACK! GASP! IT'S FULL OF GEMS!
THEY MUST BE STOLEN! BRUCE... MY BROTHER... A THIEF!
I'LL SEE WHERE HE HIDES THE LOOT... AND RETURN IT SECRETLY AS SUPERBOY! THEN MAYBE I CAN CONVINCE BRUCE TO GIVE UP CRIME!
BUT CLARK'S PLANS GO DOWN THE DRAIN, WHEN...
WHA..? TRIPPED IN THE DARK...
STUMBLING AGAINST THE WALL!
I MUST'VE HIT A SECRET BUTTON... THE WALL IS OPENING!
8

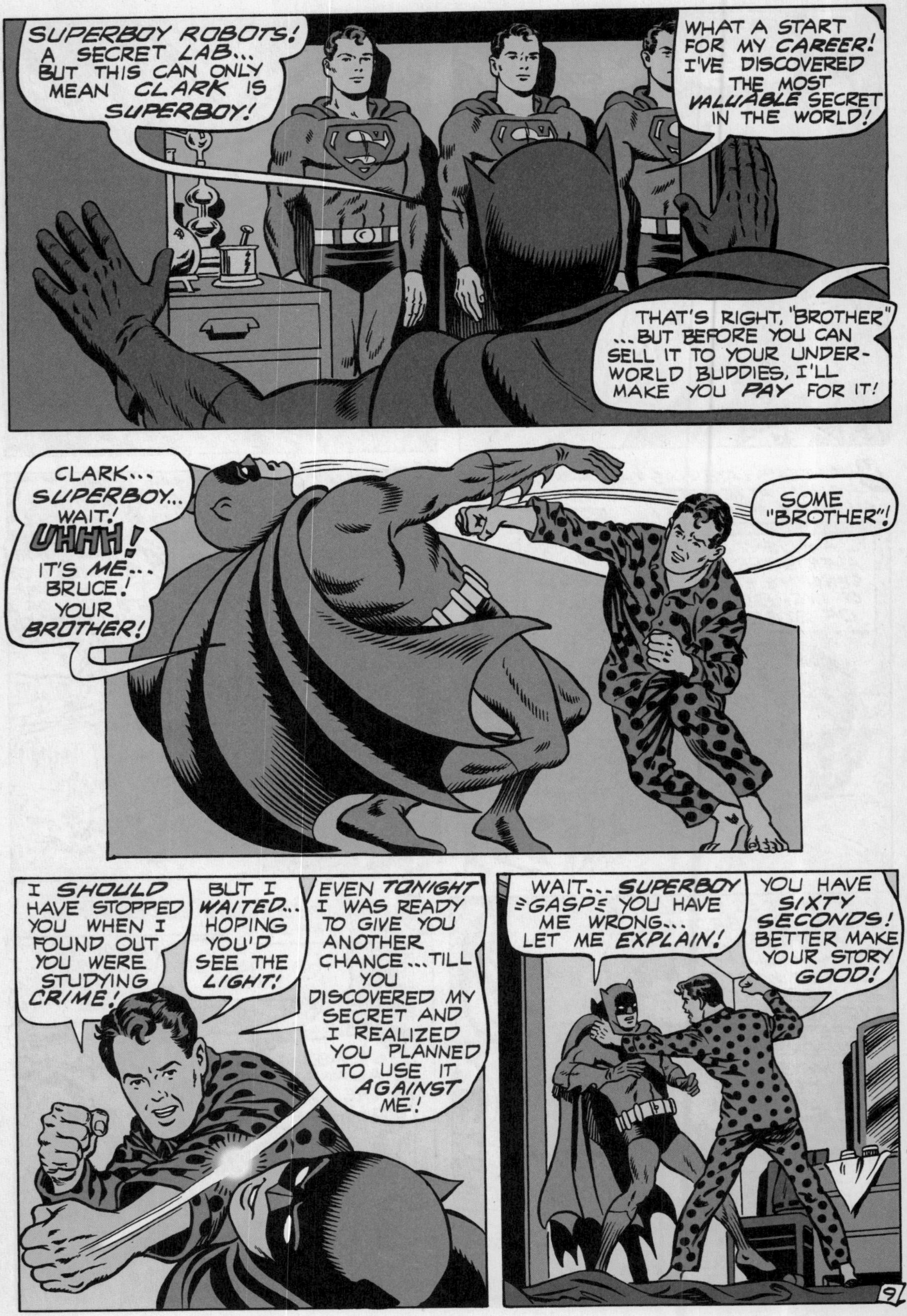
SUPERBOY ROBOTS! A SECRET LAB... BUT THIS CAN ONLY MEAN CLARK IS SUPERBOY!
WHAT A START FOR MY CAREER! I'VE DISCOVERED THE MOST VALUABLE SECRET IN THE WORLD!
THAT'S RIGHT, "BROTHER" ...BUT BEFORE YOU CAN SELL IT TO YOUR UNDER-WORLD BUDDIES, I'LL MAKE YOU PAY FOR IT!
CLARK... SUPERBOY... WAIT! UHHH! IT'S ME... BRUCE! YOUR BROTHER!
SOME "BROTHER"!
I SHOULD HAVE STOPPED YOU WHEN I FOUND OUT YOU WERE STUDYING CRIME!
BUT I WAITED... HOPING YOU'D SEE THE LIGHT!
EVEN TONIGHT I WAS READY TO GIVE YOU ANOTHER CHANCE...TILL YOU DISCOVERED MY SECRET AND I REALIZED YOU PLANNED TO USE IT AGAINST ME!
WAIT... SUPERBOY =GASP= YOU HAVE ME WRONG... LET ME EXPLAIN!
YOU HAVE SIXTY SECONDS! BETTER MAKE YOUR STORY GOOD!
9

BUT... SIXTY SECONDS WILL BE ENOUGH!

GAAAAAAA! KRYPTONITE ...FROM A LEAD POUCH IN YOUR BELT! IT CAN KILL ME... I'M GROWING WEAK!

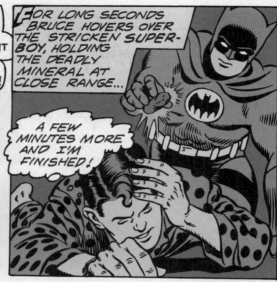

FOR LONG SECONDS BRUCE HOVERS OVER THE STRICKEN SUPER-BOY, HOLDING THE DEADLY MINERAL AT CLOSE RANGE...

A FEW MINUTES MORE AND I'M FINISHED!

BUT THEN, SUDDENLY...

HUH? YOU'RE PUTTING THE KRYPTONITE AWAY?

OF COURSE...I'M NO MURDERER, CLARK...JUST AS I'M NO THIEF!

A REAL CRIMINAL WOULD HAVE KILLED YOU WHEN HE HAD THE CHANCE!

BUT THE LOOT... THE GEMS? AND THAT EVIL-LOOKING COSTUME AND HOOD? AND WHY YOUR MIDNIGHT PROWL?

THE COSTUME IS MEANT TO STRIKE FEAR INTO MY ENEMIES' HEARTS! AND I OPERATE AT NIGHT BECAUSE THEY DO!

IN CASE YOU HAVEN'T GUESSED, MY ENEMIES ARE MUGGERS, MURDERERS AND THIEVES...LIKE THE ONE WHO KILLED MY PARENTS!

"I TRACKED DOWN MY FIRST TARGET TONIGHT...THE 'NAILS' KOKER GANG..."

THERE THEY ARE...I RECOGNIZE THEM FROM MY POLICE FILES! I FIGURED "NAILS" WOULD TRY FOR THAT JEWELRY STORE!

JEWELERS

10

"EAGER FOR MY FIRST TASTE OF ACTION, I SAILED INTO THEM, FISTS FLYING..."

Y-I-I-I! WHAT'S THAT?

THE NAME IS *BATBOY*... AND YOU'LL *REGRET* EVER HEARING IT...

UHH!

"*BUT* FISTS WEREN'T ENOUGH AGAINST SO MANY...SO I PULLED SOME TRICKS FROM MY UTILITY BELT..."

I *GAS* YOU'VE ABOUT HAD IT, FELLOWS!

"*I* DELIVERED THE THIEVES, BOUND, TO THE POLICE STATION, WITH A NOTE OF EXPLANATION, BUT..."

HMM! I CAN'T JUST LEAVE ALL THESE GEMS HERE!

I'LL TAKE THEM HOME AND RETURN THEM IN THE MORNING!

POLICE 10TH PRECINCT

WHICH EXPLAINS THE LOOT! HMM... INTERESTING!

NOW...WHAT ARE YOU GOING TO *DO* ABOUT MY NEW CAREER?

WELL, ONE THING'S SURE! I CAN'T LET YOU GO RUNNING AROUND BATTLING ANY MORE CRIMINALS...

WHAT?

11

...ALONE, THAT IS! PARTNERS, BROTHER?

SUPERBOY AND BATBOY! I LIKE IT, BROTHER!

THE *CRIME-BUSTING BROTHERS* SWING INTO *SUPER-ACTION* IN *PART II!*

Part II TRAGEDY STRIKES TWICE!

TAKE NOTICE, READERS... YOU HAVE JUST WITNESSED AN HISTORIC EVENT IN OUR IMAGINARY EPIC... THE BOYHOOD BEGINNING OF THE WORLD'S FINEST TEAM, BATBOY AND SUPERBOY! AND IN THE WEEKS THAT FOLLOW...

GAAAA! SMALLVILLE AIN'T SAFE FOR A HARD-WORKIN' CROOK NO MORE, WITH THEM BLASTED BOY BLOCKBUSTERS AROUND!

THAT'S RIGHT, BUDDY... AND WE INTEND TO KEEP IT THAT WAY!

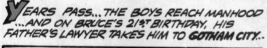

YEARS PASS...THE BOYS REACH MANHOOD ...AND ON BRUCE'S 21ST BIRTHDAY, HIS FATHER'S LAWYER TAKES HIM TO GOTHAM CITY...

HERE IT IS, BRUCE, WAYNE MANOR! IT'S ALL YOURS! NOW THAT YOU'VE COME INTO YOUR INHERITANCE!

IT WILL BE GREAT TO MOVE BACK HERE... BUT I WILL HATE LEAVING MY FOSTER PARENTS AND BROTHER!

JUST THEN, THE FRONT DOOR OPENS, AND...

WHO SAYS YOU'RE LEAVING US? I WAS GOING TO LOOK FOR A NEWSPAPER JOB IN METROPOLIS... BUT GOTHAM CITY'S JUST AS GOOD!

AND WE'D PLANNED TO RETIRE AND SELL OUR STORE! WE'D LOVE LIVING IN GOTHAM CITY IF YOU'LL HAVE US!

IF I'LL HAVE YOU! THIS IS TERRIFIC!

THAT'S RIGHT! IN THIS IMAGINARY TALE, CLARK DOES NOT WORK FOR THE DAILY PLANET, BUT FOR THE GOTHAM GAZETTE...

KENT... WE GOT A BULLETIN... A MAN IN SOME CRAZY MACHINE IS ROBBING THE WESTERN FUR WAREHOUSE!

GET OVER THERE ON THE DOUBLE!

I'M ON MY WAY!

STEPPING INTO A DESERTED STOREROOM...

MY TELESCOPIC VISION SHOWS THE REPORT WAS TRUE!

I'LL GET THERE FAST, ALL RIGHT... AS SUPERMAN!

I'D BETTER PICK UP BRUCE! HE WOULDN'T WANT TO MISS THIS!

12

AND SO, SHORTLY...
SUPERMAN AND BATMAN! WELL, YOU'VE MET YOUR MATCH IN LEX LUTHOR!
NEVER HEARD OF YOU, MISTER!
WESTERN FUR
TWIST!..IN THIS STORY SUPERMAN NEVER MET HIS ARCH-FOE WHEN THEY WERE BOYS!
NO... YOU CAN'T BEAT ME... YOU CAN'T!
THEN WHAT ARE WE DOING, LUTHOR?
THIS MINIATURE PLASTIC BOMB FROM MY GRAVITY BELT WILL PUT THE FINISHING TOUCH TO YOUR WALKING WATER TANK!
DON'T WORRY.... YOU'RE GOING TO JAIL, LUTHOR WHERE YOU CAN DO HARD LABOR!
FAT CHANCE! MY HENCHMEN WILL SPRING ME WITHIN DAYS!
BUT THOSE TWO ARE A THREAT TO ME! I MUST FIGURE OUT A PLOT TO DESTROY THEM!
WESTERN FUR SHO
13
DAYS LATER...
WE'RE OFF TO THE CHARITY BAZAAR, BOYS! LIKE TO COME ALONG AND HELP OUT?
SORRY, MOM... DAD... NO CAN DO!
WE'D LIKE TO COME, BUT WE JUST HEARD A RADIO BULLETIN ...LUTHOR BROKE JAIL!
IN THAT CASE, YOU'RE EXCUSED!

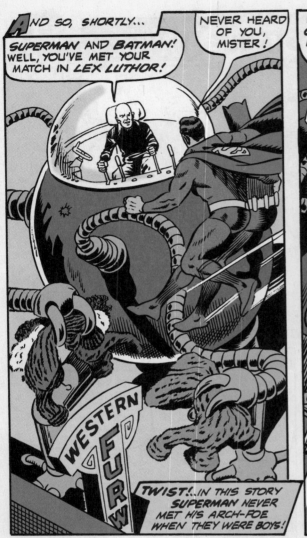

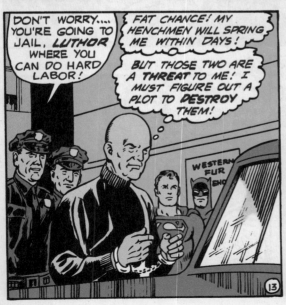

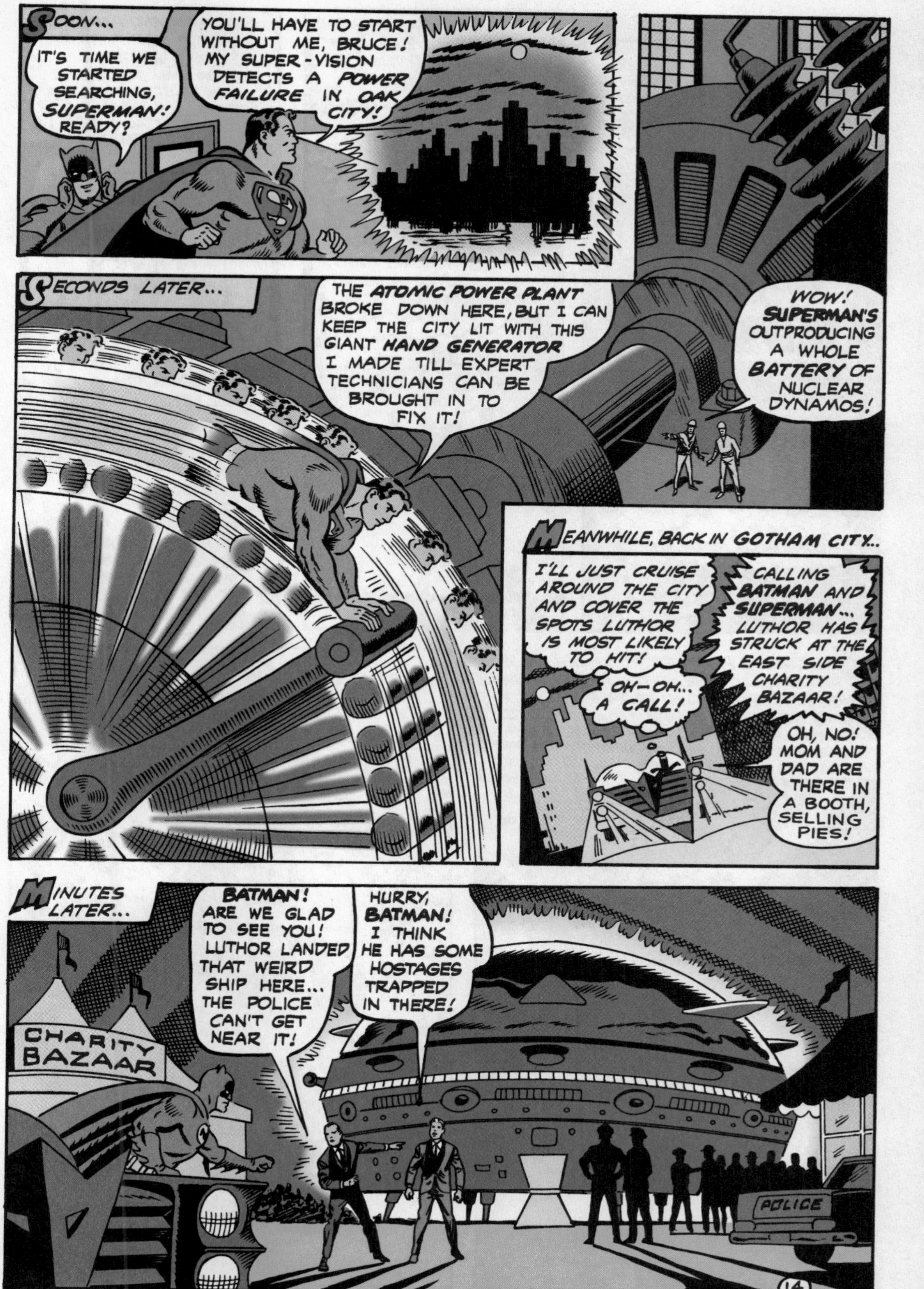
SOON...
IT'S TIME WE STARTED SEARCHING, SUPERMAN! READY?
YOU'LL HAVE TO START WITHOUT ME, BRUCE! MY SUPER-VISION DETECTS A POWER FAILURE IN OAK CITY!
SECONDS LATER...
THE ATOMIC POWER PLANT BROKE DOWN HERE, BUT I CAN KEEP THE CITY LIT WITH THIS GIANT HAND GENERATOR I MADE TILL EXPERT TECHNICIANS CAN BE BROUGHT IN TO FIX IT!
WOW! SUPERMAN'S OUTPRODUCING A WHOLE BATTERY OF NUCLEAR DYNAMOS!
MEANWHILE, BACK IN GOTHAM CITY...
I'LL JUST CRUISE AROUND THE CITY AND COVER THE SPOTS LUTHOR IS MOST LIKELY TO HIT!
OH-OH... A CALL!
CALLING BATMAN AND SUPERMAN... LUTHOR HAS STRUCK AT THE EAST SIDE CHARITY BAZAAR!
OH, NO! MOM AND DAD ARE THERE IN A BOOTH, SELLING PIES!
MINUTES LATER...
BATMAN! ARE WE GLAD TO SEE YOU! LUTHOR LANDED THAT WEIRD SHIP HERE... THE POLICE CAN'T GET NEAR IT!
HURRY, BATMAN! I THINK HE HAS SOME HOSTAGES TRAPPED IN THERE!
CHARITY BAZAAR
POLICE
14

SUDDENLY, A SCREEN LIGHTS UP...

AH...YOU'VE ARRIVED, *BATMAN*! I'VE BEEN WAITING!

I USED MY MACHINES TO TAKE *TWO* HOSTAGES...THESE ELDERLY PEOPLE WHO WERE WORKING IN A BOOTH!

≈ *GASP!* ≈ MOM...AND *DAD*!

IN SIXTY SECONDS THESE PEOPLE *DIE* WHEN THAT *BOMB* BEHIND THEM EXPLODES...UNLESS YOU PREVENT IT!

HA, HA! THEIR LIVES ARE IN YOUR HANDS...COME ON IN...TRY TO *RESCUE* THEM!

IT'S A TRAP...THAT PASSAGE IS UNDOUBTEDLY LINED WITH *WEAPONS*!

BUT MOM AND DAD KENT! I *CAN'T* LET THEM DIE! I'LL TAKE ANYTHING LUTHOR CAN DISH OUT...I WON'T LET HIM KILL THEM!

IT'S WORKING! DIVIDE AND CONQUER! WHILE *SUPERMAN* IS HANDLING ANOTHER EMERGENCY I CREATED, *BATMAN* WILL THROW AWAY HIS LIFE TRYING TO SAVE TWO *NOBODIES*!

NOBODIES? PERHAPS YOU'D FEEL LESS SECURE, *LUTHOR*, IF YOU KNEW YOU WERE THREATENING THE TWO PEOPLE ON EARTH DEAREST TO THE *MASKED MANHUNTER*...CAUSING HIM TO FIGHT WITH A *GRIM DETERMINATION* AS HE NEVER HAS BEFORE!

AGGH! HEAT RAYS...SEARING ME! BUT I CAN'T LET THEM STOP ME!

NOW...POWERFUL *ANDROIDS*! UFF! -UHHH! BUT I *MUST* BEAT THEM! TIME IS RUNNING OUT!

15

As LUTHOR WATCHES, BATMAN BARRELS THROUGH THE ANDROIDS, AND...

ANTI-MATTER BLASTS... AUTOMATIC DEATH TRAPS...HE'S DODGING THEM ...SMASHING PAST EACH ONE IN TURN ...GETTING NEARER TO THE GOAL... WHAT MANNER OF MAN IS HE?

THE BLAST-RAY ON THE DOOR TO THE HOSTAGES' CHAMBER IS MY LAST HOPE... NOW!

ARRRGH!

BUT... HE LIVES!

HE'S GETTING UP... USING AN ACID FROM HIS UTILITY BELT TO CUT THROUGH THE DOOR...

HE'S GOING TO MAKE IT!

NO! I WON'T LET HIM WIN AGAIN! I'LL SET OFF THE BOMB PREMATURELY... DESTROY THE WHOLE CHAMBER! HE MUST DIE!

BOOM!

SECONDS LATER, AS LUTHOR ENTERS THE CHAMBER...

HA... I DID IT! FINALLY! I KILLED THEM ALL!

BUT THEN, FROM THE WRECKAGE...

AIE-E-E! IT CAN'T BE...

AARRGH!

16

WHAM

ARRR-RHH!

YOU KILLED THEM... MURDERER!

BATMAN! BATMAN! STOP! HOLD IT!

WOW... A FEW MORE MINUTES AND YOU'D HAVE KILLED HIM, BATMAN!

TOO BAD ABOUT THOSE TWO OLD FOLKS, EH, BATMAN?

BATMAN?

BATMAN?

LATER...

I CAME AS SOON AS I HEARD, BATMAN! I KNOW HOW YOU FEEL--THEY WERE MY PARENTS, TOO!

YOU... COULDN'T POSSIBLY KNOW, SUPERMAN! THIS IS... THE SECOND TIME!

TWO SETS OF PARENTS... MURDERED BY CRIMINALS!

I CAN'T STAY HERE! I'LL DISPOSE OF MY PROPERTY... LEAVE GOTHAM CITY!

NO, BATMAN! YOU'RE STILL IN SHOCK! YOU NEED MEDICAL CARE! LATER...

IT WOULD BE THE SAME! THERE ARE TOO MANY MEMORIES HERE! I'M LEAVING ...FOR GOOD!

17

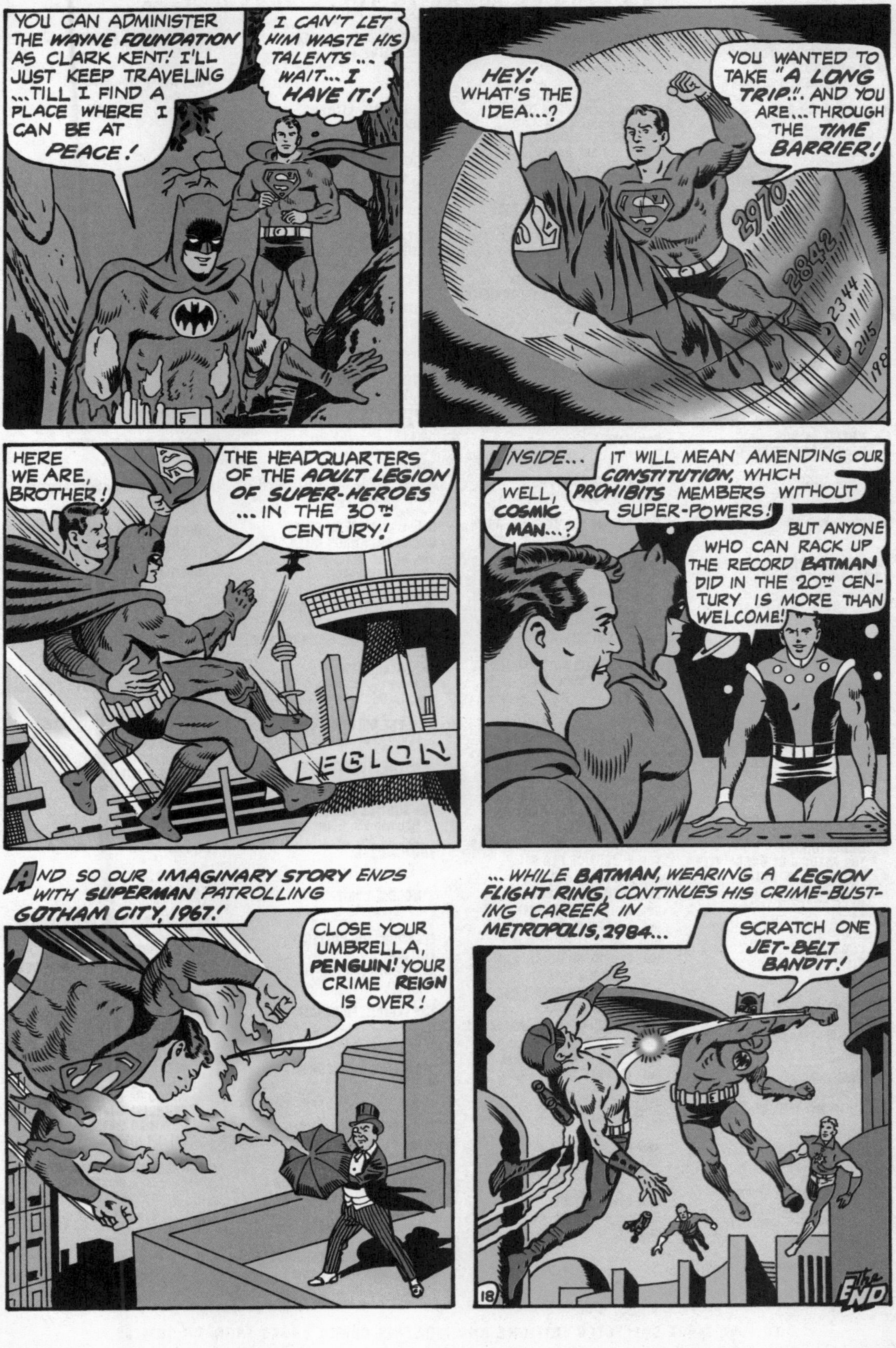
YOU CAN ADMINISTER THE WAYNE FOUNDATION AS CLARK KENT! I'LL JUST KEEP TRAVELING ...TILL I FIND A PLACE WHERE I CAN BE AT PEACE!
I CAN'T LET HIM WASTE HIS TALENTS... WAIT... I HAVE IT!
HEY! WHAT'S THE IDEA...?
YOU WANTED TO TAKE "A LONG TRIP!". AND YOU ARE... THROUGH THE TIME BARRIER!
2970
2842
2344
2115
HERE WE ARE, BROTHER!
THE HEADQUARTERS OF THE ADULT LEGION OF SUPER-HEROES ... IN THE 30TH CENTURY!
LEGION
INSIDE...
IT WILL MEAN AMENDING OUR CONSTITUTION, WHICH PROHIBITS MEMBERS WITHOUT SUPER-POWERS!
WELL, COSMIC MAN...?
BUT ANYONE WHO CAN RACK UP THE RECORD BATMAN DID IN THE 20TH CENTURY IS MORE THAN WELCOME!
AND SO OUR IMAGINARY STORY ENDS WITH SUPERMAN PATROLLING GOTHAM CITY, 1967!
CLOSE YOUR UMBRELLA, PENGUIN! YOUR CRIME REIGN IS OVER!
...WHILE BATMAN, WEARING A LEGION FLIGHT RING, CONTINUES HIS CRIME-BUSTING CAREER IN METROPOLIS, 2984...
SCRATCH ONE JET-BELT BANDIT!
18
THE END

THE STARS OF THE DC UNIVERSE
CAN ALSO BE FOUND IN THESE BOOKS:

**ACROSS THE UNIVERSE:
THE DC UNIVERSE STORIES
OF ALAN MOORE**
A. Moore/D. Gibbons/various

BATGIRL: YEAR ONE
S. Beatty/C. Dixon/M. Martin/
J. Lopez

**BATMAN/SUPERMAN/
WONDER WOMAN: TRINITY**
M. Wagner

**BATMAN BLACK AND WHITE
Vols. 1-2**
Various

BATMAN: HUSH Vols. 1-2
J. Loeb/J. Lee/S. Williams

BATMAN: YEAR ONE
F. Miller/D. Mazzuchelli

BIRDS OF PREY
C. Dixon/G. Simone/G. Land/
E. Benes/various
    **BIRDS OF PREY
    OLD FRIENDS, NEW ENEMIES
    OF LIKE MINDS
    SENSEI AND STUDENT**

BIZARRO COMICS
various

BIZARRO WORLD
various

CRISIS ON INFINITE EARTHS
M. Wolfman/G. Pérez/J. Ordway/
various

**CRISIS ON MULTIPLE EARTHS
Vols. 1-3**
G. Fox/D. O'Neil/L. Wein/
M. Sekowsky/D. Dillin/various

FALLEN ANGEL
(SUGGESTED FOR MATURE READERS)
P. David/D. Lopez/F. Blanco

THE FINAL NIGHT
K. Kesel/S. Immonen/J. Marzan/
various

THE FLASH
M. Waid/G. Johns/G. Larocque/
S. Kollins/various
    **BORN TO RUN
    THE RETURN OF BARRY ALLEN
    TERMINAL VELOCITY
    DEAD HEAT
    RACE AGAINST TIME
    BLOOD WILL RUN
    ROGUES
    CROSSFIRE
    BLITZ
    IGNITION**

**FORMERLY KNOWN AS THE
JUSTICE LEAGUE**
K. Giffen/J.M. DeMatteis/
K. Maguire/J. Rubinstein

GOTHAM CENTRAL
E. Brubaker/G. Rucka/M. Lark
Vol. 1: IN THE LINE OF DUTY

GREEN ARROW
K. Smith/B. Meltzer/J. Winick/
P. Hester/A. Parks
**Vol. 1: QUIVER
Vol. 2: SOUNDS OF SILENCE
Vol. 3: ARCHER'S QUEST
Vol. 4: STRAIGHT SHOOTER
Vol. 5: CITY WALLS**

**GREEN LANTERN/GREEN ARROW
Vols. 1-2**
D. O'Neil/N. Adams/various

GREEN LANTERN
J. Winick/G. Jones/R. Marz/
D. Banks/M.D. Bright/
D. Eaglesham/various
    **EMERALD DAWN
    EMERALD DAWN II
    THE ROAD BACK
    EMERALD TWILIGHT/
    A NEW DAWN
    BAPTISM OF FIRE
    EMERALD ALLIES
    EMERALD KNIGHTS
    NEW JOURNEY, OLD PATH
    THE POWER OF ION
    BROTHER'S KEEPER
    PASSING THE TORCH**

**GREEN LANTERN: LEGACY —
THE LAST WILL AND TESTAMENT
OF HAL JORDAN**
J. Kelly/B. Anderson/B. Sienkiewicz

GREEN LANTERN: WILLWORLD
J.M. DeMatteis/S. Fisher

HARD TIME: 50 TO LIFE
S. Gerber/B. Hurtt

HAWKMAN
G. Johns/J. Robinson/R. Morales/
M. Bair/various
**Vol. 1: ENDLESS FLIGHT
Vol. 2: ALLIES AND ENEMIES**

HISTORY OF THE DC UNIVERSE
M. Wolfman/G. Pérez/K. Kesel

JACK KIRBY'S FOURTH WORLD
Jack Kirby/various
    **FOREVER PEOPLE
    FOURTH WORLD
    NEW GODS
    MISTER MIRACLE**

**JIMMY OLSEN ADVENTURES BY
JACK KIRBY Vols. 1-2**
J. Kirby/V. Colletta/M. Royer

JLA
G. Morrison/M. Waid/J. Kelly/
J. Byrne/C. Claremont/H. Porter/
B. Hitch/D. Mahnke/J. Ordway/
various
**Vol. 1: NEW WORLD ORDER
Vol. 2: AMERICAN DREAMS
Vol. 3: ROCK OF AGES
Vol. 4: STRENGTH IN NUMBERS
Vol. 5: JUSTICE FOR ALL
Vol. 6: WORLD WAR III
Vol. 7: TOWER OF BABEL
Vol. 8: DIVIDED WE FALL
Vol. 9: TERROR INCOGNITA
VolL. 10: GOLDEN PERFECT
Vol. 11: THE OBSIDIAN AGE
    BOOK ONE
Vol. 12: THE OBSIDIAN AGE
    BOOK TWO
Vol. 13: RULES OF ENGAGEMENT
Vol. 14: TRIAL BY FIRE
Vol. 15: THE TENTH CIRCLE
Vol. 16: PAIN OF THE GODS**

JLA: EARTH 2
G. Morrison/F. Quitely

JLA/JSA: VIRTUE & VICE
D. Goyer/G. Johns/C. Pacheco/
J Meriño

JLA: ONE MILLION
G. Morrison/V. Semeiks/P. Rollins/
various

**JLA/TITANS: THE TECHNIS
IMPERATIVE**
D. Grayson/P. Jimenez/P. Pelletier/
various

**JLA: WORLD WITHOUT
GROWN-UPS**
T. Dezago/T. Nauck/H. Ramos/
M. McKone/various

JLA: YEAR ONE
M. Waid/B. Augustyn/B. Kitson/
various

**JUSTICE LEAGUE:
A MIDSUMMER'S NIGHTMARE**
M. Waid/F. Nicieza/J. Johnson/
D. Robertson/various

**JUSTICE LEAGUE: A NEW
BEGINNING**
K. Giffen/J.M. DeMatteis/
K. Maguire/various

**JUSTICE LEAGUE OF AMERICA:
THE NAIL
JUSTICE LEAGUE OF AMERICA:
ANOTHER NAIL**
Alan Davis/Mark Farmer

JSA
G. Johns/J. Robinson/D. Goyer/
S. Sadowski/R. Morales/L. Kirk/
various
**Vol. 1: JUSTICE BE DONE
Vol. 2: DARKNESS FALLS
Vol. 3: THE RETURN OF
    HAWKMAN
Vol. 4: FAIR PLAY
Vol. 5: STEALING THUNDER
Vol. 6: SAVAGE TIMES
Vol. 7: PRINCES OF DARKNESS**

JSA: ALL STARS
D. Goyer/G. Johns/S. Velluto/
various

JSA: THE GOLDEN AGE
J. Robinson/P. Smith

JSA: THE LIBERTY FILES
D. Jolley/T. Harris/various

THE JUSTICE SOCIETY RETURNS
J. Robinson/D. Goyer/various

THE KINGDOM
M. Waid/various

KINGDOM COME
M. Waid/A. Ross

**LEGENDS: THE COLLECTED
EDITION**
J. Ostrander/L. Wein/J. Byrne/
K. Kesel

THE LEGION: FOUNDATIONS
D. Abnett/A. Lanning/T. Harris/
T. Batista/various

**MAJESTIC: STRANGE NEW
VISITOR**
D. Abnett/A. Lanning/K. Kerschl

THE NEW TEEN TITANS
M. Wolfman/G. Pérez/D. Giordano/
R. Tanghal
    **THE JUDAS CONTRACT
    THE TERROR OF TRIGON**

OUTSIDERS
J. Winick/T. Raney/Chriscross/
various
**Vol. 1: LOOKING FOR TROUBLE
Vol. 2: SUM OF ALL EVIL**

PLASTIC MAN: ON THE LAM
K. Baker

THE POWER OF SHAZAM!
J. Ordway

RONIN
F. Miller

STARMAN
J. Robinson/T. Harris/P. Snejbjerg/
W. Grawbadger/various
    **SINS OF THE FATHER
    NIGHT AND DAY
    INFERNAL DEVICES
    TO REACH THE STARS
    A STARRY KNIGHT
    STARS MY DESTINATION
    GRAND GUIGNOL
    SONS OF THE FATHER**

**SUPERGIRL: MANY HAPPY
RETURNS**
P. David/E. Benes/A. Lei

SUPERMAN/BATMAN
J. Loeb/E. McGuinness/D. Vines/
M. Turner/P. Steigerwald
**Vol. 1: PUBLIC ENEMIES
Vol. 2: SUPERGIRL**

SUPERMAN FOR ALL SEASONS
J. Loeb/T. Sale

SUPERMAN: BIRTHRIGHT
M. Waid/L. Yu/G. Alanguilan

SUPERMAN: GODFALL
M. Turner/J. Kelly/T. Caldwell/
P. Steigerwald

SUPERMAN: RED SON
M. Millar/D. Johnson/
K. Plunkett/various

**SUPERMAN: UNCONVENTIONAL
WARFARE**
G. Rucka/I. Reis/various

TEEN TITANS
G. Johns/M. McKone/T. Grummett
**Vol. 1: A KID'S GAME
Vol. 2: FAMILY LOST**

UNDERWORLD UNLEASHED
M. Waid/H. Porter/P. Jimenez/
various

WATCHMEN
A. Moore/D. Gibbons

WONDER WOMAN (early years)
G. Pérez/L. Wein/B. Patterson
**Vol. 1: GODS AND MORTALS
Vol. 2: CHALLENGE OF THE GODS**

WONDER WOMAN
G. Rucka/P. Jimenez/J. Byrne/
W.M. Loebs/D. Johnson/
M. Deodato/various
    **THE CONTEST
    SECOND GENESIS
    LIFELINES
    PARADISE LOST
    PARADISE FOUND
    DOWN TO EARTH
    BITTER RIVALS**

WONDER WOMAN: THE HIKETEIA
G. Rucka/J.G. Jones/
W. Grawbadger

ZERO HOUR: CRISIS IN TIME
D. Jurgens/J. Ordway/various

**TO FIND MORE COLLECTED EDITIONS AND MONTHLY COMIC BOOKS FROM DC COMICS,
CALL 1-888-COMIC BOOK FOR THE NEAREST COMICS SHOP OR GO TO YOUR LOCAL BOOK STORE.**